ENDORSEMENTS

Deliverance from demonic torment, oppression, and possession is a trending topic right now. Candidly, it's been a relevant topic since Jesus walked the earth and made it a sizable portion of His ministry emphasis. But there is something better than deliverance: demon-proofing your life! Jareb Nott presents a book that will truly demon-proof your life through an ancient secret that gives you an upper hand over the powers of darkness: biblical meditation. *The Science of Supernatural Thinking* gives you the practicals on how to protect your mind from the enemy and walk in the power of the Holy Spirit.

Larry Sparks
Publisher, Destiny Image

Jareb has given the Body of Christ a transformative gift in *The Science of Supernatural Thinking*. In this book, he is writing from his daily practice and experience of genuine biblical meditation. I kept hearing Holy Spirit say, "This is the ancient pathway to intimacy, glory encounters, healing, deliverance, and the abundant life Jesus promises us." Jareb has taken back pure Scriptural meditation from the counterfeit, secularized hands of the enemy. In this book, he has gathered over 250 passages of Scripture, showing us how to maintain a healthy thought life in our walk with God. I encourage you to read this meditatively, practicing, developing, and experiencing the depths of God's presence and transformation. You will never be the same!

Michael Peterson
Senior Pastor, Maranatha Glory Apostolic Center

We are in a language war. Taking back language is a component of God's Kingdom. Joshua asked God to stop the sun, and He did. Joshua did not understand how the planets rotated around the sun, but his words changed biblical history. In this book, Jareb causes us to reconsider a practice of worship that we have given over willingly to the secular world. It is time to take back the intimacy of meditation. In a black-and-white manner, he addresses the truth of the gospel of Christ and the falseness the enemy has attempted to perpetrate in culture. This is an awesome read for the serious believer who wants to draw close to Jesus.

Greg Greenwood
Co-Founder, Christian Harvest International

In a unique blend of wellness and spiritual expertise, Jareb skillfully weaves together the ancient wisdom of biblical meditation with cutting-edge insights from the realms of science and spirituality. He provides a profound exploration of the synergy between prayer and biblical meditation, offering a road map to enhance mental and physical well-being and exposing the counterfeit models prevalent in secular society. From current research, he illuminates the science behind thoughts, beliefs, sounds, and engaging all five senses. He emphasizes the breath of God and its role in our abiding time with a unique focus on meditation's role in deliverance and inner healing. This book is a comprehensive guide for those seeking a holistic path to spiritual and mental wellness—a harmonious integration of physical and spiritual dimensions.

Dr. Rimoun Hanna
Founder, Triumph Physical Therapy and Wellness Center,
Dallas, Texas

We believe that the revelation that is being released in this book, *The Science of Supernatural Thinking*, is key to transformation. Jareb Nott brings biblical truths and practical application so that you can have access to the presence of God in a personal and deep way. As you grow and increase in this practice, it will deepen your faith, you will grow and be led in new ways, and you will hunger for His presence like never before. We highly recommend that you read through and step into a new dimension.

Pasqual and Norma Urrabazo
Founders, Beautiful Life Global

This book beautifully intertwines the biblical foundations for meditation with the science behind it, offering practical insights and guidance. Jareb brings his years of experience in inner healing and deliverance ministry to demonstrate the transformative practice of biblical meditation. He makes the case for the restoration of true biblical meditation to the people of God, recognizing that it has been counterfeited and stolen by the enemy. I have a new understanding of the distinctions between prayer, intercession, and meditation. I look forward to using his practical meditation guides in my work as a Christian counselor and coach!

Kristen Owen, LPC, BCPCC
Professional Christian Counselor and Coach
Owner, Flourish Coaching, Consulting and Training, LLC

The Science of Supernatural Thinking is another breakthrough work by Jareb Nott. Jareb's grace gift for connecting spiritual realities to physiological data is a much-needed discipline in the church today because it helps Western Christians more easily embrace the supernatural. This book is a master class on intimacy with the Godhead and will surely bless the reader.

Dr. Rob Covell, DMin
Wagner University

We love to think about the Lord and contemplate his love and glory. Jareb Nott's book, *The Science of Supernatural Thinking,* provides a pioneering on ramp to connect with God in the exhilarating capacities of biblical meditation. Any serious reader of the Scriptures readily acknowledges God's call to this form of communion with Him. Biblical meditation is one of His most powerful weapons. But until now, the whole subject has seemed "without form and void," shrouded in darkness for the majority of believers. The enemy loves to steal the Lord's most effective weapons. But God commissioned this book to bring clarity and understanding with a holy fire that separates light from darkness. Thank you, Jareb, for a sound approach to restoring one of the Lord's sweetest gifts—with healing and deliverance saturating the very pages!

Jon & Jolene Hamill
Lamplighter Ministries
Washington DC

There are so many powerful Kingdom principles that I believe the church has abandoned. We've been deceived into thinking that certain practices were first implemented by the occult or by the devil. The principle and practice of meditation is one of those. In this book, *The Science of Supernatural Thinking,* Jareb Nott takes us on a journey through the Scriptures, current scientific research, and his personal testimony to lay out what I believe to be an irrefutable treatise to the life-changing power of meditation. I believe the Lord has mantled Jareb in this era to be one of the voices He has empowered to restore lost Kingdom treasures to the church; I believe *The Science of Supernatural Thinking* is one of those Kingdom treasures.

Anthony Turner
Destiny Ministries International

JAREB NOTT

the SCIENCE *of* SUPERNATURAL THINKING

How Biblical Meditation
Fills Your Life with the Peace,
Power, and Purpose of Heaven

DESTINY IMAGE® PUBLISHERS, INC.
P.O. Box 310, Shippensburg, PA 17257-0310

"Publishing cutting-edge prophetic resources to supernaturally empower the body of Christ"

This book and all other Destiny Image and Destiny Image Fiction books are available at Christian bookstores and distributors worldwide.

For more information on foreign distributors, call 717-532-3040.

Reach us on the Internet: www.destinyimage.com.

ISBN 13 TP: 978-0-7684-7694-1

ISBN 13 eBook: 978-0-7684-7695-8

For Worldwide Distribution, Printed in the U.S.A.

1 2 3 4 5 6 7 8 / 28 27 26 25 24

DEDICATION

I want to dedicate this project to my beloved family, who made tremendous sacrifices to make it a reality. My wife, Petra, and my three children, Joash, Judah, and Moriah, deserve special recognition for their unwavering support. I understand that I was absent for four months during the project, and I am grateful for your kindness and patience as each of you listened to and advised me on various concepts in this book. I cannot express how much I appreciate your understanding and assistance. I love you all.

ACKNOWLEDGMENTS

Undertaking a major project always necessitates assistance from others. This book project is a perfect example of that concept. Though I may have written the words, I couldn't have brought this book to life without the incredible people who worked alongside me and supported me. Their help and support were invaluable in making this project a success, and I'm grateful for their contributions.

My family played an indispensable role in supporting me during prolonged writing periods. My fantastic wife went through each and every draft of this manuscript with a fine-tooth comb, providing invaluable feedback and corrections along the way. With her support, I was able to achieve what I did! My children, who fully understood the project and tasks I was working on, patiently waited for completion before demanding a vacation. Joash, Judah, and Moriah were frequently part of my testing group. We would all practice together as I introduced meditation ideas, concepts, and methods. It was a great time of learning to meditate and rest together and demonstrate the power of the presence of the Holy Spirit with my children.

Thanks to the unwavering commitment of my intercessors, Joyce Nicodin, Kara Puckett, and Jane Suits, and the power of prayer, this project had a blessed journey. Though he tried, the enemy could not interrupt this message.

I am genuinely grateful to Becca Greenwood, whose prophetic words over me have led me to this moment. She prophesied and imparted in me the capacity to host the glory and presence of the Holy Spirit during Awakening the Wells of Revival in Kansas City 2021. I am thankful for her friendship and leadership all these years.

To everyone at Christian Harvest Training Center and Engage Ministries: You supported me well as we walked together through this journey of understanding and re-learning the ancient principles of biblical meditation. I believe we all have experienced new heights and new depths in our experiences with the Holy Spirit. Thank you all for your support and prayers.

CONTENTS

SECTION THREE
PRACTICAL GUIDES *for* MEDITATION
− 219 −

FOREWORD

*Finally, brethren, whatsoever things are true, whatsoever
things are honorable, whatsoever things are just,
whatsoever things are pure, whatsoever things are lovely,
whatsoever things are of good report; if there be any
virtue, and if there be any praise, think on these things*
(Philippians 4:8, American Standard Version).

Peace involves the heart and the mind. To experience God's peace, freedom, and supernatural thinking, we must do what Paul teaches. The Greek word used for *think* in this verse is *logizomai*. It means "to reason about, ponder, think on, reflect on." It implies concentrated, focused effort (Strong's #G3049). Paul is telling us that we must intentionally fix our minds on those things that reflect the truth of who God is and what He thinks about us, His dearly loved children.

This means we are to think on whatever is reliable and honest. We must direct our attention to the noble, those things that are worthy of respect. We are to meditate on what is righteous—that which conforms to God's standards and which merits approval. We need to uphold all that is pure, those things that are moral and chaste. We are called to see the lovely—all that is pleasing and agreeable—and to behold what is admirable and worthy of praise.

The following quote by Ralph Waldo Emerson creates a profound picture of what can develop in our lives as a result of what we choose to think or meditate on:

> *Sow a thought, reap an action.*
>
> *Sow an action, reap a habit.*
>
> *Sow a habit, reap a character.*
>
> *Sow a character, reap a destiny!*[1]

The prophet Isaiah tells us how to prepare our minds to sow right thoughts, where we are then empowered and aligned to walk a life supernaturally blessed in His perfect and constant peace: *"You will guard him and keep him in perfect and constant peace whose mind [both its inclination and its character] is stayed on You, because he commits himself to You, leans on You, and hopes confidently in You"* (Isaiah 26:3, Amplified Bible). The Hebrew word for *stayed* is *samak*. It means "to sustain, uphold, support, to cause a state to continue and to have a focus on whatever is necessary to remain in that state" (Strong's #H5564).

These are powerful scriptural and spiritual truths. Friends, our minds, our thoughts, what we believe and hold true must be stayed on Him. Why? When we welcome Holy Spirit into our time of studying His Word, our times of worship, and our times of prayer and intercession, He empowers and gives us the increased capacity within His presence to set our minds on good things, on the truth of God's Word, and on God Himself. Here is where we will experience the beauty and greatness of who He is, and our minds, thoughts, souls, and bodies

---

1.   Ralph Waldo Emerson as quoted in Stephen R. Covey, *The 7 Habits of Highly Effective People: Powerful Lessons in Personal Change* (New York: RosettaBooks, 2013).

encounter perfect peace. Not only that, but we will be strengthened to walk according to His Word in our full identity as sons and daughters of our Heavenly Father, no matter how many obstacles are set in our way.

Jesus teaches us in John 15:

> *Dwell in Me, and I will dwell in you. [Live in Me and I will live in you.] Just as no branch can bear fruit of itself without abiding in (being vitally united to) the vine, neither can you bear fruit unless you abide in Me* (John 15:4 AMPC).

> *If you live in Me [abide vitally united to Me] and My words remain in you and continue to live in your hearts, ask whatever you will, and it shall be done for you* (John 15:7 AMPC).

Upon hearing the word *abide*, our minds quickly go to the normal steps we have been taught and know to be true. But let's take a closer look at this word, *abide*. As Jareb shares, the Greek word is *meno*. It means "to remain, dwell, continue, endure, not to depart from, to continue to be present (continually), to be held and kept" (Strong's #G3306). In other words, when we abide, we become so in tune with His presence from the dedicated times of entering beyond the veil and encountering Him in His Word, greatness, presence, and glory that we grow into the ability to remain in existence with Him. We know who we are in Him. He is very real and close to us. We are not separate or apart but vitally united. The following is an incredible promise that Jesus shared:

> *No one has greater love [no one has shown stronger affection] than to lay down (give up) his own life for his friends. You are My friends if you keep on doing the things which I command you to do. I do not call you servants (slaves) any longer, for*

*the servant does not know what his master is doing (working
out). But I have called you My friends, because I have made
known to you everything that I have heard from My Father.
[I have revealed to you everything that I have learned from
Him.] You have not chosen Me, but I have chosen you and I
have appointed you [I have planted you], that you might go
and bear fruit and keep on bearing, and that your fruit may
be lasting [that it may remain, abide], so that whatever you
ask the Father in My Name [as presenting all that I AM],
He may give it to you* (John 15:13-16 AMPC).

Such an awesome Kingdom promise. He is stating that you and I
can be vitally united to Him, His friends to whom He reveals everything. I believe He hears all of our prayers. The beautiful truth is when
we are vitally united to Him, we come into unison and agreement with
His heart over a matter.

My husband, Greg, clearly states, "We are in a language war." And
this is so very true. We are also in a spiritual war. You see, the enemy
comes to kill, steal, and destroy. And he has truly acted as the illegal
squatter in twisting and robbing our understanding of what scriptural
meditation is and how we are to intentionally engage in our Kingdom
of Heaven inheritance of supernatural thinking, living, and healing. As
we read and meditate on the Scriptures—as we encounter Him—our
Heavenly Father affirms His word to us, confirming His truth to our
hearts. As He does so, He affirms us with His words, His love, His presence, and His healing.

Jareb has done a wonderful job scripturally and biblically laying a
true foundation on supernatural thinking and meditation. He has
created solid avenues through Scripture to explore our Kingdom inheritance in drawing close to Him through meditating on His truths, His
Word, His presence, His holiness, His love, His healing, and His greatness. And as a result, we are welcomed and ushered into a dynamic,

life-altering, spiritual awakening and intimate relationship with the Lord. That which is made evident and manifest in our spirit, mind, body, will, and emotions. Let's begin the journey of learning about meditation as Jareb clearly teaches what it is, what Scripture reveals to us concerning meditation, and the transforming benefits and healing awaiting each of us on this journey.

Rebecca Greenwood
Cofounder Christian Harvest International
Strategic Prayer Apostolic Network
International Freedom Group
Christian Harvest Training Center
Author of *Defeating Strongholds of the Mind, Glory Warfare,*
and *Discerning the Spirit Realm*

SECTION ONE

FOUNDATIONS *of* BIBLICAL MEDITATION

MIRACLES *of* DESTINY

Surrender your anxiety! Be still and realize that I am God.
I am God above all the nations... (Psalm 46:10 TPT).

The Bible no longer commands us to meditate. However, when we come across an instruction to cast off anxiety and be still, we pause to recognize the weight of the message and its intent. And rather than abiding by the practice of the law, biblical meditation becomes a choice as we partner with God's greatest commandment to love God and to love each other, as recorded in Matthew 22:33-40. Our meditation becomes a partnership with that command, and we now meditate in alignment with the great commandment.

Psalm 46:10 begins to lay the foundational message of biblical meditation. We are encouraged here to surrender, be still, and focus our thoughts on God's greatness. The words *be still* comes from the word *raphah,* and in this context means to sink down, to relax, and hang limp.[1] This is a picture of our purposeful meditative posture before God. The word *realize* or *know* in other translations comes from the word *yada,* meaning to acknowledge, to be aware, and to be concerned with.[2] Our meditative approach will always be to focus our thoughts on God and His goodness, then partner with Him in our pursuit of His revelation in our lives, which brings restoration, vitality, energy, and healing.

MY MIRACLE

During the writing of this book, I found myself sitting in my doctor's office for an annual physical, something that many of us do to maintain our optimum performance. This was just like any other visit. I waited and waited and waited. Once the doctor entered, it was all fairly routine: the same questions, the same tests, and the same instructions, including a typical blood test. I completed the exam with flying colors, and like usual, we said goodbye and good riddance to each other until next year. I felt pretty good and moved on with my day.

Three hours later, my phone rang. It was the doctor's office. I was hesitant to answer because I was knee-deep into a busy day and did not figure that the doctor's office had anything important to tell me. I assumed it had something to do with billing or medications, but I answered the phone anyway. The nurse on the other end was dry and quick to the point. "Mr. Nott, your blood glucose levels were dangerously high, and we need to see you again right away because you have diabetes." *Wow!* I thought, *What a great way to introduce a difficult topic to someone.* Anyway, I scheduled an appointment to see the doctor again the next morning at her urging.

Here I am again, sitting in the doctor's office, waiting to be seen. This time, the doctor sat down and began to explain that I am now one among 37.3 million other Americans who have type 2 diabetes.[3] He asked if I had any questions. I sat in stunned silence and with a blank mind. I had no questions. I sat with absolutely no idea how something like this could happen to me. There must be a mistake, and I thought this did not make sense. There must be an environmental or some other natural explanation. Yet that day, I walked out with a piece of paper that said I was diabetic. I was also prescribed a healthy new medication concoction to go with my diagnosis. My mind was swirling, and I needed time to think and seek understanding. I was shaken, but also, I was convinced that this diagnosis was not my destiny. I have witnessed and experienced the healing power of God, and I have learned too much about how the spiritual realm operates to accept this as the next step in the aging process. In a later chapter, I will detail several things that I immediately began doing in order to manifest my complete healing.

Why am I telling this story? What does diabetes have in common with biblical meditation? As you will soon learn, meditation is a big part of a healthy spiritual and physical lifestyle. I received my total healing, and I received it prior to the completion of this book and without taking any of the pharmaceuticals recommended for this disease. I practiced biblical meditation and breathwork along with physical activity and proper eating, and my healing arrived.

The following chart shows the exact moment my healing was manifested in my life. In a literal instant, I was healed. The dramatic dip seen in this image represents the levels of glucose in my body normalizing at 3 p.m. on May 6, 2023, and was later confirmed by an A1C test confounding my doctor.[4]

DESTINY

I have been practicing and teaching biblical meditation for many years. It's a strange story of destiny that took me on a journey of awakening in my spirit, my mind, and my body. I was raised, like many believers, with a doctrine and worldview that disallowed anything that had the appearance of evil. If a belief or practice was not fully biblically grounded, it was not given a second thought. So naturally, things like drugs, pornography, and anything having to do with any form of witch-craft are some of what God rightly disallows for believers. Engaging in those practices invites the demonic realm through open doors in our lives and our generational lineage. Consequently, these open doors grant the tormenting demons the legal right to set up residence within the temple of God, our minds, and bodies.

However, there are biblical topics among believers that are well documented in Scripture yet are not afforded much, if any, attention in the body of Christ. Meditation and our supernatural thought life is one such topic and is the journey on which we will engage together in this book. Many of us, myself included, were raised to believe that the practice of meditation was directly associated with various antichristian and atheistic religions throughout the world. And sadly, in most cases, that's true.

Many religions around the globe incorporate meditation into daily worship as part of their growth or enlightenment rituals. It is because of the adoption of the practice of meditation into these religious cultures that Christianity has disregarded the practice of all forms of meditation. We should recognize, however, that the Bible speaks extensively concerning the practice of meditation in daily living. David wrote in Psalms many times concerning his personal experiences with meditation and even provided us with a road map by which to learn from him in his meditations. In a later chapter, I will address the Davidic meditation model from the book of Psalms.

The principle of biblical meditation exists in Scripture and is confirmed by research. Meditation is necessary, fundamental, and vitally important for the body of Christ to align our thoughts and engage with the Holy Spirit as we pursue the depths of God's Kingdom naturally and supernaturally. Meditation combined with a supernatural thought life is the key that unlocks the manifestation of glory and the presence of God within the personal lives of each believer.

Find your delight and true pleasure in Yahweh, and he will give you what you desire the most (Psalm 37:4 TPT).

The Bible contains so much wisdom on the procedures of meditation that we cannot set it aside and relegate it under the auspices of prayer. The practice of meditation is not the same as prayer or intercession, and I will demonstrate the core differences and importance of each as you read on. My hope is that through this teaching, more believers will come to see the gift of biblical meditation, enrich their abiding time, and experience a new dimension of freedom in God's Kingdom.

Meditation, when approached from a biblical worldview and practiced with the guidance of the Holy Spirit, will lead you to physical healing and spiritual freedom. Recalling my testimony, you might be thinking, what does meditation have to do with diabetes and lowering blood glucose levels? That's a fair question, and the answer may surprise you. In 2018, a six-month study was published through the National Library of Medicine concerning the effect of meditation and its direct impact on blood glucose levels. The study concluded that "there is a significant decrease in the blood sugar and glycosylated hemoglobin levels in patients practicing meditation for a period of 6 months and [a] significant increase in fasting serum insulin levels in patients not practicing meditation."[5]

This study, and many others like it, demonstrates the connection between our bodies and our spiritual health. These studies were not performed using any biblical approach. Quite the opposite, these studies used widely accepted forms of meditation, thus proving the principles of meditation work despite the religious association. How much more effective will meditation be when practiced from a biblical worldview and while in alignment with the Holy Spirit's guidance? The healing I have received is due in part to a lifestyle of biblical meditation.

You will read how a meditation lifestyle helps heal the body, and you will also read how it heals the mind, reduces stress and anxiety, and welcomes the peace of the Holy Spirit. You will also learn how biblical meditation will elevate your relationship with God. You will hear God's voice in a new way, with more clarity and understanding than ever before.

Are you waiting for an answer? Do you have a tough dilemma? Approaching God through biblical meditation will fine-tune your mind to hear His voice more accurately.

HE'S MINE!

In 2012, I was standing in the basement of a shop well known for its occult and pagan associations. The store's purpose was the sale of paraphernalia and teaching of occultic and satanic practices. I was there for reconnaissance, to gather information to be used later in prayer. Suddenly, while observing a display cabinet filled with different types of incense, I heard a nearly audible voice say to me, "This is what I had planned for you." The voice I heard was clearly not the Holy Spirit, and the implication was that an assignment was placed on my life to entice me into the dark power of the enemy.

I knew instantly that by the blood of Jesus, I had escaped the snare of the enemy. Engaging in occultic practices is not only forbidden, but it serves as an invitation into our lives for the demonic and the resulting torment. Those who engage in all forms of witchcraft actively invite the demonic to take residence in and torment what is designed to be the temple of the Holy Spirit.

> *In whom the whole structure, being joined together, grows*
> *into a holy temple in the Lord. In him, you also are being*

built together into a dwelling place for God by the Spirit (Ephesians 2:21-22 ESV).

After hearing those words, I felt the presence of the Holy Spirit and the assurance that came when He replied, "He's redeemed, and he's Mine." Right and true biblical meditation will supernaturally tune your thoughts and bring your mind, will, and emotions into alignment with the Holy Spirit.

As we move through this book, I will demonstrate how meditation and a supernatural thought life are both biblical and backed by modern science as a benefit to our lives. I will show that meditation can enhance your quality of life, healing in your body, peace to your mind and heart, and a deeper relationship with God our Father. Many of the insights throughout this book are directly acquired by way of the Holy Spirit's voice in my life through meditation and prayer.

As I began many years ago to learn as much as I could about this topic, I soon realized that the only sources of knowledge came from people who do not believe in Jesus and have no desire to pursue a relationship. I could not incorporate wisdom from these practitioners and thus began my own learning journey with the Holy Spirit teaching me and guiding me in the proper and most freeing aspects of meditation.

I do not cast off all secular knowledge of meditation, however. So much scientific research has been done in this field that demonstrates its effectiveness that it cannot be ignored. I have invested hours spent with the Holy Spirit and buried in deep research to compile techniques that you now hold in your hand. You will see that research aligns with what we already hold true from Scripture. The Bible needs no confirmation. It stands on its own and always will. Yet, the evidence provided through modern technology increases our faith and enables us to understand biblical application more effectively.

NO COMPROMISE

While meditation is wholly biblical and meant for use by all believers, the world has already perfected an understanding of demonically influenced "enlightenment" meditation. The religions of the world incorporate various techniques to achieve higher levels of consciousness, transcendence, enlightenment, and states of physical being. One example is the four spiritual exercises compiled by the founder of the Jesuit order, Don Inigo Lopez, and currently accepted by many as a pure approach to meditation.[6] These meditative exercises were given to him through demonic inspiration over many months while in solitude in a cave in Spain.[7] This is an example of compromise and mixing the holy with the profane. I will not accept any form of meditation that does not agree with the entirety of the Bible. Meditation originating from practices such as those commonly found in Buddhism, Hinduism, or the New Age cannot be redeemed.[8]

While I reject meditation practices from these ungodly religions, I also recognize that the rudimentary principles of meditation exist and are fundamentally proper, biblical, and effective in spite of demonic influence.

Above all, let our meditations bring glory to God. As you read these pages, I challenge you to a meditative and supernatural thought life enhanced, enriched, and manifesting renewal, joy, healing, and peace that only comes through a deep relationship with the Holy Spirit.

Now, please take a deep *Ruach* breath, let it out slowly, and let's get started.

BIBLICAL MEDITATION—
FOUNDATION *for*
SUPERNATURAL THINKING

This Book of the Law shall not depart from your mouth,
but you shall meditate on it day and night so that you
may be careful to do according to all that is written in
it. For then you will make your way prosperous, and
then you will have good success (Joshua 1:8 ESV).

The Bible contains an abundance of references central to the practice of meditation. So many that God provided us with a road map concerning its exercise. A road map that fully connects us to embrace the intimate, one on one, pure, profound relationship with the Father. Each meditative encounter brings us into the throne room and envelops us with the glory of God. These encounters are precious and deeply personal, leading to personal growth, healing, and inward and outward restoration of our minds and bodies. Through the years, I have compiled more than 250 passages in Scripture relating to the practice of meditation and the directive of maintaining a healthy thought life.

In Joshua 1:8, God issued the command to meditate on the law day and night. He promised a result of prosperity and good success. We are no longer under the law since Jesus made a new covenant for us, yet the principle of meditation lives on because God first established it. As believers in Christ, we are now living in the fulfillment of the promise made to Joshua. To experience this rest and success, we must give our all and eagerly engage in meditation. This helps us stay away from doubt and unbelief, which can corrupt the thought life of God's children.

Now if this promise of "rest" was fulfilled when Joshua brought the people into the land, God wouldn't have spoken later of another "rest" yet to come. So we conclude that there is still a full and complete "rest" waiting for believers to experience. As we enter into God's faith-rest life we cease from our own works, just as God celebrates His finished works and rests in them.

> *So then we must* [give our all and] *be eager to experience this faith-rest life, so that no one falls short by following the same pattern of doubt and unbelief* (Hebrews 4:11 TPT).

The practice of meditation is often misunderstood and even disregarded because of the relationship it holds in our world as either belonging to New Age, Buddhist, or Hindu spiritual practices. Despite its extensive biblical and historical connection, meditation remains uncharted territory for pragmatic Christianity. Believers should only undertake a prayer assignment of uncharted spiritual territory after receiving a direct mandate from God. The difference with meditation is not that it is altogether uncharted. Instead, it is unknown and misunderstood.

Many books and researched theologians and pastors have attempted to provide the church with guidance on the topic of meditation. A cursory search for Christian-based guidance on meditation reveals literature that proposes to define and explain the boundaries of biblical meditation while providing safe advice and instruction. These well-meaning practices only serve as a starting point but rarely expand into meaningful, mindful thoughts or more profound meditative moments with the Holy Spirit. I will not blur the lines to redeem Buddhism or any other ungodly religious practice. Yet, we must be willing to go deeper into the fullness of what God intended meditation to be. We will remain faithful to biblical standards, and as God promises, we will be prosperous and successful.

This book is the result of an assignment God gave me when He revealed to me how satan had asserted control and brought corruption where Kingdom purity and power once dominated. Meditation is one principle in God's Kingdom that has been hijacked, counterfeited, secularized, and fully integrated into the strategies of the enemy. Why? Because the practice of meditation is robust to the believer and is one of the most incredible ways to walk in freedom and wellness, bring glory to God, and deepen the relationship with the Holy Spirit. No wonder satan has worked so hard to corrupt and eliminate the practice from churches.

It would be like taking everyone's cell phone away and proclaiming that cell phones are only for non-believers to connect with and receive enlightenment from the spirits of cell phone towers. It's a limited power, but power, nonetheless, because meditation is a Kingdom principle. Whereas believers should not only have cell phones but also use them to communicate with the ultimate Authority, the Creator of the entire system. This is an analogy, but we must look further at how satan's power works, so we can understand better how meditation became so corrupted.

LUCIFER'S LIMITED POWER

God created satan as Lucifer, a high-ranking angel who carried significant power and authority in the Kingdom of God. Lucifer was designed to fulfill a role within God's divine plan:

> *You were an anointed guardian cherub. I placed you; you were on the holy mountain of God; in the midst of the stones of fire you walked. You were blameless in your ways from the day you were created, till unrighteousness was found in you* (Ezekiel 28:14-15 ESV).

Lucifer's title and role afforded him significant power granted to him by God Himself. His power was a pure form, created to bring glory to God and to fulfill his purpose within God's ultimate plan. The Bible does not explicitly outline the scope of Lucifer's power. But we can ascertain from Scripture that Lucifer and now satan wields the following powers:

- Authority and influence as a high-ranking angel and anointed cherub (Ezekiel 28:14).

- Beauty and splendor as being full of wisdom, perfect in beauty, captivating and charismatic (Ezekiel 28:12).

- Music and worship were created within him, implying that he was a worship leader built for praising God (Ezekiel 28:13).

It is important to note here that the fall of Lucifer, due to his own rebellion, did not entirely strip him of his power and authority but instead corrupted them. Satan's reign is now limited to operating within the kingdom of darkness—and the good news is that God has dramatically diminished his power.

He disarmed the rulers and authorities and put them to open shame, by triumphing over them in him (Colossians 2:15 ESV).

While his power was greatly diminished, he also retained an amount of authority within the realm of darkness. He is the "god of this world" and the "prince of the power of the air." This limited authority allows satan to exert his influence and promote his deception to deceive humanity.

In their case the god of this world has blinded the minds of the unbelievers, to keep them from seeing the light of the gospel of the glory of Christ, who is the image of God (2 Corinthians 4:4 ESV).

And you were dead in the trespasses and sins in which you once walked, following the course of this world, following the prince of the power of the air, the spirit that is now at work in the sons of disobedience (Ephesians 2:1-2 ESV).

As we continue to discuss this topic, understand that satan is an expert manipulator who has used his ability to influence and deceive. That manipulation and influence is precisely what he has sought after and primarily accomplished concerning meditation and the thought life of many believers. Satan and his demonic forces can only manipulate humanity through suggestion and thoughts, making our thought life the foremost battleground.

THE BATTLEGROUND OF THE MIND

God endowed humanity with the capacity to think, reason, and make decisions. Meditation aligns our thoughts with God's and propels us forward in our pursuit of living according to Jesus's example. Our thoughts are where satan and his demonic forces wage war. Because of satan's limited power and authority, he is reduced to influence and dominance over the minds and thoughts of God's children, believers and non-believers. Knowing this, we can even see how mental illness is such a devastating problem in our society, affecting more than eighteen million adults each year in America. It is the leading cause of depression-based disabilities leading to suicide.[9]

All people have the capacity to be extraordinary in God's Kingdom. Satan's demonic forces are highly tuned to this fact and specifically target thoughts, hearts, and minds because of our capacity to disrupt the kingdom of darkness and bring glory to God.

The Bible has taught us to take every thought captive, destroy arguments and lofty opinions, be transformed by the renewing of our minds, and center our thoughts on righteousness. This control over our thought life is important because, as previously mentioned, this is where satan's attacks are focused in the lives of humanity.

> *But I am afraid that as the serpent deceived Eve by his cunning, your thoughts will be led astray from a sincere and pure devotion to Christ* (2 Corinthians 11:3 ESV).

Paul, in his second letter to the Corinthians, expressed his fear over how easily the thought life of the people can be influenced by the demonic. So much so that he acknowledged how they had been deceived already by saying, *"For if someone comes and proclaims another Jesus than the one we proclaimed...you put up with it readily enough"* (2

Corinthians 11:4 ESV). These Scriptures all confirm that satan can and does manipulate thoughts to draw people away from truth and understanding.

That said, the good news is the Bible defines the strategy for our thoughts and how to stop the enemy's advance on our minds. This book details that strategy, instructing you in making meditative practices a natural part of your life. We will cover the following areas and much more:

- Spend time with God's word (Deuteronomy 11:18; Psalm 119:11).

- Practice renewing the mind, reject lies of the enemy, and always allow God to adjust our beliefs (Romans 12:2).

- Do not be anxious. Pray and meditate with thanksgiving, and peace will guard our hearts and minds. Focus your thoughts on all things righteous (Philippians 4:6-8).

- Actively take every thought captive and destroy every idea antithesis to God (2 Corinthians 10:5).

- Guard your heart and mind because everything comes from them (Proverbs 4:23).

- Maintain a steadfast mind and trust in the Lord (Isaiah 26:3).

- Focus our minds on things of heaven (Colossians 3:2).

- Always seek guidance from the Holy Spirit (John 14:26).

As we have discussed and will further demonstrate, we persistently guard our minds and hearts through biblical meditation and a deliberate focus concerning all things righteous. Through the practice of meditation, deliverance, and inner healing, we renew our minds and become transformed inwardly and outwardly, stepping into our rightful identity. The enemy's currency is lies and wrong beliefs.

Discarding false beliefs and coming out of agreement with the lies brings renewal, healing, and total transformation. Then we take every thought captive, replacing it with the truth, and make it obedient to Christ. In the book of Psalms, David's writings provide us with a meditative strategy. Our meditation should focus on God's wonderful works, His statutes, promises, mighty deeds, and His ways. This focus on God is how we intentionally guard our minds against demonic corruption and focus on righteousness. Scientific findings concerning our thoughts support the biblical model by demonstrating how the way we think affects our worldview and our physical, emotional, and spiritual selves:

> Our brain contains a massive network of nerve cells...connecting across synapses. Those neural connections both are how we think and shape how we think. Those connections produce memories of the past, and predict the future; we can think of these memories and predictions as stories. Those stories inform how we see the world and act within it, including how we pursue our goals.[10]

BIBLICAL MEDITATION DEFINITION

Let us begin with a definition of biblical meditation. I have practiced biblical meditation for many years and gained the experiential knowledge to understand what meditation is. I have meditated, prayed, and sought after God's heart concerning this topic. As I studied the Bible and vast amounts of literature, a biblically informed and God-inspired definition for all believers began to take shape. This definition will establish the foundation and set guidance for how we proceed.

Biblical meditation is the intentional, private, and intimate act of thinking and being—a moment to quietly listen and engage with the Holy Spirit, emotions, and thoughts. Meditation is an act of worship, surrendering the entirety of our person to be enveloped by the majestic glory of God. Meditation is a release of all anguish, pain, trauma, and sorrow, welcoming the flood of God's love and grace, which brings healing, restoration, and total transformation to the mind, body, and spirit. Meditation creates a stillness and quiets the mind and body, providing the richness and depth of connection with the Holy Spirit. Meditation builds us up and creates space for the Holy Spirit to speak truth and guidance. He takes us to the mountain of the Lord to be still and realize that He is God, He is love; and in meditation, His glory becomes a tangible garment surrounding us as we draw deeper and closer to Him. Meditation primes the pump for unhindered two-way communication with God as He reveals His plans and purposes to each of us, ultimately strengthening, healing, and renewing our mind, body, and spirit and paving the way for us as we seek to model Jesus.

In short, *meditation is an intentional moment of stillness within our mind and body, focusing on our thoughts and the Holy Spirit, resulting in mental and physical transformation.* The word *meditate* comes from two Hebrew words *hagah* and *siah*. Siah means to meditate, muse, commune, complain and to ponder. *Hagah* means to muse, consider, and ponder with wonder and elation often while making a sound.[11] In meditation, we intentionally create space and time to give thoughtful attention to our minds. We muse on the things within our lives that we are working toward or problems we are attempting to solve. We ponder the possibilities of what could be, and we learn from the decisions of the past. These holy contemplations build stories in our minds stored as thoughts, awaiting fulfillment as we ponder with wonder and elation the glorious things of God in our lives and the lives of those we love.

This act of meditation is further understood as an utterance or a sound originating from deep within the soul as David often demonstrated throughout the book of Psalms. I will address the topic of sound later. Suffice it to say that we are encouraged to engage with the Holy Spirit through the gift of tongues, song, or an utterance. These words appear in Scripture so many times that it becomes evident that the practice of meditation and the practices of *hagah* and *siah* are to be incorporated into the daily lives of all believers.

This process can be described as divine contemplation, which means we intentionally focus our minds and align our thoughts to Heaven. When we do, we are actively inviting and allowing the Holy Spirit to navigate our flow of ideas and emotions in a transformative way, bringing new life and purpose. The great stoic Aristotle argued that contemplation is proper to humans and devoid of divine influence.[12] This argument assumes that when we think, we are essentially satiating our own selfish needs and emotional stability. If we believe the Bible is accurate, and we do, then we can apply scriptural evidence to the contrary.

> *For who knows a person's thoughts except the spirit of that person, which is in him? So also no one comprehends the thoughts of God except the Spirit of God. Now we have received not the spirit of the world, but the Spirit who is from God, that we might understand the things freely given us by God* (1 Corinthians 2:11-12 ESV).

As believers in Christ, we are indwelt with His Holy Spirit, guiding us through His never-ending presence in our lives. When we invite His guidance and turn our attention to Him, our thoughts cannot help but become saturated with His thoughts. His presence shapes the stories we build in our minds during meditation.

> *Delight yourself in the Lord, and he will give you the desires of your heart* (Psalm 37:4 ESV).

When we meditate on the things of God, we tune our flow of thoughts to Him. As we do, He begins to unfold the longings and desires within us as meditative contemplations. The Hebrew word for *delight* is *anog,* which means to gently and delicately take pleasure in your identity as He unfolds your inheritance as a child of God.[13] The atheist approach of stoic philosophers is hereby rejected, choosing instead to rely entirely on the Word of God in our lives, proved through experiences and encounters with our Lord. It is my desire that through this book, you will encounter Jesus through right and proper meditation that brings you closer to the throne room and brings healing and transformation to your mind, body, and spirit.

IS IT OKAY FOR CHRISTIANS TO MEDITATE?

I hope you have seen by now that meditation as a practice is not only permissible for Christian believers but necessary for our continued growth, health, and sustained relationship with the Holy Spirit. Meditation is not evil, nor does it belong to the enemy. However, the enemy has stolen and counterfeited the purity and power for secular gain. Today, in the secular, non-believing world, meditation is used to "create a healthy space between you and your thoughts and emotions." Yet another secular definition states that "meditation provides a moment in time where you are focused on the here and now."[14]

These definitions are not fundamentally wrong. Yet they are missing one of the most important aspects of what meditation provides us. A direct connection to the throne room of Heaven, a relationship with the Holy Spirit, which provides the foundation for how to handle the here and now, process emotions, and plan for the future. Yes, meditation is for every believer, and the Bible has created boundaries for us and a framework from which to get started. Let us take a deeper look at the notable verse in Philippians.

> *Rejoice in the Lord always. I will say it again: Rejoice! Let your gentleness be evident to all. The Lord is near. Do not be anxious about anything, but in every situation, by prayer and petition, with thanksgiving, present your requests to God. And the peace of God, which transcends all understanding, will guard your hearts and your minds in Christ Jesus. Finally, brothers and sisters, whatever is true, whatever is noble, whatever is right, whatever is pure, whatever is lovely, whatever is admirable—if anything is excellent or praiseworthy—think about such things. Whatever you have learned or received or heard from me, or seen in me—put it into practice. And the God of peace will be with you* (Philippians 4:4-9 NIV).

As we break down this Scripture passage, understand there is no linear approach or rule. The important thing is to flow in your meditation with freedom.

- Rejoice with joy and thankfulness. "I love You, Lord. I thank You for Your presence, and I thank You for aligning my thoughts with Yours as I meditate with You."

- Invite the peace of God, which dispels all stress and anxiety. As we focus our thoughts and breath, peace begins to fall.

"Holy Spirit, I welcome the tangible manifestation of Your Spirit. Join me now."

- Tune your thoughts and surrender all ideas that disagree with your identity or with Scripture. Instead, choose to intentionally train your thoughts on all things pure, right, excellent, praiseworthy, lovely, admirable, and noble. (PREPLAN your thoughts.)

- You may expect to hear directly from the voice of God; He will teach you and reveal answers for which you've been searching. He may also allow you to rest in perfect peace, soaking up the presence of the Holy Spirit.

- Perfect peace is reached when you fully surrender all thoughts and invite Him to shape your mindsets.

David, whom I consider the expert meditator, detailed his meditations so precisely that we have a beautiful framework for our meditation from which we will learn. I will provide the Davidic model for meditation later in this book. Let me now, though, explain David's meditative approach in various psalms.

"May my meditation be pleasing to him, as I rejoice in the Lord" (Psalm 104:34 ESV). David begins his meditations with an attitude of humility and a desire to bring glory to God.

> *I said, "I will watch my ways and keep my tongue from sin;*
> *I will put a muzzle on my mouth while in the presence of the*
> *wicked"* (Psalm 39:1 NIV).

David begins with focus, aligning his thoughts rightly, *"I will watch my ways...."* He moves into the quietness of mind and speech, *"I will put a muzzle on my mouth while in the presence of the wicked."* He acknowledges his thoughts are wicked and must be brought into obedience.

Psalm 39:2 (NIV), *"So I remained utterly silent, not even saying any-thing good. But my anguish increased."* David approaches his meditation with silence, *"I remained utterly silent."* But then he acknowledges his increasing anguish to the Lord.

Psalm 39:3 (NIV), *"my heart grew hot within me. While I meditated, the fire burned; then I spoke with my tongue:"* His thoughts became passionate within him, so intense that he felt the need to release his voice. This example of vocalizing during meditation is typical and encouraged. It is never healthy to suppress emotions, and meditation is a healthy outlet for those utterances. Notice that David released his anguish with God.

Psalm 39:4 (NIV), *"Show me, Lord, my life's end and the number of my days; let me know how fleeting my life is."* David then vocalizes his anguish and submits them to God. In this way, God will gently counsel and will bring healing.

Psalm 40:1-3 (NIV), *"I waited patiently for the Lord; he turned to me and heard my cry. He lifted me out of the slimy pit, out of the mud and mire; he set my feet on a rock and gave me a firm place to stand. He put a new song in my mouth, a hymn of praise to our God. Many will see and fear the Lord and put their trust in him."* Finally, David returns to his quietness, waiting patiently on the Lord who lifted him up, built him up, and replaced his anguish with a song of praise and honor to God.

David further explains the topics he uses to focus his meditation. These are good places to begin for anyone new to biblical meditation:

- God's attributes: Psalm 103:8

- God's word and statutes: Psalm 119:15,78,99; Psalm 1:2

- God's mighty deeds and wonders: Psalm 119:27; Psalm 145:5

- Personal experiences and emotions: Psalm 39

- Sin and forgiveness: Psalm 51:1-7
- God's presence and refuge: Psalm 16:1,11
- God's promises: Psalm 119:148
- God's decrees: Psalm 119:23
- God's ways: Psalm 119:15

Engage deeper by pondering the following questions in your life:

- What are God's defining qualities that minister to you?
- What has He asked of you?
- What are you reading in Scripture that resonates?
- What has He done for you that seemed impossible?
- What are you currently experiencing?
- What are you thankful for?
- What areas do you need forgiveness?
- To whom do you need to extend forgiveness?
- Focus on the strength and goodness of God in your life.
- Find peace in the fact that you are redeemed as a born-again child of God.[15]
- What are God's promises and prophetic words? Both fulfilled and unfulfilled.
- What has God decreed in your life?
- What has God decreed for your purpose and next steps in life?
- Revel in His goodness and soak in the presence and glory of the Holy Spirit.

The Davidic model of meditation allows for freedom of emotions, thoughts, and expressions while focusing on the preceding list for alignment in thinking, restoration, and healing of the mind.

To directly answer the question, is it suitable for a Christian to meditate? My answer is a resounding YES! Not only is it okay, but I hope that as you make your way through this book, you will also see how important meditation is in the life of every believer. I have ministered to many hundreds of people throughout my ministry career. I have always had the pleasure of partnering with God as He brought healing into the lives of those I ministered to.

However, it was not until I began incorporating the principle of meditation that I began witnessing a higher-level breakthrough in people's lives. It was as though a barrier holding their thoughts and emotions down was suddenly released, and healing followed. Further, those who maintained a lifestyle of biblical meditation sustained their freedom far more significantly than those who returned to a normal lifestyle.

THE PRINCIPLE OF MEDITATION

Years ago, on a prayer assignment on a warm summer afternoon. I led a group of prayer warriors to visit and pray on location at a Tibetan Buddhist meditation temple in Colorado. There are numerous Buddhist temples in Colorado, and we saw as many as possible, but this visit was memorable. We parked our cars about a block away so that we could walk in while praying and blessing these monks to encounter the love of Jesus. We were shocked at what we encountered as we walked onto the property. Two monks with giant goofy grins walked out to meet us, beaming with joy and excitement. They shook our hands and greeted us warmly and with the traditional *namaste,* which means, "I salute the god within you"; it is a recognition of the divine light that is said to exist in all things. After removing our shoes, we were welcomed to come inside the temple. Once inside, we were quickly seated, and the monks sat around us.

One exceedingly kind monk named Yut took an interest and sat very close and began having conversations with us. We started to ask questions about the Buddhist tradition. I asked, "Who do Buddhists worship and pray to as God?" Having researched, I was prepared with a basic understanding that Buddhists do not believe in any deity or god. My inquiry was a leading question to discover why they pray if there is no god. I would not be disappointed.

Yut eagerly acknowledged my question, and as expected, he said, "As Buddhists, we do not believe in or acknowledge any deity or god. Alternatively, we are on a journey of enlightenment through the path of reincarnation."

"Very interesting," I acknowledged and went in for a follow-up question. "I have seen you pray; who do you pray to?"

He answered, "Buddhists pray to the image of Buddha, spiritual leaders, and other icons."

I said, "Okay," and looking confused, I asked, "So if you pray to the Buddha, is the Buddha god?"

"No," he responded and, seeing my confusion, attempted to explain. "The Buddha represents attained enlightenment. When we bow or pray before an image or statue of the Buddha, we must visualize enlightened qualities in our own hearts. This is because the Dharma object, statue, or image is nothing more than a symbol, regardless of its material or size. The one who bows and the one who is bowed to are both, by nature, empty."

"Very interesting." I acknowledged and continued questioning, "When you meditate, what do you focus on, and how do you become enlightened?"

Yut explained that "Meditations are a series of chants and mantras designed to focus the mind and clear out all distractions with the goal of eventually reaching enlightenment or awakening, which is known as the end of the cycle of death and rebirth, and ending what is known as *dukkha.*"

Dukkha is one of the four noble truths at the core of Buddhism and Buddhist meditation and essentially means life is suffering, anguish, and pain. There is little hope provided for the ending of *dukkha* aside from walking a perfect path of emptiness and living a life of works-based struggle. As we continued our visit, I was intrigued by these monks' warmth and welcoming nature. They were kind and gentle and radiated an unusual calmness that was very inviting to an undiscerning mind. They laughed and generally appeared to be having a wonderful time. Some of them were working, others were cooking, and most were milling around, paying little notice to our group. I was left with more questions.

How could a group of people whose primary belief is that life is suffering and there is little hope for reprieve outside of death be so happy? I had to know. I asked one last question: "How are you so happy, and where do you get your joy?"

Smiling, Yut said, "Through our meditation and chanting, we seek peace, fulfillment, and happiness on the journey of enlightenment and awakening."

That is remarkably interesting, I thought. I love our Buddhist friends and pray that they each receive an encounter with Jesus.

This story demonstrates one critical aspect of meditation. It proves that the practice of meditation exists as a principle of our world despite who is practicing or the focus and intent. Yut appeared happy and full of joy, yet the joy and happiness he was experiencing were not life-giving in his spirit. Nor can this joy last, as he intends to suppress the feelings of suffering and anguish to generate the emptiness required for his enlightenment. There can be no joy of the Lord, no focus on the promises of God, and no communication from the Holy Spirit, bringing lasting peace and comfort. Only striving and empty hope that suffering may eventually cease with enough effort.

Joy and happiness attained while focusing on the emptiness of life cannot produce life in our spirits. Yet for those to choose to meditate without the Holy Spirit, emptiness is sought after and is attainable only through a personal struggle. But God says He fills us up with joy, inspiration, hope, peace, fulfillment, and the power of the Holy Spirit.

> *Now may God, the* [inspiration and] *fountain of hope, fill you to overflowing with uncontainable joy and perfect peace as you trust in him. And may the power of the Holy Spirit continually surround your life with his super-abundance until you radiate with hope!* (Romans 15:13 TPT)

Becoming empty is a practice endorsed by the adversary. God's plans are to fill us completely with uncontainable joy that surrounds us and emanates from us, and because He bestows so much joy, it spills out of our lives, radiating the glory of God.

Amy Semple McPherson captured this concept best when she said, "What is my task? First of all, my task is to be pleasing to Christ. To be empty of self and be filled with Himself. To be filled with the Holy Spirit; to be led by the Holy Spirit."[16]

Research in the field of meditation has shown that long-term repeated meditation creates an environment where our behavioral traits are positively changed, resulting in lasting transformation. Qualities like gentleness, kindness, joy, general happiness, low stress, and increased tolerance become subject to conversion. These ongoing changes in the brain produce higher qualities of feeling, thinking, and acting.[17]

If you have ever encountered someone who exuded a calming peace that was inviting and created an atmosphere of peace, you know what I am referring to. The difference with secular meditation is that peace is not a lasting peace that comes from the love of God. And as such cannot fully transform the mind, body, and spirit into the identity as sons and daughters of the King.

NED'S STORY

Meet Ned, a rock-solid, sold-out believer in Jesus. He is a son, husband, father of three, a leader in his church community, and a professional in a fast-paced and demanding industry. He didn't start out this way. While Ned was raised in a Christian community, he doubted God's goodness and truth throughout his teens. However, in his late teens, he felt the void in his heart where Christ should be. Ned found himself searching and looking for answers to fill the gaps in his life that he felt God had not yet touched. This led him to search for truth through diligent study of the Bible and to search for an authentic connection to God.

Ned's search led him toward a meditative exploration to find answers, and in the coming months, Ned began to learn and practice transcendental meditation. I will discuss transcendental meditation a bit later in this book. As Ned practiced transcendental meditation, he would enter into meditative moments, not necessarily a trance but a stillness. He would posture himself in the traditional manner, sitting comfortably, eyes closed, while mentally repeating his chosen mantra. While in a meditative state, Ned would petition God to reveal His truth and provide the answers for which he was searching.

During one session, while Ned was meditating, Jesus Himself interrupted his session and vividly appeared to Ned in his meditative state.

As Ned looked at Jesus, he was overcome with overwhelming peace, love, and acceptance that completely surrounded him spiritually, physically, and emotionally.

Jesus approached Ned and, taking him in His arms held him and in his ear, said, "I am here, and I will never abandon you. I love you." As Ned sunk in and rested in the arms of Jesus, his entire perspective on his life was forever changed. He belonged to Jesus, and in that moment, his identity became synchronized with God's plans for his life. Right there, without hesitation, sinking into the loving arms of Jesus, his doubts melted away, and he fell apart weeping in an indescribable ecstasy. He committed himself and his life to Jesus right there. Ned explains it this way. "After that experience, there is literally nothing that could tear me away from loving Jesus and my commitment to Him and His purpose for me and my life."

Secure in Jesus's love, salvation, and guidance, Ned continued in his meditations with a new mantra in Christ and began to grow in his skill of the practice of meditation. Knowing that he was secure in Jesus's salvation, his participation in transcendental meditation would forever change his life and solidify his identity as a child of God with a purpose and identity from Heaven. He began to experience the benefits of meditation in his life, experiencing peace and an overall calming within his mind. Transcendental meditation practitioners often describe these benefits as expectations of the practice.

Ned's story does not tell us that transcendental meditation is a good practice. Quite the opposite, in fact. Ned's story proves two things. First, when we ask for truth to be revealed, Jesus always answers. In Ned's case, he showed up in a very personal way. Second, the principle of meditation works in spite of any additional Eastern mysticism.

I will not endorse transcendental meditation as its practice is contrary to the Word of God. Ned would have had his encounter with Jesus outside of his meditation practice as well because he asked and was hungry. The benefits Ned received from his participation in transcendental meditation were solely physical, mental, and emotional, all positive benefits in the natural, which further demonstrate the principle of meditation. But these effects were limited without God engaging with his spirit. The moment Jesus appeared to Ned was the moment described in Romans 12:2, where he was entirely and forever transformed, both in his natural state and his supernatural state.

Today, Ned no longer practices transcendental meditation. Instead, he chooses to engage in biblical meditation, where he meets God and receives all of the natural and supernatural benefits.

Let me highlight a few Scriptures here that demonstrate the principle of biblical meditation for believers.

> *May these words of my mouth and this meditation of my heart be pleasing in your sight, Lord, my Rock and my Redeemer* (Psalm 19:14 NIV).

David meditates with a free flow of thoughts from his mind and from the overflow of his heart, demonstrating the freedom we have as we meditate. No script, format, method, or instruction book is required. Once the basic principles have been understood, meditation is a free-flow exercise.

> *My heart became hot within me. As I mused, the fire burned; then I spoke with my tongue* (Psalm 39:3 ESV).

The passion within David's heart grew while he meditated (mused) until he released his heart in a fury of emotion to the Lord.

> *Come to me, all who labor and are heavy laden, and I will give you rest. Take my yoke upon you, and learn from me, for I am gentle and lowly in heart, and you will find rest for your souls* (Matthew 11:28-29 ESV).

God promises when we approach Him in our struggle, in moments of stress and anxiety, He will bestow peace and rest. Our times of meditation are times to reset and allow our minds to refocus.

Several names for meditation, which are commonplace in religious contexts outside of Christianity, bear a striking resemblance to truths taught in Scripture. For example, let me break down the following well-known meditation models. While each of these is well known in the secular world of meditation, the biblical application and benefits of each are reserved for believers.

"Mindfulness" is defined by the American Psychological Association as an awareness of one's internal state and [external] surroundings. Mindfulness is an intentional observation of thoughts, emotions, and experiences.[18] In this context, the word *observation* is essential as it highlights the importance of noticing their presence without reacting or judging.

> *So then, prepare your hearts and minds for action! Stay alert and fix your hope firmly on the marvelous grace that is coming to you. For when Jesus Christ is unveiled, a greater measure of grace will be released to you* (1 Peter 1:13 TPT).

Compassion, as defined by Compassion International, means to empathize with someone who is suffering and to feel compelled to reduce the suffering. It is a fuller, more authentic definition than feelings alone, and it is a very biblical understanding.

> *You are always and dearly loved by God! So robe yourself with virtues of God, since you have been divinely chosen to be holy. Be merciful as you endeavor to understand others, and be compassionate, showing kindness toward all. Be gentle and humble, unoffendable in your patience with others* (Colossians 3:12 TPT).

Loving-kindness is similar in ideology to compassion, yet it is offered as unconditional love for another person or yourself. (The meditation known as *metta sutta* or Loving Kindness is demonic. This is covered in further detail later.)

> *So I give you now a new commandment: Love each other just as much as I have loved you. For when you demonstrate the same love I have for you by loving one another, everyone will know that you're my true followers* (John 13:34-35 TPT).

Thankfulness and gratitude are defined by the American Psychological Association as "a type of meditation that focuses on expressing gratitude for the things in your life."[19] In the case of biblical meditation, we focus our thoughts on the blessings and favor of God in our lives.

> *We know that all creation is beautiful to God and there is nothing to be refused if it is received with gratitude* (1 Timothy 4:4 TPT).

> *Since we are receiving our rights to an unshakeable kingdom we should be extremely thankful and offer God the purest worship that delights his heart as we lay down our lives in absolute surrender, filled with awe* (Hebrews 12:28 TPT).

COMMON MYTHS OF MEDITATION

While supernatural thinking and the application of meditative practices are beneficial to life and health, we must not view them as a miracle cure-all from life's daily challenges or an escape from life. Placing your meditation in the proper space during your day will prepare you for the challenges the day brings. Bringing clarity to the following common misconceptions should help clear up any misgivings.

Myth: There is only one way to meditate properly.

Jesus said in His own words, "*Come to me, all who labor and are heavy laden, and I will give you rest. Take my yoke upon you, and learn from me, for I am gentle and lowly in heart, and you will find rest for your souls. For my yoke is easy, and my burden is light*" (Matthew 11:28-30 ESV).

This Scripture passage shines a light on the freedom we have in meditation. Jesus said, "Come to Me." This invitation is free of any requirement of heart posture or perfection of our thoughts. Next, He promises when we do come to Him, "I will give you rest." Simply pausing and thinking about Him for a moment is sufficient to reset our minds and allow God to adjust our mindset and our feelings.

The end of this book contains several methods for meditation and supernatural thinking. While there is no rulebook, best practices are built into these methods that will enable you to succeed. In an article published by Bangor University, they documented that meditation is beneficial even when practiced in many forms. Sitting quietly, crossed legs, focusing, gentle breathing, visualization, sounds, focused thought, and even daily activities can become meditative moments.[20]

Myth: Meditation is only about being motionless and quiet.

Quite the opposite, Dr. Duncan Riach, a clinical psychologist, clarifies in a recent article, "If anything, meditation is about noticing what's happening: the struggling, the attempt to control, the thoughts, the feelings, the resistance. Meditation is not about searching for or finding some kind of peace. Meditation is about discovering the truth of what's actually happening."[21]

Myth: Meditation is only about silencing our thoughts and emptying the mind.

"You cannot stop your mind as an act of will. Instead...you intently focus your mind on one thing [or activity] to the exclusion of all others, as your mind becomes fully engaged in that one thing."[22]

The Bible teaches us not to empty our minds but to constantly prepare, stir up, and renew them.

> *Therefore, preparing your minds for action, and being sober-minded, set your hope fully on the grace that will be brought to you at the revelation of Jesus Christ* (1 Peter 1:13 ESV).

Myth: Meditation must be free from distraction.

Supernatural thinking is not about removing all distractions but training the mind to focus while in the midst of chaos. Distraction-free meditation is lovely, and I recommend setting aside time for distraction-free moments. But bringing your supernatural thinking into moments of distractions will bring peace and calm. Meditation is not about suppressing the noise but allowing the mind to drift naturally.

> *Peace I leave with you; my peace I give to you. Not as the world gives do I give to you. Let not your hearts be troubled, neither let them be afraid* (John 14:27 ESV).

> *You keep him in perfect peace whose mind is stayed on you, because he trusts in you* (Isaiah 26:3 ESV).

Myth: A wandering mind leads to a rested mind, a rest that is deeper than sleep.

This falls under the classification of "more than the sum of its parts." A wandering mind does inspire rest and deep relaxation. However, this is a myth because of the disservice caused by the belief that simply allowing the mind to wander and become more restful is the only benefit or end goal of meditation. "Meditation is more than just a way to calm our thoughts and lower stress levels: our brain processes more thoughts and feelings during meditation than when you are simply relaxing."[23]

Meditation is the only activity scientifically known to reduce brain age. In a study compiled across four international universities, the following conclusions were observed:

> We observed that, at age fifty, brains of meditators were estimated to be 7.5 years younger than those of controls. While brain age estimates varied only little in controls, significant changes were detected in meditators: for every additional year over fifty, meditators' brains were estimated to be an additional one month and 22 days younger than their chronological age. Altogether, these findings seem to suggest that meditation is beneficial for brain preservation, effectively protecting against age-related atrophy with a consistently slower rate of brain aging throughout life.[24]

Myth: Meditation is a new-age occultic practice that cannot be redeemed.

As demonstrated earlier in this chapter, the practice of supernatural thinking is for believers in Jesus and was commanded by God to Joshua under the original covenant. Meditation has since become commonplace and corrupted by religious and new-age secularization. Nonetheless, the righteous practice of meditation does not need to be redeemed as the practice was established for God's children and has always belonged to us. It was never stolen, only imitated in a corrupt manner for corrupt purposes. Forms of meditation involving worship toward and focus on other spirits, emptiness, or pagan worshipful poses are evil and cannot be redeemed. Biblical meditation does not require these expressions.

SO WHY SHOULD BELIEVERS MEDITATE?

We've already established that God's principle of meditation was handed to Joshua in Joshua 1:8. Its practice is no longer commanded under the original covenant. Yet the principle lives on; and as I will demonstrate, God still instructs us to meditate under the new covenant. God declares that He will go in front and fight for us in our silence (Exodus 14:14). When Moses was leading the people through the desert and as Pharaoh pursued them, they complained, were ungrateful, and were unable to see the favor of God. Moses's response to the people was essentially to take a pause, stop acting in fear, and watch what the Lord was about to do if they remained silent and rested in Him.

> *And Moses said to the people, "Fear not, stand firm, and see the salvation of the Lord, which he will work for you today. For the Egyptians whom you see today, you shall never see again. The Lord will fight for you, and you have only to be silent"* (Exodus 14:13-14 ESV).

Paul instructs Timothy to practice, or *meletaō*[25] the teachings he has heard. The Greek word *meletaō* means to ponder, meditate, and practice. Timothy was being instructed here: First, don't just let these words be clever ideas. Next, meditate on them with intentional focus and let them become part of your character. And finally, when you do, others will see how well you have done.

> *Practice these things, immerse yourself in them, so that all may see your progress. Keep a close watch on yourself and on the teaching. Persist in this, for by so doing you will save both yourself and your hearers* (1 Timothy 4:15-16 ESV).

We receive wisdom, understanding, peace, clarity, energy, focus, and healing in our minds and bodies through our meditations. But perhaps most importantly, as we explore the depth of His presence, we cultivate a relationship with the Holy Spirit. And through the cultivation of this relationship, we learn to hear His voice, feel His expressions, and engage with the One who first loved us.

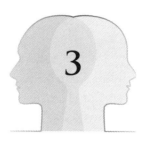

3

The SYNERGY *of* PRAYER *and* MEDITATION

I have had the great honor and pleasure of accompanying my friend Becca Greenwood as we placed boots on the ground and executed incredible prayer and intercession strategies worldwide for the Kingdom.

In 2022, during the early stages of writing this book, I was struck with awe as we were in the country praying at the Bible College of Wales. We were not there for any events or invitations. We were not there to speak or gain attention. No, our assignment was to spend the week approaching the throne room in pure intercession. God had called this band of prayer warriors to uproot and fly to Wales to do nothing more than devote our time to prayer and intercession.

As we entered the prayer room at the Bible college, I was struck at how minimal the décor was; very little attention was given to decoration or creating an atmosphere of warmth. I know that those treatments are not necessary and do nothing to welcome the Holy Spirit. Yet it stuck with me. As we settled in and began to worship, my friend Anthony Turner took us right into the throne room with his first note on his keyboard.

We were immediately caught up in a spiritual moment, where prayer and intercession flowed. It flowed as freely and timelessly as though we had been plowing in prayer for years. It was unlike any other moment of intercession I had ever encountered. The Holy Spirit was speaking assignments, granting wisdom, and showing His love for us and those for whom we were interceding. Over the next eight hours, deep, uninterrupted intercession was lifted in that little undecorated room at the Bible College of Wales.

At one moment during a time of deep intercession, not one of us was seated. All were standing in worship, kneeling, or lying down in reverence to the Lord. The Holy Spirit spoke to me, "Look around; what do you see?" As I raised my eyes, I scanned the room, observing every person, their posture, and expressions. I had seen it a hundred times, but this time the reality of what I was seeing landed. In the stillness of the moment, with quiet worship music radiating from Anthony's keyboard, every person in the room was lost in various states of deep meditation. It felt as though time came to a stop as everyone in the room simultaneously touched the glory experienced through the offering of heartfelt intercession. It was so pure and right; I could see that God was present with each of us in this moment of corporate meditation.

I believe that God highlighted that moment to me because of my assignment to write this book and teach this message. He needed me to understand the righteous connection between intercession, prayer, and meditation. Meditation is not performed in a vacuum; God does not operate in a vacuum. Everything He does and everything He inspires has a purpose. Meditation, intercession, and prayer are no different. All are needed, all are necessary, and all can stand on their own; but when combined, it's as though a spiritual power implosion of God's goodness has just occurred, which leads to the outward explosion of worship and joy.

Corporately, these are the moments when worship meets meditation, encounters intercession wrapped in prayer, and returns back to worship and meditation, repeating the process over and over as the Holy Spirit moves. That is what the Holy Spirit wanted me to see. After all, our posture in worship led to our spiritual preparation in meditation, thereby allowing the Holy Spirit to speak directly to us as we speak out the heart and plans of God in prophetic intercession. Intercessors and prayer warriors get it. We may not have always labeled these moments as "meditation," yet that is precisely what is happening: a focus on whatever the Holy Spirit desires while resting on God, focusing our thoughts, and seeking the heart of the Father for the matter.

As these meditative moments flowed, some people in the room were prostrate. Some were kneeling, and some sat with arms raised. Others stood with eyes heavenward. Still, others were on their hands and knees with groanings too deep for words, as described in Romans 8:26. It's worth noticing here that this flow I've just described happens at different times and at various intervals for each person in attendance. Worship has a way of directing the atmosphere. Still, our intentional surrender to follow the Holy Spirit will naturally take us through these flows as we devote ourselves to the movement of God within the moment.

A PRECURSOR TO INTERCESSION OR PRAYER

As you can see, biblical meditation is one way the Holy Spirit brings us into moments of prayer or intercession. What I've just described explains how prayer, intercession, and meditation operate mutually. Yet prayer and intercession can and do work just as effectively independently. Biblical meditation, however, always includes prayer.

I once attended an intercession event in Colorado led by other ministry leaders and prayer warriors from the area. The purpose of that intercessory event was to gather and pray for the city, the cultural changes happening, and the political firestorm we've all been experiencing. This type of intercession functions more like a corporate prayer meeting, yet the intercessors were present and operating in their gifts.

During this meeting, we encountered a flow of the spirit where individuals would be handed a microphone and would then release a prayer placed on their hearts from God. Anyone was encouraged to declare a prayer regardless of church affiliation or position. This gathering did have soft worship as a background accompaniment, which was helpful to help set the atmosphere. But it did not have a prominent place in the meeting. As each person released their prayer, we could feel the atmosphere in the room become charged, and more people began to pray and release prophetic words and visions.

This type of intercessory event did not include a flow of meditation, as that was not the purpose. God moved mightily, and in this case, prayer and intercession was the assignment. Would it have been wrong for someone to enter into a meditative moment during the meeting? Not at all! And unlike times when the natural flow of the spirit moves everyone corporately through meditation, intercession, prayer, and worship, this was more prescribed, planned, and directed. In this example, any meditation occurs at the private and personal level rather than the corporate level, as the Holy Spirit leads.

Remember from earlier that our meditations are enriching to us at an individual level and strengthen our relationship with the Holy Spirit. Meditations will generate an outward expression of some sort. Corporately, that expression might be a prayer. Privately, it might be a passionate release of emotions as the Holy Spirit ministers. What I am saying here is to be sensitive to the atmosphere and the purpose of the corporate gathering. Meditation may not always be an appropriate expression. At other times, it becomes an integral part of what God is doing. When that happens, let it flow!

It's easy to see prayer and meditation as mutually exclusive. But the truth is that they are designed to operate together. As I have demonstrated, our thoughts can be turned toward God as meditative moments during any form of prayer in which we participate. Meditation always requires prayer, but prayer does not require meditation. In the coming chapters, I lay the groundwork explaining how we are to meditate biblically. Private meditation will always begin with a prayer welcoming the Holy Spirit's tangible Spirit to fill the room. Then, during meditation, expect to connect with God as He speaks to you through thoughts, visions, and ideas.

Let me stress here that prayer, intercession, and meditation do flow well together. Prayer and intercession are capable of standing on their own. Prayer joins with our meditation, which fully connects us to the throne room of God. The Hebrew words *sichah* and *siach* translate as both meditation and prayer, demonstrating the unity of the practices. David uses these two meditative concepts prolifically throughout the psalms.

> *I have more understanding than all my teachers, for your testimonies are my* [sichah] *meditation* (Psalm 119:99 ESV).[26]

> *On the glorious splendor of your majesty, and on your wondrous works, I will* [siach] *meditate* (Psalm 145:5 ESV).[27]

As we encounter the presence of God during our meditative moments, we may engage with our gift of tongues, a sound, or even a vision. Additionally, we may rejoice or release a prayer of thanksgiving according to 1 Thessalonians 5:18. These moments when our meditation is focused on God become flashes of time when we can hear His voice and speak with the Holy Spirit with clarity because our minds and environment are filled with His presence.

BRIEF CONTRAST BETWEEN MEDITATION AND PRAYER

Meditation

The Bible has many varying descriptions of meditation. Each example further exemplifies the depth of importance given to the practice of meditation in our lives. What follows is a short primer on the biblical meanings of meditation.

To Ponder and Devote Time to Thinking

Our ability to ponder comes from a place of deep personal meditation and welcomes peace, vitality of life, and great joy. The Greek word *meletaō*, used at the beginning of this verse, means to practice with intention and meditate with purpose.[28]

> *Make all of this your constant* [meletao] *meditation and make it real with your life so everyone can see that you are moving forward. Give careful attention to your spiritual life and every cherished truth you teach, for living what you preach will then release even more abundant life inside you and to all those who listen to you* (1 Timothy 4:15-16 TPT).

> *We have thought on your steadfast love, O God, in the midst of your temple* (Psalm 48:9 ESV).

To Abide

At this moment of abiding, we are called to be still, to wait and lean in on the moment. The Greek word for *abide* is *menō,* which means to be still and to wait.[29]

> *Abide in me, and I in you. As the branch cannot bear fruit by itself, unless it abides in the vine, neither can you, unless you abide in me. I am the vine; you are the branches. Whoever abides in me and I in him, he it is that bears much fruit, for apart from me you can do nothing. If anyone does not abide in me he is thrown away like a branch and withers; and the branches are gathered, thrown into the fire, and burned. If you abide in me, and my words abide in you, ask whatever you wish, and it will be done for you. By this my Father is glorified, that you bear much fruit and so prove to be my disciples. As the Father has loved me, so have I loved you. Abide in my love. If you keep my commandments, you will abide in my love, just as I have kept my Father's commandments and abide in his love. These things I have spoken to you, that my joy may be in you, and that your joy may be full* (John 15:4-11 ESV).

Imagination and Sound Within Our Meditation

We are encouraged to muse and engage with sound. Sounds of meditation will be covered in-depth in a later chapter. However, praying in tongues or even the sounds made during intense experiences in the glory are all normal and encouraged. Adding the sound of pleasant worship music in the room sets the right atmosphere for meditation. The Hebrew word for *meditate* in these Scriptures is *haga,* which means to muse and meditate with a sound or utterance.[30]

In Psalms, David is also seen imagining the law of the Lord and good food and remembers God during his meditations in the night. David's imagination is easily discernable when he says how he meditates on the thoughts of God and how they compare to the grains of sand on the earth. He provides us with a beautiful example of imagery applied to our times of meditation.

> *But his delight is in the law of the Lord, and on his law he meditates day and night* (Psalm 1:2 ESV).

> *My soul will be satisfied as with fat and rich food, and my mouth will praise you with joyful lips, when I remember you upon my bed, and meditate on you in the watches of the night* (Psalm 63:5-6 ESV).

> *How precious to me are your thoughts, O God! How vast is the sum of them! If I would count them, they are more than the sand. I awake, and I am still with you* (Psalm 139:17-18 ESV).

Be Still

> *Be still, and know that I am God. I will be exalted among the nations, I will be exalted in the earth!* (Psalm 46:10 ESV)

This command to be still only touches the surface of what this verse in Psalms is instructing. "Be still" comes from the Hebrew word *rapa* which means to sink down, to be completely relaxed, and to let go of all of the burdens of the mind.[31] So that when we meditate, our posture is to be fully and intentionally relaxed and withdraw into the arms of the Lord.

Intentionally Posture Our Bodies and Minds

We are to posture ourselves worshipfully before the Lord and be humbled in our minds. The Hebrew word for *meditate* in Genesis is *suah,* which means to meditate, commune, and speak with God.[32] The Hebrew word *nāśā* is used here to illustrate that Isaac was postured low in meditation and that he lifted his head at the sound of camels.[33] *"And Isaac went out to meditate in the field toward evening. And he* [nasa] *lifted up his eyes and saw, and behold, there were camels coming"* (Genesis 24:63 ESV).

To Commune and Ponder

We get to meet with the Holy Spirit in these moments, where He guides our thoughts. The Hebrew word for *meditate* in the following Scriptures is *siah,* which means to meditate, to commune, and to speak with God.[34]

> *When I remember God, I moan; when I meditate, my spirit faints. Selah* (Psalm 77:3 ESV).

> *I will ponder all your work, and meditate on your mighty deeds* (Psalm 77:12 ESV).

> *I will meditate on your precepts and fix my eyes on your ways* (Psalm 119:15 ESV).

Just as with meditation, Scripture eloquently captures the richness of prayer. What follows are contextual references and contrasts encapsulated from the Bible.

Prayer

The Bible is rich with encouragement for us to pray. Prayer unlocks guidance and wisdom from God. It brings transformation, healing, and blessings. But above all, prayer allows us to develop deeper relationships with God. The following are a few examples of biblical prayer to contrast meditation.

Make a Request and Ask[35]

> *Therefore pray earnestly to the Lord of the harvest to send out laborers into his harvest* (Matthew 9:38 ESV).

Request the Presence of the Lord

We call on the Lord, speak with Him, and make requests known. The Hebrew word for *implored* in the following verse is *parakaleo,* meaning to call for or to request the presence of the Lord.[36] *"And implored him earnestly, saying, 'My little daughter is at the point of death. Come and lay your hands on her, so that she may be made well and live'"* (Mark 5:23 ESV).

Engage in Meaningful, Life-Giving Conversations Through Prayer

As the deepest of emotions are released during prayer, God responds with incredible mercy and patience, fully satisfying our need as children of God to be connected to Him:

> *O Lord, how long shall I cry for help, and you will not hear? Or cry to you "Violence!" and you will not save? Why do you make me see iniquity, and why do you idly look at wrong?*

Destruction and violence are before me; strife and conten-
tion arise. [And the Lord answers] *Look among the nations,*
and see; wonder and be astounded. For I am doing a work
in your days that you would not believe if told (Habakkuk
1:2-3,5 ESV).

In Genesis 18, Abraham and God are engaging in a conversation.
Abraham is interceding for the city of Sodom, requesting, if any righteousness is present, to spare Sodom. This level of dialogue with God
has not ceased to exist. We have simply forgotten how to be still and
know. I have experienced it, and you will, as well.

But Abraham still stood before the Lord. Then Abraham
drew near and said, "Will you indeed sweep away the
righteous with the wicked? Suppose there are fifty righteous
within the city. Will you then sweep away the place and not
spare it for the fifty righteous who are in it? Far be it from
you to do such a thing, to put the righteous to death with
the wicked, so that the righteous fare as the wicked! Far be
that from you! Shall not the Judge of all the earth do what is
just?" And the Lord said, "If I find at Sodom fifty righteous
in the city, I will spare the whole place for their sake" (Genesis 18:22-26 ESV).

The minimalist room I spoke of in Wales earlier was an obvious lesson for me. One might think that the barrenness of the room represents
humility and humbleness. Instead, the Lord showed me that the room
was wide open, ready to be filled and decorated with the meditation
and intercession of the people—the kind of decorations we cannot see
with natural eyes. As we prayed, the room was revealed as beautiful
and full of joy, and inside was an incredible weight of God's presence.
Let this be a metaphor for our thought life. The Holy Spirit indwells
in each of us, and our mind space is not bare and undecorated. The

more time we devote to meditation, the more we decorate that space. Outwardly our lives reflect the beauty and the glory of God.

We are instructed in Scripture to get wisdom, but the acquisition of understanding is even more significant than that. It is wise to devote ourselves to meditation, and it becomes understanding when we comprehend why God instituted the principles of meditation through our supernatural thought lives.

The SCIENCE of MEDITATION

"Repeated practice of meditation results in lasting traits."[37]

E arly research in the field of meditation may have been lackluster and even a bit deceptive in some cases. To quote a study published in the National Library of Medicine, "Something has gone wrong with the science of mindfulness."[38] On one hand, meditation is presented in a narrow box, and little acknowledgment is given to its efficacy. On the other hand, meditation is presented as a panacea for all of life's ailments. The truth is camped right between these polar extremes. It's worth noting that meditation is associated with a wide range of benefits, including the reduction of stress and anxiety, as well as the promotion of physical healing.

In this chapter, I present the science of meditation, looking through legitimate research and science performed from an objective perspective. It is essential to acknowledge that while biblical meditation can be helpful, it is not a cure-all solution for all challenges in life, nor is it the fountain of youth. I believe and will aim to demonstrate that biblical meditation can heal, reduce stress, and bring lasting change. Because we are the temple of God, the Holy Spirit indwells us, and when invited to our meditation, He permeates our thoughts and emotions as we abide with Him.

Meditation has the capacity to produce lasting changes in our minds and our bodies when we give time and focus to its practice. Remember, as I taught earlier, meditation is a partnership with the Holy Spirit within us as believers. It is an abiding call to rest in Him as He partners with our thoughts. Through that partnership, something happens in our bodies and our minds. Through biblical meditation, a shift happens, righting our emotions, thoughts, and outward expressions. For the change to be lasting, it must produce changes within us, both spiritually and physically.

Harvard University conducted a study that examined the meditation practices of individuals, both those who have been meditating for a long time and those who have just started. The question was whether a meditation state called "relaxation response" caused any physical changes. Remarkably, the study concluded that "meditation—short or long term—causes hundreds of genes to turn on or off." Further, it is believed that meditation "may counteract cellular damage due to chronic psychological stress." "Now, we have solid scientific proof of the positive genetic effects of meditation in that it affects genes that positively influence cell metabolism and the response to oxidative stress."[39,40]

This study is important as it highlights vital physical observations regarding the benefits of incorporating meditation into our daily lives. Oxidative stress is linked directly to several diseases, such as Parkinson's and Alzheimer's, and is known to accelerate aging at the cellular level. That is to say, cells, tissues, and organs break down more quickly through a process called entropy. Entropy is defined in the most basic way as a measure of disorder or chaos.[41]

MENO

Earlier, I taught that meditation is a principle created by God that produces life-changing results for the meditator. These results impact both the religious and non-religious, spiritual and non-spiritual meditators. The previous study and others reinforce meditation as a principle, demonstrating that it just works. However, for believers in Jesus, God is glorified when we receive an inheritance of added life transformation and the gift of His tangible presence.

> *Abide in me, and I in you. As the branch cannot bear fruit by itself, unless it abides in the vine, neither can you, unless you abide in me. I am the vine; you are the branches. Whoever abides in me and I in him, he it is that bears much fruit, for apart from me you can do nothing. If anyone does not abide in me he is thrown away like a branch and withers; and the branches are gathered, thrown into the fire, and burned. If you abide in me, and my words abide in you, ask whatever you wish, and it will be done for you. By this my Father is glorified, that you bear much fruit and so prove to be my disciples* (John 15:4-8 ESV).

Likewise, we see this parallel in this Scripture. "To abide" is the Greek word *meno,* which means to tarry, to wait, to be present, and not depart.[42] Just as science demonstrates a lasting physical change, the Bible noted it first when Jesus said, *"Whoever abides in me and I in him, he it is that bears much fruit."*

Our participation in meditation is an abiding time that transforms our minds and bodies from the outside in and inside out. Jesus continues by stating that those who do not abide with Him will not receive this added blessing. Believers! Biblical meditation has been given to us as an inheritance. As the secular world spins in darkness around us, we are called to be a light. Time spent in *meno* meditation with the Holy Spirit produces that light that emanates from each of us relative to the measure of time spent.

Recent scientific studies have demonstrated a link between meditation and the improvement of common disorders related to epigenetics and gene expression. We see the following conclusions in a study titled "The Molecules of Silence" published at the National Library of Medicine:

> Surprisingly, meditation practices seem to act on gene targets, such as FKBP5 [the link between stress and cancer],[43] SLC6A4 [linked to OCD and anxiety],[44] and BDNF [linked to learning and memory],[45] and promote [positive] endocrinal, neuronal, and behavioral functions.
>
> ...the achievement of a state of inner silence through the practice of meditation can prevent or reverse the detrimental effects of a stressful environment.
>
> It is conceivable that, by improving the immune system, metabolism, and stress–response pathways and by promoting neuroplasticity, meditations of several kinds could affect mechanisms of energy saving, promote homeostasis, and potentiate the reciprocal mind and body's relaxation abilities, with a positive impact on psychology.[46]

To summarize this amazing study, meditation, specifically silence and allowing the mind to wander, reduces stress and anxiety and promotes a decrease in stress-induced cancer cells while improving the immune system and areas in the brain responsible for metabolism, stress response, stability of the mind, and increases the body's natural relaxation abilities.

How is that for bearing good fruit!? Jesus promised our abiding *meno* moments would produce health through the adoption of quiet meditation. Knowing now what we know lets us grow in our desire to partner with the Holy Spirit in our stillness and allow His natural principle of meditation to restore our health.

DAMAM

I am standing in absolute stillness, silent before the one I love, waiting as long as it takes for him to rescue me. Only God is my Savior, and he will not fail me (Psalm 62:5 TPT).

I have now demonstrated how the abiding *meno* benefits our lives. However, this study showed another critical aspect of meditation that we cannot overlook. *Damam* is the Hebrew word for "silence, stillness, and rest."[47] All of these benefits I've taught so far have two things in common. First is *meno* meditation, the abiding moment with the Holy Spirit. The second is *damam,* which is to pursue your *meno* meditation in rest and silent stillness.[48] We could say that this form of meditation is a *meno* in *damam* meditation, a silent, still, and abiding moment that removes the stress of life, restores health to the body, and encounters the Holy Spirit. In a later chapter, I have provided a meditation based on the principle of *damam* and *meno*.

Silence and speech are inseparable, inescapably intertwined. Silence is simply the void in which speech occurs.[49]

As we slow ourselves down intentionally and relax into a *meno* in *damam* moment with the Holy Spirit, our minds are never void of communication with him. Quite the opposite, as documented in an article published at Arizona State University, "silence or speech may co-occur with voiceless forms of language."[50] Our mind intentionally and organically engages in a dialogue with the Holy Spirit in our quiet moments. Of course, natural verbal expressions of communication also occur during these times, but here we are addressing the principle of silent communication. The following well-known story of Elijah learning to hear God's voice demonstrates this principle.

> *And he said, "Go out and stand on the mount before the Lord." And behold, the Lord passed by, and a great and strong wind tore the mountains and broke in pieces the rocks before the Lord, but the Lord was not in the wind. And after the wind an earthquake, but the Lord was not in the earthquake. And after the earthquake a fire, but the Lord was not in the fire. And after the fire the sound of a low whisper. And when Elijah heard it, he wrapped his face in his cloak and went out and stood at the entrance of the cave. And behold, there came a voice to him and said, "What are you doing here, Elijah?"* (1 Kings 19:11-13 ESV)

Elijah expected to hear God in the context of his mind's understanding. God equals big; therefore, I'll wait for the dramatic eruption of God's voice. This is an oversimplification to enhance the point. It was not until Elijah became silent and rested that the whisper of the Lord's voice came to him. This word *whisper* is the Hebrew word *demamah,* which originates from the word *damam* addressed earlier, meaning silence.[51] We need to slow down and wait. When we do, God will speak within the silence.

IMAGINATION

> *"The soul without imagination is what an*
> *observatory would be without a telescope."*
>
> –Henry Ward Beecher

Western Apache Native Americans in Cibecue, Arizona, have an intriguing form of communication they refer to as "speaking with names." This communication style involves speaking to one another by only saying the names of a place or local landmark. A long pause follows this in silence until another member speaks of another location or landmark. These moments of silence are not empty flashes in time. Instead, when the name of a place is spoken, each person is instantly transported in their imagination. It is as though they are standing in that place, observing, reliving, and, in their case, connecting with history.[52]

This story illustrates how powerful our capacity for imagination and visualization is. Our minds are wired for imagination and creativity, and it is fundamental to human life.[53] And not just for our enjoyment and entertainment either. Amazing research is only now uncovering how much our minds need and thrive on our God-given gift of imagination. Children are masters of imagination and crafting mental realities. Observing children reveals that the function of creative imagination does not stop for serious moments. Sometimes, to the chagrin of their parents, toys and stuffed animals make their way to the dinner table, where they become part of the evening's events.

I recall many times when a two-foot-tall Spiderman would be seated in my chair at the dinner table, having been invited by my seven-year-old to accompany him to dinner. Naturally, I graciously moved to a different seat at the table. Spiderman was our guest, after all. As dinner was served and everyone began to eat, my son would hold bites to Spiderman's mouth before feeding himself. Each of my children would engage in similar forms of healthy imagination, and I was happy to participate.

Yet somewhere in our departure from adolescence, most of us put aside or lose as much as 96 percent of our creativity simply by growing up. That may sound disheartening, but as with most skills, it is the lack of practice that causes the decline. But there is hope! Children feed their creativity, which inspires more creativity, and so on. According to the Public Relations Society of America, "As adults, we have less freedom than when we were five years old. Life gets stressful, responsibilities stack up, and our daily checklists can take us out of a creative headspace. But even small changes and mindset shifts can help us channel childhood imagination, lose some of our creative inhibitions, and think in a way that can help us."[54]

FIND YOUR FIVE-YEAR-OLD MIND

Okay, so do children have a better imagination? Not remotely! The difference is that children routinely engage in repetitive practices involving imagination, whereas adults reduce their engagement in the imaginative process, leading to a creative decline. Divergent and convergent modes of thinking help to explain what is occurring. *Divergent* thinking is spontaneous, non-linear, creative thought that produces many ideas. *Convergent* thinking is the ability to reach a solution through logic rather than creativity. As we grow up, we actually learn our way out of the creative mind. While divergent thinking is the creative accelerator in our mind, convergent thinking becomes the brakes.

Over time, children are taught to do both types of thinking simultaneously. This creates a dichotomy in the mind. What happens is our neurons fight one another, "actually diminishing the power of the brain."[55] Sadly, as the creativity of a child is exposed, it becomes met with the following responses, either from other adults, peers, themselves, or demonic influence: "That's a dumb idea," "You can't do that," "That's crazy," "That won't work." All of this criticism leads to a fear of failure, which leads to low self-esteem and pressure to conform, all while planting the root system for complete rejection and a suppression of creativity and imagination.

In a study conducted for NASA, 1,600 four and five-year-olds were tested for creativity. Ninety-eight percent of five-year-olds scored as a "creative genius." Furthering the study as longitudinal, researchers found that the number had been reduced to 12 percent over the next ten years. And by the time they reach adulthood, the number is only 2 percent still scoring as creative genius. This study has since been replicated more than a million times.[56]

So, what is the solution to our lost imagination? We have to rediscover our five-year-old. I'm not talking about a return to an adolescent mindset. We already engage in divergent thinking every night while we dream. I'm talking about giving intentionality to our imagination and allowing our God-given creativity to flow. Imagination is crucial as we continue to discuss the use of ideas, creativity, and visualization in our meditation.

VISUALIZATION

"It all depends on what you visualize."

–Ansel Adams

At first glance, visualization might seem synonymous with imagination. Where imagination is the creative process of coming up with ideas or concepts, visualization is the formation of a mental image and imagining that it is real. When we visualize an image or a task, our brains perceive the image or task as a reality, part of the physical world. All of this is happening in the thalamus, the part of the brain responsible for the formation of reality.

Neuroscientists have discovered that visualization establishes neural pathways in the brain, which act as a blueprint to be followed in the actual performance. When we visualize, our brain engages and begins creating the same neural pathways that it would create as though we are actually performing the action.

This concept is beneficial for everyone. The most noticeable application of this can be seen in athletics and public speaking. Athletes will visualize their performance, perfecting every move in their imagination prior to the big game. Public speakers will envision themselves on stage in front of the people presenting their talk, correcting errors and addressing challenges in the mind long before the live performance.

The benefits gained through visualization are not limited to high-profile public speakers or athletes. Everyone benefits from visualization in all aspects of life. From marriage and raising children to the desk job at work. However, the most restful and beneficial moment occurs when relaxation becomes the focal point of the visualization. Try closing your eyes and visualizing yourself surrounded by the place or activity that brings you great joy. Engage with that moment and lose yourself in the enjoyment of your creative imagination. Welcome back to your five-year-old mind.

Not surprisingly, the same process just described can also be used to bring healing to the body. For example, knowing how visualization works, and as I walked through my own victory from diabetes, I used the principle of visualization to engage my brain to accept a new reality.

First, I learned what a healthy pancreas and liver look like, so I had an image to work with. Then, during my meditations, I would visualize my healthy pancreas and liver. I also imagined an image of my healthy blood cells traveling through my body, as represented by smiley faces. My mind and body quickly began to align with the new reality of a healthy body that I was visualizing. My complete restoration manifested! Meditation using visualization played a prominent role.

This practice is one that I have used in the Ministry of Deliverance and Counseling for many years. Neuroscience has identified two fundamental principles of the brain that explain why visualization works. First, "the brain thinks in pictures," and second, the "brain often cannot distinguish whether you are imagining something or actually experiencing it."[57] People everywhere have begun to adopt the principle of visualization as a method to prepare for a task. Athletes, public speakers, doctors, and more use visualization to hone skills, relax, and overcome fear.

Further, according to Johns Hopkins, "By creating images in your mind, you can reduce pain and other symptoms tied to your condition. The more specific the visualization, the more helpful it will likely be."[58] The journal *Basic and Applied Social Psychology* concludes in a study that "pursuing both a mastery goal and a performance goal is more beneficial when using imagery, compared with pursuing only one of these goals."[59] This is supported by a study explicitly examining the mastery of action-based performance activities. "During early phases of skill acquisition, motor learning is associated with order formation of action-related knowledge in long-term memory, and this order formation seems to be promoted by mental practice."[60]

As we use the power of our minds to envision the outcomes we desire, we open ourselves up to the potential of transforming those visions into tangible realities. Research demonstrates that with no physical exertion, the visualization of strength training produces a 35 percent increase in physical strength.[61] Combining visualization with physical training and that number continues to grow. Using the mind to visually train and ultimately restore health is quite well documented. Elite athletes regularly use visualization to improve performance.[62] Successful public speakers visualize the ideal conditions for the event.[63] Visualization is preparation, training, and exercise for the mind and body. Visualization meditation instructs your brain that you are already successful in these areas, and when the time comes, you will be!

This sounds good, but is it biblical?

The practice of visualization is not only biblical, but Scripture encourages our vivid imagination in many ways.

Meditation is a form of worship; remember earlier when you read about David's meditations, he was guiding us through his worship, meditation, and now his visualizations.

"Oh, taste and see that the Lord is good! Blessed is the man who takes refuge in him!" (Psalm 34:8 ESV). Here, we see an interesting use of the word *taste*. When we look at the Hebrew meaning, it becomes clear. Taste, in this instance, means to perceive and to engage the senses.[64] Looking further, the word *see* means to consider, to have a vision, and to observe.[65] This beautiful verse is David's instruction to intentionally take a moment to visualize and focus on the goodness of God, reflecting on the blessings from Him.

> *Now to him who is able to do immeasurably more than all we ask or imagine, according to his power that is at work within us* (Ephesians 3:20 NIV).

No matter how creative our imagination is, God is infinitely greater than the breadth, length, height, and depth that we could possibly imagine. Be encouraged that as you explore visual meditations, focus on the greatness of God, how big and how wonderful He is, and know that as amazing as those thoughts are—He is magnitudes greater yet!

BENEFITS OF MEDITATION

"First, I do the meditation, then I do all the things."

–Unknown

This is a suitable quote that serves as a healthy starting point for discussing the benefits of meditation and cleansing our supernatural thought life. Please take a quick inventory of your current task list; I'll wait. Whew, okay, breathe and relax.

People often tell me, "I'm too busy to pursue the passions of my heart. Between my career, children, and daily demands of life, I struggle to devote time to the desires of God in my life." These statements are all true, and I'm sure they resonate with most who read this book. Amazingly, by investing a small, almost insignificant amount of your time, meditation can bring peace and power, reset your thought life, and achieve all the things you are called to accomplish.

Let me poke a nerve: Try substituting a moment of doom or zombie scrolling on your cell phone, choosing instead to meditate and allow your mind to reset and be restored. Mindlessly scrolling through social media, also known as zombie scrolling, can have negative impacts on both our mental and physical health. This habit can lead to eye strain, brain fatigue, difficulty concentrating, and emotional detachment, among other unpleasant symptoms.[66]

Although numerous benefits demonstrate the efficacy of meditation, I believe the benefits to our thought life outweigh and overshadow other benefits we also experience. As a result of my own experience and having conquered my own thought life, I now lead people frequently in ministry through a supernatural cleansing and reset of their own thought life. Doing this serves to bring restoration to our thought life and resets our belief system, which brings new life to our spiritual and physical well-being.

A study conducted at the New York Academy of Science with over 20 randomized controlled trials involving more than 1600 participants shows "evidence that mindfulness meditation is associated with changes in select immune system processes involved in inflammation, immunity, and biological aging." According to this study, practicing meditation can have positive effects on the body's biological systems. This includes boosting the immune system, which can help protect against viruses and bacterial infections. The study continues to show that certain diseases, such as cardiovascular disease, osteoporosis, arthritis, type 2 diabetes, and cancer, can be mitigated through meditation.[67] Let's look at how a meditative lifestyle can positively affect some of the most common health challenges we face today, especially in a post-pandemic world.

DEPRESSION

The most recent data demonstrates that nearly four in ten, or 39.3 percent of adults, experience forms of anxiety and depression. That number increases to nearly 50 percent for young people between 18-24. These feelings of hopelessness and sadness lead an unacceptable number of these people to consider suicide.[68] There is good news! We know now that stress and anxiety are triggers for depression. Implementing a lifestyle of meditation has been shown to physically change the brain, targeting areas linked directly to depression. Specifically, researchers are able to watch as a section of the brain known as the medial prefrontal cortex, or "me-center," begins to show hyperactivity in depressed people.

Thinking about things such as the stress of life can cause the me-center to go into overdrive, releasing cortisol from the amygdala and contributing to the depression cycle and, ultimately, a spiral downward if unchecked. By engaging in regular biblical meditation, we retrain our thoughts, take them captive, and, through meditation, break the connection between these two brain regions responsible for depression. Other notable benefits related to depression include providing protection for the hippocampus, or the primary memory center of the brain, by actually increasing the volume of gray matter.

ANXIETY

No good medications exist for the long-term treatment or cure of generalized anxiety disorder. In fact, some of the most frequently prescribed medications designed to alleviate anxiety actually increase depression, feelings of confusion, and dizziness. The statistical numbers for anxiety are the same as those reported for depression earlier.[69] Friends, that's no way to live a redeemed life!

So, what is the common thread? All of this data points to our ability to take power and authority over our thought lives. The moment we abdicate our thought life to demonic advances, our stress increases, heart rate increases, body temperature rises, cortisol releases in a fight or flight response, and we spiral into anxiety and depression. Oh, but the good news is that, as with depression, we must change our thinking and align fully with the biblical standard for our thoughts. Thinking only of whatever is pure, righteous, excellent, pleasant, lovely, admirable, and noble.

Pause now, place a bookmark here, close your eyes, and take a deep breath through your nostrils. Imagine something, someone, or a place that brings you great joy. Stay there in that moment of pleasure for as long as you want; there is no timer. You can even invite the Holy Spirit to join you in this visualization as a traveling thought Companion.

Reduce stress and regulate emotions. Regular biblical meditation brings an alignment to our emotions and helps to regulate emotional health. The Mayo Clinic confirms the benefits to our mental health. "Meditation can give you a sense of calm, peace, and balance that can benefit both your emotional well-being and your overall health. You can also use it to relax and cope with stress by refocusing your attention on something calming."[70]

CHILDREN

> [Jesus says,] *"I want little children to come to me, so never interfere with them when they want to come, for heaven's kingdom realm is composed of beloved ones like these! Listen to this truth: No one will enter the kingdom realm of heaven unless he becomes like one of these!"* (Matthew 19:14 TPT)

"There is no junior Holy Spirit." That message has been preached many times over the last decade, and rightfully so. Children have the total capacity to experience the presence and power of God. Everything in this book can introduce our children not only to the biblical practice of meditation but also to the Holy Spirit Himself through powerful encounters. It is concerning to note that anxiety and depression are becoming increasingly common among children.

The number of children displaying symptoms of these conditions in the United States has risen significantly. The trend toward mental health concerns in kids was already rising before the pandemic, but it has spiked even more.[71] This is truly an urgent issue and must be addressed by the family by welcoming the Holy Spirit into the home. Teaching our children biblical meditation techniques to connect with the Father's heart is essential. It equips them with valuable tools to handle the constant influx of emotions and thoughts they experience, making them stronger and better prepared for life's challenges.

Over the years, I have had the pleasure of watching my children develop their own meditation practices. Initially, I would sit with them at bedtime and lead each one through a nighttime meditation. I would encourage them to grab their favorite stuffed animal and hold on to it for comfort. Then, lying or sitting in bed, I would have them close their eyes and begin breathing. We would start out breathing deeply through their nose and letting it out very slowly through their mouth. I would tell them to "exhale like you are blowing through a straw." Immediately, the calming nature of the breath would settle in. We would then pray and invite the Holy Spirit to speak to and guide them both now and in their dreams.

Next, I would have them ask the Holy Spirit for a picture to show them something that brings them great joy. Children are incredible seers and, with their imaginative capacity, will always see something unique. I would let them explore the moment with the Holy Spirit. Sometimes, He would play soccer with them or ride skateboards together. Their happiness in the moment was tangible. After a minute or two, I would have them talk to the Holy Spirit. "Ask the Holy Spirit, what does He want to tell you today?" In their small voices, each of them would instantly say, "I heard something." And they each would proceed to tell me what the Holy Spirit told them. Usually, it was an encouraging word or a deposit of love in their spirit. Sometimes, they would say, "We had fun together." After that, they would quickly fall into a peaceful sleep free from any pressure or stress that might have followed them to their beds.

We still do that occasionally, but they now prefer to do it independently as they have matured in their meditative capacity. Children need to be taught how to connect with the Holy Spirit through biblical meditation for many reasons. First, to develop a lifelong relationship with the Holy Spirit that is lifegiving to their mind, body, and spirit. And second, as a coping mechanism by which they can handle the stress of life as they mature and grow. Whenever my children come to me with concerns or something bothering them, I ask them, "Have you meditated?" And if not, I encourage them to breathe and meditate, asking the Holy Spirit for guidance. This parental skill can be used for accidents as well.

One of the most effective tools in my parenting arsenal is guiding my children to breathe through pain or a moment of high stress. I usually say, "Take a deep breath." I then mirror the action with them by breathing deeply into my belly and exhaling. When they do this, a message is sent to their brain with instructions to calm down and relax.[72] This simple technique switches them from a state of high anxiety to a present state of calm, allowing us to talk and reason. I will include in a later chapter a meditation for children. I urge parents to inspire their children to meditate biblically and connect with the Holy Spirit early in their lives. What better gift can we give them than direct communication with God?

MEMORY COGNITION

Recent studies have concluded that regular meditation not only lowers stress and anxiety but is also known to improve memory and cognition significantly. Some participants showed an impressive tenfold improvement in memory, and some studies even showed significant improvement within two weeks of faithful meditation. This is confirmed in Scripture when Jesus says, *"But the Helper, the Holy Spirit, whom the Father will send in my name, he will teach you all things and bring to your remembrance all that I have said to you"* (John 14:26 ESV).

When we invite the Holy Spirit into every moment of our meditation, it is He who restores our memory to righteousness.

OVERALL PHYSICAL HEALTH

We clearly see many benefits gained by devoting time to regular meditation. Each of the benefits we've discussed is amazing, and we could stop there, but the intrinsic benefits of meditation, along with a redeemed thought life, continue. For example, meditation also helps restore health to people with asthma, cancer, chronic pain, heart disease, high blood pressure, IBS, sleep problems, and headaches, to name a few.

Groundbreaking scientific research has also demonstrated just how large an impact meditation has on our physical brains. A study performed over fourteen years was able to measure the decline in age-related grey matter density and demonstrate the results of long-term meditation impacts. One lifelong meditating test subject in particular named Mingyur, who chronologically is forty-one years old, has a brain whose chronological age is determined to be thirty-three. This study demonstrated "an underlying change in the structure of the brain."[73] Additional research shows that meditation actually leads to a thickening of the pre-frontal cortex. This is the part of the brain that is responsible for higher-level executive functions such as language, memory, decision-making and personality, and self-control.[74,75]

When we are instructed by God in Psalm 46:10 to *"be still, and know that I am God,"* He intentionally built our bodies with the capacity to reset and restore us to health through the embracing of the stillness and the knowing. Isn't it amazing that all of this time, God, our Creator, built in simple systems designed to connect with Him and restore our lives and bring order from the chaos?

MBSR, MBCT, CBT

Three methods currently in use successfully for treating high stress, anxiety, and depression bear a review for their efficacy and effectiveness. MBSR, or Mindfulness-Based Stress Reduction, is a meditation-based model designed in 1979 as a clinical model for stress management.[76] Over the years, achievements in the study of stress management have led to its development in the successful treatment of health disorders, as described earlier in this chapter. MBCT, or Mindfulness Based Cognitive Therapy, was developed later to address recurrent stress management specifically.[77] And CBT, Cognitive Behavioral Therapy, was developed to treat depression, anxiety, mental illness, and relationship problems.[78]

While each of these meditation therapies stands on their own for the targeted healing of specific areas, they all share one commonality. Each of them addresses our lifestyle of thinking and the resulting behaviors. The reason this works is due to the principle of meditation addressed earlier. God effectively created biblical meditation to "change how you feel by changing the way you think."[79] For the non-believer, the results are tangible: physical health and restored mental health. For the believer, the benefits are innumerable, with the gift of a relationship with the Holy Spirit, which creates lasting change resulting in the outflow of God's grace in our lives.

STRESS

We are no stranger to stressful living. That's a sad realization, but as of 2022, the following statistics confirm we are operating under too much stress:

- 33% of people report extreme stress.

- 77% experience health issues related to stress.

- 73% experience mental health-related problems.

- 48% have difficulty sleeping due to stress.[80]

There are four different types of stress as defined by the American Institute of Stress. Only one is considered a benefit:

1. **Acute stress:** This is what we know as fight or flight. If a bear is chasing me, acute stress is good. But if acute stress becomes a norm, it turns into chronic stress.

2. **Chronic stress:** The demands of life. Bills, career, family, etc. Chronic stress is what we typically suppress and ignore, leading to a plethora of health concerns, namely a compromised immune system.

3. **Distress:** Another form of daily stress that can become chronic. It includes things such as relationships, punishments, fear, injury, negative thought patterns, finances, and work challenges.

4. **Eustress** is a form of positive stress. This might entail a healthy marriage/relationship, promotions, a new baby, new friends, etc. This form of stress does wonders for our emotional, psychological, and physical health.[81]

Aside from eustress, all forms of enduring stress prove harmful to the body. Higher levels of cortisol in the body ramp up the heartbeat and rush blood through the body in response to a perceived emergency. This is a normal response, but if the stress is left unaddressed and persists, it can become chronic physical stress. Chronic stress negatively impacts several systems in our bodies. The system responsible for regulating cortisol is called the Hypothalamus Pituitary Adrenal

Axis (HPA). A complex system within the body that is responsible for regulating the immune system, among other essential things. Stress is what activates the HPA, and enduring stress causes higher than normal levels of cortisol, which leads to a host of physical and mental problems such as:

Respiratory and cardiovascular systems cause a change in breath rate and oxygen intake. The heart works harder, and blood pressure is elevated. These lead to headaches, stroke, and heart attacks.

Digestive systems increase glucose production in the liver, contributing to ongoing type 2 diabetes. Breathing problems, digestive problems, heartburn, and acid reflux due to increased stomach acids.

Muscular systems remain constricted and under tension as a physical effort by the body to protect itself. Experiencing chronic stress means that the muscular system is never relaxing.

Sex and reproductive systems in men are impacted by lower levels of testosterone and risks to the prostate. For women, physical symptoms of menopause are increased. And for both men and women, a loss of sexual desire.

The immune system is constantly stimulated by stress. As in the situation of being chased by a bear, the immune system can provide protection. But as time progresses, stress defeats the immune system, which makes it susceptible to illness. Common viruses like the cold and flu are not as easily defended or recovered from when the immune system is weakened under stress.[82]

Adopting a lifestyle of biblical meditation and a renewed thought life will reduce stress and encourage our bodies to reset and be at peace. Biblical meditation is not mystical, and there is no magic. It cannot make the stressors disappear. But better than that is having a mind and body that can withstand the stressors of life as we position ourselves within the explosive power of God flowing through us, as Paul writes to the Ephesians:

> *Now my beloved ones, I have saved these most important truths for last: Be supernaturally infused with strength through your life-union with the Lord Jesus. Stand victorious with the force of his explosive power flowing in and through you* (Ephesians 6:10 TPT).

THE DARK SIDE OF MEDITATION

Taking a purely holistic view of biblical meditation requires us to also look at the potential pitfalls of the meditation and inner healing process. Some people refer to it as the downside of meditation. During meditation, it is common and even healthy to engage with deep emotions, feelings, and long-buried wounds of the past. Secular meditation has demonstrated that privately engaging with these deep hurts and buried wounds can lead to deeper states of depression, anxiety, and even psychosis.[83] Examples include confronting unhealed, forgotten childhood traumas or inner hurts and wounds held by unforgiveness.

Understand this is not the rule but the exception. As you follow the guidance in this book and adopt a lifestyle of meditation partnered with the Holy Spirit, the wounds of the past can be healed, and those areas in your life can be restored. Secular meditation has no answer outside of professional clinical therapy to heal wounds. There is nothing wrong with professional therapy, and it is often an excellent addition to leading an optimistic and healthy lifestyle.

Biblical meditation, as is taught in this book, demonstrates that we do not seek to empty ourselves; emptying offers no way of dealing with unearthed traumas. Instead, we aim to be filled with the glory of God as the Holy Spirit ministers to us through our stillness. And when we release trauma, the Holy Spirit is always faithful to bring healing and restoration. The practice of inner healing was developed for this, to invite the Holy Spirit to reveal and heal the lies and false beliefs we acquired at the moment of trauma. Buddha can't do that; Kundalini meditation can't do that; yoga can't do that, etc. Only when we invite the Holy Spirit can we safely walk through healing with him as we meditate. Please hear this caution: If at any time during peaceful biblical meditations, you experience trauma so great that it consumes you, I want to encourage you to do three things.

First, realize that pain and suffering do not come from God. He will never cause you trauma, nor will He manipulate your meditations to become painful. When you are ready, He may walk with you through past hurts and trauma but will always guide you through the healing process painlessly.

Second, immediately invite the Holy Spirit into your room and mind to manifest in a tangible way (goosebumps are okay!) "Holy Spirit, I thank You for Your presence; please join me now and heal me in my weakness." Wait as the Holy Spirit ministers to you and restores your peace.

Third, please pause and seek inner healing ministry from a credible deliverance and inner healing ministry or biblical professional counselor. These ministries specialize in restoration through inner healing.

Let's consider more of the fantastic benefits of biblical meditation.

Meditation is non-linguistic. When we engage in biblical meditation, we are focusing our thoughts on things of God by allowing Him to take us on a thought journey. During this time, our mind is experiencing a non-linguistic moment. Remarkably, our mind communicates spirit to Spirit with God during these moments.[84]

Meditation can be as effective as medication. In a study published by the Journal of the American Medical Association, research concluded that meditation is as effective as medication when treating anxiety disorders.[85] My own story of overcoming type 2 diabetes stands as an example of how meditation can bring healing without medication.

I am encouraged by the incredible body of evidence demonstrating what has been documented in Scripture all along. We don't need science to prove the Bible, and we don't worship at the altar of science. Our faith is enriched when scientific discoveries align with the teachings of Scripture, affirming what God has provided us.

MENO IN DAMAM MEDITATION

(short version)

Purpose: A quiet, still, Holy Spirit encounter

Let's begin by taking a deep breath in through your nostrils, holding it in for several seconds, and slowly exhaling through your mouth for several seconds. Now, do it two more times with your eyes closed. As you do, allow your mind to go wherever it wants to go. Don't try to push nagging thoughts away or silence the noises in the room. Just let your mind process and jump from one thought to another.

Now, ask the Holy Spirit, what do You want to tell me? Have a short conversation with the Holy Spirit and go to whatever thought He takes you.

Now, take a moment to notice what your current state feels like intentionally. How does your head feel? How does your body feel? How about your mind? Did you notice anything different about the atmosphere in the room? Did you notice an increase in peace and calm within your mind? Perhaps you are feeling uncomfortable and strange. All of these feelings and questions are perfectly normal and are precisely how our minds and bodies are designed to process this experience.

Perhaps you were raised in a church where you were taught that being alone with your thoughts is sinful and an open door for the enemy. You may have been told, "Idle hands are the devil's playground," an unfortunate misinterpretation and paraphrase of Proverbs 16:27. Quite the opposite is true in Scripture. Our silence moves us closer to holiness.

> *I am standing in absolute stillness, silent before the one I love, waiting as long as it takes for him to rescue me. Only God is my Savior, and he will not fail me* (Psalm 62:5 TPT).

> *When words are many, transgression is not lacking, but whoever restrains his lips is prudent* (Proverbs 10:19 ESV).

5

HISTORY *and* PRIMER *on* the COUNTERFEIT

ORIGINS

Now Isaac had returned from Beer-lahai-roi and was dwelling in the Negeb. And Isaac went out to meditate in the field toward evening. And he lifted up his eyes and saw, and behold, there were camels coming (Genesis 24:62-63 ESV).

This is the first mention in the Bible of meditation. Understanding the value of a supernatural thought life, Isaac sequestered himself in private meditation. Look at his posture; during his meditation, he looked up. This was a posture of reverence to God. He was gazing heavenward as a natural expression of his worship. However, his time in the field was not coincidental, and God used this moment. While Isaac was looking heavenward, he saw his future in Rebekah approaching him. At this moment, during his meditation, Isaac received the revelation of his future in a very tangible manner. The Bible tells us that Isaac immediately married Rebekah and loved her. Likewise, we can expect revelations from Heaven to flow as we practice the art of supernatural thinking in our meditative moments.

It is important to understand the history and origins of meditation practices before we move on. By understanding how far back in human history meditation is practiced, we can understand how and when this righteous practice lost its place among believers.

Meditation as a practice has been part of human culture as far back as the history of humanity on earth. It was God who first established meditative moments with Adam and Eve in the garden. God begins by modeling a meditative moment. First, at the conclusion of the sixth day, God entered a reflective moment. He took a pause to look at everything He had made and, in that moment, focused His attention on what He had created and concluded that "It was very good." The precise Hebrew words used are *tob mod,* which means exceedingly beautiful.[86] God's reflection was a meditation focusing on the beauty of His creation.

"And God saw everything that he had made, and behold, it was very good" (Genesis 1:31 ESV). *"By the seventh day Yahweh had completed his work of creation, so he rested from all his work..."* (Genesis 2:2-3 TPT). God has no need of rest, yet being God, He knew humanity does, so it became incumbent upon Him to demonstrate and create an entire sabbath day for the purpose of rest, meditation, and supernatural thinking.

According to archaeological studies, the practice of meditation "has been a spiritual practice of human beings since our beginnings." Research indicates that meditation has roots in the practices of early human societies, often occurring during communal activities like fire-gazing around campfires. Psychologist Matt J. Rossano's work suggests that these early forms of meditation might have played a role in "shaping the human brain's capacity for symbolism and language development."[87]

These findings amazingly demonstrate how the practice of contemplation, meditation, and supernatural thinking has been intertwined with the development and creation of humanity. When David wrote

Psalms, these practices were well known, understood, and practiced widely. As we've already seen in the book of Psalms, we can surmise that David became a master meditator by watching and learning from his leaders throughout his life.

FAST-FORWARD

Meditation practitioners have a well-documented history. Now I will present a short, simplified timeline showing how meditation has traveled and impacted cultures through time.

- God created the earth and appointed Adam and Eve as guardians and stewards. He first demonstrated for us the act of rest, focus, and reflection.

- Satan enters the garden, and the world is forever changed following the fall of Adam and Eve. While in the garden, Adam and Eve developed a deep, intimate relationship with God. It's likely that they spent time in contemplation and meditation while in the presence of God. We believe this because Genesis 3:8 states that they recognized the sound of the Lord.

- The earliest forms of meditation and yoga began in ancient Egypt and later spread to India. Early Buddhist writings record that Hindu travelers visited Memphis, the old kingdom of ancient Egypt, and developed the practices now known as Buddhism. It is from the Egyptian influences that Buddhism acquires knowledge of the divine and the lotus flower, among other iconographies.[88] These original forms of meditation and yoga are called Kemetic yoga or Smi Tawi, which means the unification of the upper and lower parts of humanity. More concisely, Smi Tawi yoga and meditation practices are believed to reunify the soul and the original divine source.[89] Worship of ancient demonic deities is deeply rooted in these early practices.

- 5000 BC – Wall art was discovered in the Indus Valley, South Asia, depicting early forms of meditation and yoga.[90]

- 1500 BC – 500 BC – Documented forms of yoga, Taoism, and Buddhism become written forms of meditation.

- 20 BC – 325 AD –Greek philosophers Zeno of Citium (Cyprus), Socrates, Marcus Aurelius, etc., brought stoicism and secular meditation into popularity.

- 300 AD – 1200 AD – Christian mysticism brings meditation and divine contemplation into the church. Religious monks widely adopted its practice.

- 500 AD – 1400 AD – Zen Buddhism, Sufism, Sikhism, and the Jewish Kabbalah all become accepted forms of secular meditation practices.

- 1800 – present time – A wide adoption of all practices mentioned were incorporated into Western secularism. Today, meditation, mindfulness, and forms of contemplation are widespread and mainstream. The explosion of thinking and meditating in Western culture is largely due to advancements in research showing the benefits to the mind, body, and spirit.[91]

- Recent years – In limited streams of Christianity, yoga has been adopted in the form of Christian Yoga, Holy Yoga, Biblical Yoga, and Original Yoga.

- 2019 – The Covid pandemic led to a rapid acceleration of acceptance of meditation and mindfulness practices.[92]

- Present day, 2023 – Supernatural thinking and holy forms of biblical meditation are being reintroduced to the body of believers as a righteous inheritance, to bring glory to God, and for the enrichment of our lives and well-being. J.I. Packer wrote concerning meditation in his book, *Knowing God:* "Meditation is a lost art today, and Christian people suffer grievously from their ignorance of the practice. Meditation is the activity of calling to mind, and thinking over, and dwelling on, and applying to oneself, the various things that one knows about the works and ways and purposes, and promises of God. It is an activity of holy thought, consciously performed in the presence of God, under the eye of God, by the help of God, as a means of communion with God."

As we look through history, we can see how satan has intentionally orchestrated practices of meditation, twisting them and crafting a fascination designed to draw people toward it. Why does he care about meditation? Because it's through secular meditation that he gains unrestrained access to the thoughts and minds of the people. Once he gains a controlling interest in their thought life, he has the ability to control the person.

The positive aspect is that engaging in biblical meditation, which is pure and righteous, prevents the enemy from making progress and firmly grounds us in supernatural thinking aligned with Heaven.

The remainder of this chapter provides a primer on the most prevalent forms of demonic meditation practices used throughout the world. These are surging through the world's population because people are desperately searching for ways to overcome stress and anxiety, reduce fear, and maintain good mental health. We should also acknowledge that these forms are highly fascinating and enticing. That is precisely what the Bible teaches us to *turn away from.*

*When you are tempted, don't ever say, "God is tempting me,"
for God is incapable of being tempted by evil, and he is never
the source of temptation. Instead, it is each person's own
desires and thoughts that drag them into evil and lure them
away into darkness...* (James 1:13-14 TPT).

*Do not detour into darkness or even set foot on that path.
Stay away from it; don't even go there!* (Proverbs 4:14-15
TPT)

YOGA

Yoga has enjoyed a largely uncontested journey through several
of Earth's cultures. In the United States, yoga is described by the
National Center for Complimentary and Integrative Health as an
"ancient and complex practice, rooted in Indian philosophy. It began
as a spiritual practice but has become popular as a way of promoting
physical and mental well-being."[93] Unfortunately, that definition is
precisely what has desensitized yoga for much of American society.
Having attempted to strip away the spiritual significance of the
practice has created a physical exercise seemingly void of spiritual
significance. Let us look deeper at the origins and intent of yoga as
the truth is revealed.

The word *yoga* is a Sanskrit word that translates to yoke or union.
"Yoga is a method joining the individual self with the divine, univer-
sal spirit, or cosmic consciousness. Physical and mental exercises are
designed to help achieve this goal, also called self-transcendence or
enlightenment."[94] The Bible offers clear guidance that we should not be
unequally yoked with unbelievers. By its own name, yoga is a covenantal

act of marital union designed to yoke oneself to the demonic spirits in association with the practice.

Each of the movements within yoga is called *asana*. An *asana* is a deliberate and worshipful posture designed to induce different states of mind and being. For example, asana postures are frequently used to invoke the spirits of trees, animals, and demonic gods. Specifically, each asana is a worshipful position, ultimately honoring the demon god shiva. Shiva is honored through each yogic posture, saying, and hand gesture, which represents a physical prayer offering given by the body to a demon god. Yoga comes from the Bhagavad Gita, written around 400 BCE by a man named Veda Vyasa. Veda Vyasa was believed to be the avatar of the demon god Vishnu, who imparted the sacred written texts of Hinduism, including yoga and the worship of shiva.

Along with asana postures, the yogic tradition includes the repetition of specific sounds called mantras, hand gestures called mudras, and postures called asana. The practice of yoga always involves asana, and the inclusion of mudras and mantras varies by style and purpose.

Biblical Response to Yoga

No biblical evidence exists supporting the practice of yoga. Christian yoga does not and cannot exist despite the moniker, as the two directly oppose each other. The church of believers is called the bride of Christ, and Jesus is the Bridegroom. Believers cannot be yoked in union with God and shiva simultaneously. This is why it is written that we are not to be unequally yoked because light cannot exist with darkness.

> *Do not be unequally yoked with unbelievers. For what partnership has righteousness with lawlessness? Or what fellowship has light with darkness? What accord has Christ with Belial? Or what portion does a believer share with an unbeliever? What agreement has the temple of*

God with idols? For we are the temple of the living God... (2 Corinthians 6:14-16 ESV).

For more understanding and thorough research, I highly recommend David Hunt's book titled *Yoga and the Body of Christ*.

Is Yoga Redeemable?

Make no mistake: Yoga is a profoundly religious practice that cannot be separated from its demonic origins. Yoga in all aspects, asana (body postures), mantra (sayings), and mudra (hand postures), are irredeemable and unsuitable for believers in Jesus. Wisdom concerning how we are to steward our bodies is made clear by Paul as he wrote in 1 Corinthians 6:19-20 (ESV), *"Do you not know that your body is a temple of the Holy Spirit within you, whom you have from God? You are not your own, for you were bought with a price. So glorify God in your body."* Matthew 6:24 (ESV) tells us, *"No one can serve two masters, for either he will hate the one and love the other, or he will be devoted to the one and despise the other."* Yoga was created to bring people into unity with false gods, and it is for this reason that all forms of yoga are irredeemable. If you have participated in any form of yoga, I urge you to pray the prayer of release from yoga and meditation located at the back of this book.

TRANSCENDENTAL MEDITATION, MANTRA, AUM (OM)

Transcendental Meditation, or TM, is a meditation technique using sound, mantras, or Om. The focus of transcendental meditation is to induce a state of consciousness often referred to as bliss or inner peace. A mantra is defined as a repeated sound, word, or utterance. The most famous mantra is the sound, Om. Om is a sound made from three sylla-bles, AUM, and is pronounced as AaaaaUuuuuuMmmm. The purpose of Om is to create a vibration that moves throughout the body. The meaning of OM is said to represent birth, life, and death. Practitioners believe this is the original and most primal sound that created the uni-verse. The famous symbol, ॐ, is a representation of the sound of Om. Notice the three segments; each represents the movement through dif-ferent states of consciousness, from waking to the unconscious to the dream state, in cyclic repetition.

Biblical Response to Transcendental Meditation

For a believer in Jesus, this type of meditation is unbiblical and is an open door to demonic influence in our lives. The proper expression of sound in biblical meditation is the use of a blessing, the name of Yahweh, the gift of tongues, or through song. In a later chapter, I pro-vide meditations that involve sound from a biblical perspective. It is also important to note that nowhere in Scripture are we encouraged to recite sounds or phrases in a repeated fashion. Although referring to prayer, Jesus told us not to pray with repetition or empty phrases. I believe the same applies to our meditations.

> *When you pray, there is no need to repeat empty phrases, praying like those who don't know God, for they expect God to hear them because of their many words* (Matthew 6:7 TPT).

Is Transcendental Meditation Redeemable?

Transcendental meditation is not redeemable as it is commonly prac-ticed. Biblical meditation involving the use of sounds such as tongues or a prayer is a beautiful expression that does not require repetitive sound to benefit the believer.

KUNDALINI

Kundalini meditation and yoga refer to a meditation that is designed to invoke the power of a sleeping serpent that lies coiled dormant at the base of the spine. The word *kundalini* means coiled serpent. The root word "kund" means a deep pit or cave. And "lini" means to be overcome with energy.[95] Principally, the purpose of kundalini meditation is to invoke the serpent energy from the deep pit within and encourage it to flow up the spine until it reaches the crown of the head. As the serpent spirit rises up the spine, it awakens the seven spiritual chakras (or energies) throughout the body. Each chakra represents a different focus for awakening as the serpent rises. Those who practice this form of meditation state that "It feels like the life force has amplified itself and has suddenly become even more alive. This is felt in its movement up the spine and sometimes as an electrical or radiating feeling in every cell. This sensation can be uncomfortable or terrifying. Nothing prepares us for this eruption."[96] Manifestations such as tremors, involuntary movement, and multisensory hallucinations leading to mood swings, grief, fear, and depression are reported as typical.[97]

A story documented in a psychological case review describes the decline of a 24-year-old man who became involved in kundalini. During his treatment, he would present himself as delusional, in poor self-care, and with disorganized speech. He would tell his medical team that his condition was due to his kundalini awakening. Within two years, he had deteriorated so severely that he was forcibly detained in an adult psychiatry ward.[98] According to prominent kundalini instructor

Sadhgru, "When kundalini goes bad, it goes bad in ways that cannot be fixed. Kundalini is the most dangerous of all."[99]

Ava's Story

Let me introduce you to Ava. Ava is a believer in Jesus and attends church regularly. Her family history and upbringing were like so many: a tumultuous time filled with hardship, trauma, and pain. Along her journey, Ava devoted herself to practices and belief systems that appeared to help her maintain a healthy mental state. She explored Yoga, Catholicism, Christianity, Buddhism, Kundalini, and Transcendental Meditation. Of all of the things that Ava explored, her involvement in kundalini meditation and yoga has had the most profoundly damaging impact on her life.

She described to me the various states of awakening she encountered. "I felt like waves of electrical energy surging through me, causing my body to convulse and tremor." Ava's participation in kundalini grew more intense as time passed, and deeper connections were experienced. One of the reasons she pursued this was the promise of mental health restoration and healing in the body. This is one of the false claims of kundalini yoga when, in fact, the opposite is true, as I've previously taught. Not long ago, during a particularly hard time in Ava's life, she found herself addressing past traumas and settling complicated family concerns. She turned to her kundalini instructor for guidance. Then, after intense periods of kundalini meditation, Ava found herself drowning in a state of mental despair.

Suddenly, she was spinning out of control, unable to focus or maintain even a healthy conversation without mentally breaking down. Her mental stability and physical condition only declined as a result of her involvement in kundalini meditation and yoga. Eventually, her ability to maintain a healthy mental state was so significantly impacted that she was no longer able to fulfill her obligations at work. I had the good fortune of speaking with Ava during this time in her life. I began to explain the root of kundalini yoga and meditation and exposed everything she has invited into her life. Seeing the truth in what I was saying, Ava immediately stopped her involvement in kundalini and began speaking with a professional counselor. Ava is now doing great and on the road to recovery, and though she has a lot of work ahead, her future is bright.

Ava's story exemplifies the principle of opening doors to the enemy through participation in unrighteous and evil activities. Ephesians 5:11 from the Passion Translation teaches us, *"And don't even associate with the servants of darkness because they have no fruit in them; instead, reveal truth to them."* In Ava's case, once the truth was revealed and the Gospel was made known in her life. Her decision to turn away and accept God's gift of freedom led to her victory.

Biblical Response to Kundalini Meditation

For the believer, any willing participation with any demonic spirit, such as kundalini, opens the gates for demonic torment. When we accept the free gift of salvation, the Holy Spirit indwells us, and we have His presence always guiding us. This is how Christians should approach meditation, in partnership with the Holy Spirit, not through serpent spirit demons. Reject all teachings that desensitize and normalize kundalini meditation among believers in Jesus. Kundalini masters and practitioners widely caution that it is the most dangerous of all forms of meditation. Claiming that when practiced without proper focus and discipline, it can completely dismantle your life instantly.[100] The Sai Ayurvedic Institute describes a ranging list of problems known as kundalini syndrome attributed to this type of meditation. These include Involuntary body movements, sleeping disorders, digestive system problems, numbness in limbs, pain throughout the body, random emotional outbursts, increased fear, rage, depression, hearing voices or sounds, mental confusion, and many more.[101]

Believers, we are to steer clear from anything that exalts itself against the knowledge of God. This is dangerous; do not be deceived. If you have participated in kundalini, I invite you now to repent and renounce participation with this prayer:

"Thank You, Holy Spirit, for Your presence. Lord, I invite You to fill me with Your Spirit. Jesus, I believe You are the Son of God, and I believe You died on the cross for me, cleansing me from all sin and redeeming me from death. I acknowledge my participation in kundalini practices, and I repent for and renounce all involvement in this evil practice. Holy Spirit, I invite You now to cleanse my mind, my body, and my emotions from any evil spirit that may have come into my life. I speak to my body and my mind, and I command all effects brought on through kundalini be broken off of me now through the name of Jesus. I tell my DNA to forget the trauma brought on me when I partnered with these demons. I receive the blessings of the Lord, I am created in His image, I am fearfully and wonderfully made, and I am called to righteousness. And now, I receive the freedom from demonic attachments in my life, and I command every demonic spirit to GO NOW in Jesus's name. Thank You, Jesus, I am free!"

Place your hand on the base of your spine, and in a prophetic act, pull it out, throw it to the ground, and crush its head!

Is Kundalini Meditation Redeemable?

All aspects of kundalini meditation and yoga are irredeemable. Believers must not participate in this demonic form of meditation. Some teachings have tried to link the Holy Spirit with kundalini in an effort to legitimize the practice within Christianity. Believers are indwelt with the Holy Spirit at the moment of our salvation. As we seek and receive the Holy Spirit, we can be confident that His power and glory will be evident in various ways, including the remarkable gift of speaking in tongues.

The difference is that, unlike the kundalini, the Holy Spirit is not dormant, awaiting a moment of awakening. He is always present and speaking. Additionally, the power of the Holy Spirit has been promised to all believers, not just those who choose to awaken the demonic power of a dormant spirit.

The glory of the Holy Spirit brings joy, peace, patience, kindness, virtue, faith, gentleness, and strength of spirit. In contrast, the fruits of kundalini worship manifest the opposite. For believers to truly align their minds, hearts, and bodies, it is absolutely crucial to meditate in line with the Holy Spirit. This practice allows the fruits of the Spirit to manifest in our actions and behavior, ultimately leading to a fulfilled life of purpose.

> *Even the Spirit of truth, whom the world cannot receive, because it neither sees him nor knows him. You know him, for he dwells with you and will be in you* (John 14:17 ESV).

> *But you will receive power when the Holy Spirit has come upon you, and you will be my witnesses in Jerusalem and in all Judea and Samaria, and to the end of the earth* (Acts 1:8 ESV).

> *Likewise the Spirit helps us in our weakness. For we do not know what to pray for as we ought, but the Spirit himself intercedes for us with groanings too deep for words* (Romans 8:26 ESV).

VIPASSANA

Believed to have origins dating back to Buddha himself, vipassana, also known as insight meditation, means clear seeing or insight.[102] It is a form of Buddhist meditation designed to restructure the personality, sense of self, and worldview of the meditator. Vipassana meditation is "the effort made by the meditator to understand correctly the nature of the psycho-physical phenomena taking place in his own body."[103] Its ultimate goal is to focus on three aspects of human existence. Suffering, transience, and unbinding. This type of meditation encourages complete silence, abstinence, fasting, and various forms of breathwork as well.[104] Vipassana meditation encourages the practitioner to take a unique inward-looking approach to awakening. Those who practice this technique report coming to the realization that they do not love anyone but themselves. This view of self-love is said to be the awakening of pure love. S.N. Goenka, the most prominent modern vipassana teacher, teaches that vipassana reveals that the love felt for others is purely dependent on what we gain in return. The goal of vipassana is to reach a place of enlightenment where the practitioner is able to express pure love as one-way traffic.[105] The sounds of a gong, or cymbals, generally accompany this form of meditation.

Is Vipassana Redeemable?

No. Vipassana meditation is irredeemable for believers in Christ. Buddhism is an atheistic spiritual path and a religion focused on self-enlightenment. Vipassana meditation emphasizes total introspection, leading to inner personal salvation.

The Biblical Response to Vipassana

Salvation is only promised through our belief in Jesus and our acceptance of the free gift of grace offered at the cross. As believers in Jesus, we cannot save ourselves by looking inward for our hope. We reject anything that raises itself against the knowledge of God; see 2 Corinthians 10:5.

> *Jesus explained, "I am the Way, I am the Truth, and I am the Life. No one comes next to the Father except through union with me. To know me is to know my Father too"* (John 14:6 TPT).

The Bible teaches us to pursue love and that if we do not have love, we are nothing more than a noisy gong or a clanging cymbal. In vipassana and other forms of meditation, the gong, cymbal, and bell are used strategically throughout the stages of meditation. Beginning with a call to meditation, followed by a call to focus, and ending with a deliberate ceasing of the meditative moment. In Buddhist meditation, the bells, gongs, and cymbals are not only pleasant sounds, but the belief is that the specific sounds clear the atmosphere of negative energy, preparing the space for ceremonial purposes and rituals. Specifically in Buddhism, the brass sounds are believed to be the actual voice of Buddha, who is speaking protection over the meditators. Additionally, the sounds are thought to unite the feminine and the masculine, ultimately leading to the purity of enlightenment.

What is impressive is that the apostle Paul knew all of this as the practices of Eastern meditation had already spread to the known world. God addressed these practices through Paul directly when he wrote the following, comparing the lack of love to the emptiness and powerlessness of the gongs and cymbals used in these forms of religious expression.

If I speak in the tongues of men and of angels, but have not love, I am a noisy gong or a clanging cymbal. And if I have prophetic powers, and understand all mysteries and all knowledge, and if I have all faith, so as to remove mountains, but have not love, I am nothing (1 Corinthians 13:1-2 ESV).

In addition to the pursuit of love, we are to eagerly desire spiritual gifts, and that we should prophesy. The use of our gifts and prophecy is an outflow of the pure love attained only through a relationship developed in the meditative abiding time with Jesus.

Pursue love and earnestly desire the spiritual gifts, especially that you may prophesy (1 Corinthians 14:1 ESV).

TAI CHI

Tai Chi, also known as shadow boxing, is a form of Taoist martial arts whose origins claim self-defense. Meaning "supreme polarity," Tai Chi meditation is practiced in a standing position in a balanced posture aiming to still the mind and body. The practice of Tai Chi involves slow, concentrated movement of the body, which is thought to inspire a sense of peace. The exercise consists of standing or balancing in a perfect position for extended periods of time. Meditators believe that this practice brings clarity and fortitude.

The origins of Tai Chi are rooted in Yijing, sometimes spelled as I Ching. Yijing is a form of divination and witchcraft involving fortune-telling and spiritism. Yijing is explained and taught through an ancient divination text called the Book of Changes.[106] This book describes the two life forces understood as Yin and Yang. Yin and

Yang are said to have been created by a creature known as Fu Xi. He is depicted conjoined with his sister/wife Nuwa as half human and half serpent. Images depicting them show them holding a compass and a square, an unexpected parallel to Freemasonry's reference to the great architect of the universe.[107] Fu Xi and Nuwa, likewise, are believed to be the first parents of humanity.[108] The practice of Tai Chi is a form of worship honoring the Yin and the Yang, which is to worship the false gods.

Is Tai Chi Redeemable?

No. Tai Chi is irredeemable due to its roots within Yijing divination, along with the balance between the opposing life forces of Yin and Yang. The practice is a form of worship that honors the demon principalities Fu Xi and his sister/wife Nuwa.

The Biblical Response to Tai Chi

The practice of Tai Chi involves slow, repetitive movements while emptying the mind of all thoughts.[109] This practice of emptying the mind opens the believer up for torment and invites demonic influences into the life of the meditator. For the believer, we are not called to empty ourselves but to be filled with the joy of the Holy Spirit.

> *You make known to me the path of life; in your presence there is fullness of joy; at your right hand are pleasures forevermore* (Psalm 16:11 ESV).

The Bible teaches us that only God created the world and humanity, and Jesus upholds the universe. He alone is who we worship.

> *Long ago, at many times and in many ways, God spoke to our fathers by the prophets, but in these last days he has spoken*

to us by his Son, whom he appointed the heir of all things, through whom also he created the world. He is the radiance of the glory of God and the exact imprint of his nature, and he upholds the universe by the word of his power. After making purification for sins, he sat down at the right hand of the Majesty on high (Hebrews 1:1-3 ESV).

We receive strength in the simple stillness of the presence of God. In biblical meditation, posture is not as crucial as the abiding time in the glory. Referring to earlier in this book, we are encouraged by God to abide in Him, and He is faithful to abide in us. *Damam,* to wait, and *meno,* to be still, are the words used to describe our perfect expression in biblical meditation.

LOVING KINDNESS (METTA)

Metta, commonly known as Loving Kindness, is a form of meditation with its roots in Buddhism. Its name is derived from the Pali language, and it focuses on the development of the divine abodes of Compassion, Altruistic Joy, Equanimity, and Loving Kindness. Together, these all seek to explore sweeping emotions in the abode of Brahma, the creator god.[110] In the Buddha's teaching called the Metta Sutta, Loving Kindness meditation focuses on thoughts of benevolence toward yourself, others, and living creatures, specifically toward serpents.[111] One sutta tells of a monk who died from being bitten by a snake. The Buddha reprimanded the monks for not loving the serpent families well enough and commanded them to increase their love for the four primary serpent families.[112] The practice of Loving Kindness involves both mantras and visualizations during the exercise.

Is Loving Kindness Redeemable?

No. Loving Kindness is irredeemable as a form of meditation. The principles of loving each other and spreading kindness are not problematic. However, they are not rooted in a belief in Christ, and the pattern of belief does not align with God's Word. Since God is love, apart from Him any understanding of loving-kindness will be distorted and corrupted; a decoy that deters us from the real thing. The concept of offering altruistic, selfless love, specifically toward snakes, is an obvious and overt contradiction to Scripture when God cursed satan in the form of a serpent; see Genesis 3:14.

> *The Lord God said to the serpent, "Because you have done this, cursed are you above all livestock and above all beasts of the field; on your belly you shall go, and dust you shall eat all the days of your life"* (Genesis 3:14 ESV).

The Biblical Response to Loving Kindness

For the believer, Jesus says, *"So I give you now a new commandment: Love each other just as much as I have loved you. For when you demonstrate the same love I have for you by loving one another, everyone will know that you're my true followers"* (John 13:34-35 TPT).

As we abide in Jesus, the pure love of the Father enriches our lives and produces a natural outflow of that same love. A love that is not manufactured or created to suppress a false reality of defilement and suffering. Through our abiding time, the Holy Spirit transforms our hearts and minds. We first love God, then our neighbor. As we abide in the love of God, we naturally love our neighbor. We focus on the Author of love rather than trying to drum up the emotion of love. These two principles are how believers exercise all prior Ten Commandments.

THE FOUR SPIRITUAL EXERCISES

As I wrote earlier, Saint Ignatius Loyola was the founder of the Jesuit order of Catholics. The four spiritual exercises were provided to him through demonic intervention in the form of a serpent while in solitude in a cave in Spain. While these exercises appear wholesome, they were provided through demonic inspiration. That alone makes them impure and ungodly. This is truly an example of mixing the holy and the profane. These spiritual exercises are to be carried out over the course of four phases called weeks.[113] I provide a simplified description here:

- Phase 1 – Pondering God's love for us and our flaws and sins.

- Phase 2 – Pondering God's mission to save the world. A focus on compassion is encouraged at this stage.

- Phase 3 – Pondering the suffering of Jesus.

- Phase 4 – Pondering the chaos, confusion, and awe of the resurrection.[114]

Are the Spiritual Exercises of Ignatius Loyola Redeemable?

Once again, the principles of these exercises are not entirely problematic. The roots and the origins are. They are what makes the entire practice unbiblical. The Bible clearly outlines how a believer is to meditate. Any teaching that attempts to reframe meditation outside of the Bible is in error and irredeemable. For example, the Bible does not teach us to devote our thoughts to our flaws and sins. Instead, we look again to Philippians 4:8 (NIV) for guidance in our thoughts from a biblical perspective:

Finally, brothers and sisters, whatever is true, whatever is noble, whatever is right, whatever is pure, whatever is lovely, whatever is admirable—if anything is excellent or praise-worthy—think about such things.

The Biblical Response to the Spiritual Exercises

It is easy to see how pondering some of these may bring a stillness to the mind. Yet, consider the conditions in which these exercises were developed. And realize that satan cannot create anything, only pervert and counterfeit. Likewise, we are given life-giving models for meditation in Scripture that produce life in the body and mind when implemented. God clearly instructs believers to think about things that are pure, right, excellent, praiseworthy, lovely, admirable, and noble. When we intentionally think about these things, our minds become renewed, and we are transformed from the inside out.

Throughout this book, we have seen the Bible is rich with various forms of contemplation and meditation. Yet even as followers of Jesus navigated life in early history, we see how satan came in and began to attack the minds and hearts of the people after the fall. Today, the idea of meditation and its various forms has been abdicated to the non-believing in our secular society. This must stop, and the practice must be restored back into the daily lives of every believer.

Meditation is wholly biblical, and I believe it should be a necessary part of the fruitful life of every believer. As such, meditation does not need to be redeemed; it is not a "new age" concept, and the demonic practitioners do not own it. I reject all meditative practices that worship another god, or another Jesus, or deity. I reject all forms of chanting and mantras. I reject the demonic postures of yoga, which invite kundalini and other demonic spirits. I reject stoic meditation as a model of mastering emotion and the contemplation over suffering and death. I reject the chant aum (ॐ, om) and its false representation of the Holy Spirit.[115] And I reject any meditation techniques revealed through demonic intervention.

Forms of meditation have been used for centuries, not merely as religious functions but as methods of restorative health. The book of Proverbs promises healing through meditative supernatural thinking.

> *My son, be attentive to my words; incline your ear to my say-ings. Let them not escape from your sight; keep them within your heart. For they are life to those who find them, and healing to all their flesh. Keep your heart with all vigilance, for from it flow the springs of life* (Proverbs 4:20-23 ESV).

This is a fun verse to analyze; the word *incline* here means to bend down, spread out, and to extend yourself in a posture to receive.[116] *"Let them not escape from your sight"* is a call to contemplation and focus on the instruction. *"Keep them within your heart"* is a call to focus the mind on the words of life.[117] All resulting in renewed life, healing, vigor, and an outward representation of God's attributes from your heart.

REPENT AND RENOUNCE

If you have participated in any form of ungodly meditation, breath-work, or pagan thinking, I urge you to pray the following prayer of repentance. Renounce all involvement, and declare your new intent to follow the biblical model for meditation and supernatural thinking:

> I repent for and renounce my participation in all forms of ungodly meditation and the worship of demons. I renounce all meditative practices that worship another

god, or another Jesus, or deity. I renounce all forms of chanting and mantras.

I renounce the demonic and worshipful postures of yoga, which invite kundalini and other demonic spirits. I renounce stoic meditation as a model of mastering emotion and the contemplation over suffering and death. I renounce the chant aum (ॐ, om) and its false representation of the Holy Spirit. I renounce the A (ah) sound meant to represent consciousness. I renounce the U (oo) sound meant to represent the dream consciousness. I renounce the M (mm) sound meant to represent the deep sleep consciousness.

Finally, I renounce the fourth sound of silence, which opens the door and invites a demonic presence. And I renounce any meditation techniques revealed to gurus, sages, monks, shamans, and wise people through demonic intervention.

I break the associated trauma resulting from my participation, and I command all trauma attached to my DNA to be removed and to fall off now. I command my genes to forget the trauma and to be healed now in Jesus's name.

I forgive myself for all my involvement in these practices. And I now break every demonic hold over my life and command every evil spirit to leave me now in the name of Jesus.

I declare from this point forward that I will engage in holy biblical meditation, bringing glory to God and drawing me deeper into my relationship with Jesus.

I receive the blessings of peace, rest, stillness, and healing in my mind and body as I engage in meditation that glorifies God and deepens my relationship with Him. Amen.

TAKE A MOMENT TO THINK SUPERNATURALLY

Biblical Grounding:

This meditation is based on Proverbs 4:20-23

Purpose:

To train the mind in supernatural thinking by intentionally focusing on God and His words. As His words penetrate your heart, new life flows from you. Repetition is the key to this meditation. As your thought life develops a habit of right thinking, the outflow of your life becomes a reflection of your heart and mind.

Environment:

This meditation is best performed in a calming space, allowing your mind to ponder. Play a soft worship song, perhaps instrumental (optional).

Posture:

Begin by bending, stretching out, extending yourself, and spreading out as your posture before the Lord. (Alternatively, remaining seated or lying down is acceptable.) Having a Bible nearby for reference may be useful.

Open with Prayer:

Thank the Holy Spirit for joining you, and ask for a tangible manifestation of His glory to fill the room. "Thank You, Holy Spirit, for Your presence; I ask You to join me with an increase of Your manifestation. May Your glory tangibly fill this room."

Breathe:

Close your eyes, take a slow, deep breath in through your nose, and hold it for five seconds.

- Exhale slowly through your mouth, speaking in tongues on the exhale.**
- Repeat five times.
- Return to normal breathing, remain silent, soaking in the presence of the Holy Spirit for 2-10 minutes.
- Open your eyes slowly when you are ready.

Meditate:

Open the Bible to Proverbs 3:13, read the words, and set it aside.*

In silent reflection, focus on the following words from this Scripture verse and contemplate them in your mind:

> *Blessed is the one who finds wisdom, and the one who gets understanding* (Proverbs 3:13 ESV).

Close your eyes once again and breathe deeply.

Say, "Holy Spirit, I'm listening; what are You saying to me in this verse?" Continue in this intimate moment with the Holy Spirit as He counsels you; remain as long as you need. These are words of instruction promising life and healing for your body.

Stay in the quiet moment of abiding for several minutes.

Having done this, you are being prepared for the outward expression of God's glory in your life resulting from your meditation.

*Later, you may choose any Scripture or prophetic word you wish to contemplate.

**Alternatively, if you do not yet have the gift of tongues, you can utter any phrase of thankfulness. Example: "Thank You, Holy Spirit, for Your presence." Or make a declaration over your life such as, "I am blessed and highly favored." Or simply, "Yahweh."

The BIBLICAL
PILLARS *of*
MEDITATION

6

BREATH *of* GOD

Then the Lord God formed the man of dust from the
ground and breathed into his nostrils the breath of life, and
the man became a living creature (Genesis 2:7 ESV).

Picture this moment: Adam is a lifeless statue lying on the dirt from which he had just been formed. God is hovering over him, admiring His work, thinking about the beautiful relationships He is about to bring forth through Adam. Then, in a moment, God leans down and, with one blast of His breath, opens Adam's nostrils, inflating his lungs and filling his body with life made possible by the Ruach Spirit of God. As Adam breathed in the breath and Spirit of God, he became awakened, self-aware, and ALIVE!

As God's breath continued to circulate through his new body, his cardiovascular system was brought to life, and his heart began to beat. Blood infused with the same essence of God began to flow rhythmically into and through each new artery, sending blood to his brain and traveling through brand-new capillaries. His blood continued its journey into his veins, returning the blood back to his heart and completing the journey for the very first time. Adam and Eve are awakened as God's first creation destined to host the Spirit of God Himself present within every single breath.

Humanity was awakened with a single breath. But not just any breath; it was the very essence of God's Spirit. And it is the same breath and the same Spirit that has awakened all of humanity since Adam and Eve took their first breath. When God breathed life into Adam and, subsequently, Eve, the Bible tells us that God breathed His breath of life into their nostrils. This act makes the nostril of great importance. Why did God not place the breath of life into their lungs or even their mouths? Why were the nostrils important?

Here, we will explore the importance scientifically and bring context to these questions, Additionally, we will explore the relevance of breathing as it pertains to meditation. But before we do, let's dive a bit deeper into the breath of God.

> The earth was without form and void, and darkness was over the face of the deep. And the Spirit of God was hovering over the face of the waters (Genesis 1:2 ESV).

As God began the days of creation, the Bible tells us that the Spirit of God hovered. This is our first encounter with the Spirit of God in breath-form. The Hebrew definition of the Spirit of God is *Ruach* or breath of God.[118] Here, in the very beginning, the breath of God is hovering, covering, and filling the earth in order to sustain life. The hovering is the Hebrew word *rachaph,* which means to brood, to grow soft, and to relax.[119] Here, God appears to be in a state of contemplation over what is to come. Over the next six days, He created everything before pausing on the seventh day to contemplate His work once again and declare, "It is good."

- Genesis 1:2: The *Ruach* breath of God hovers over the waters. *Ruach* is the breath and Spirit of God as He moves over the waters in contemplation.
- Genesis 2:7: The *Neshamah* breath, which animated Adam, also represents another form of the spirit of God.

Neshamah is the breath of God which entered Adam's nostrils flooding him with new life and the Spirit of God. Later, the same *Neshamah* spirit of God was also imbued into Eve at her moment of creation.[120]

The Hebrew definition of the "breath of God" is *Neshamah* or the Spirit of God. *Ruach* and *Neshamah* are different manifestations of the same Spirit of God. Both are powerful and creative forces responsible for the life-giving breath in all humanity. In the Bible, *Neshamah* is interpreted as the breath of God, while *Ruach* is represented as the Spirit of God. After Adam received the *Ruach* and *Neshamah* breath of life, all of creation now continues to breathe and draw life from God's Spirit. The *Neshamah* breath of God that awakened Adam is the same Spirit who gives each of us life with every breath we take.

LIFE BEGINS

Ever since Adam and Eve received their first breath in the nostrils, every child born since receives their first oxygenated breath immediately after arriving in the world from the mother's womb. Even prior to that, babies only ten weeks old in utero exhibit a unique behavior that scientists now believe is crucial to the development of their lungs and respiratory system. A behavior called "fetal breathing" stimulates neural connections and aids in the development of respiratory muscles and lung growth.[121]

While not breathing in a traditional sense, babies in the womb are "breathing" and preparing for their first blast of oxygenated air, which occurs immediately at birth. A baby's muscles, lungs, and neural pathways would not be fully formed without fetal breathing. God created fetal breathing to be a developmental process that each person experiences within the womb.[122] This is important as we understand the power of the breath and how we were designed not just to sustain life but for so much more.

JESUS'S IMPARTATION

Scripture tells us clearly that Jesus employed the power of His breath to impart and give life:

> *Jesus repeated His greeting, "Peace to you!" And he told them, "Just as the Father has sent me, I'm now sending you." Then, taking a deep breath, he blew on them and said, "Receive the Holy Spirit"* (John 20:21-22 TPT).

This is a pivotal moment in history when Jesus once again breathed His life into the disciples, completing their awakening by the impartation of the Holy Spirit.

> *I send you to preach the forgiveness of sins—and people's sins will be forgiven. But if you don't proclaim the forgiveness of their sins, they will remain guilty* (John 20:23 TPT).

But that's not all; with the impartation of the Holy Spirit through His breath, a new commissioning occurred not just for the disciples who were present that day but for all who choose to believe in Jesus.[123] Wow, each of us has been commissioned by our acceptance of Him and by the power of God's breath to bring people to the cross for their eternal forgiveness.

I once knew an amazing man, apostle, pastor, and leader from Colorado who would speak often at the church I attended in a beautiful, tiny city called Green Mountain Falls. His name was Dave Duell, founder of Faith Ministries International. During his life, Dave worked many miracles under the power of the Holy Spirit, including personally praying for and healing PLO leaders while Yasser Arafat watched in amazement.[124] During his ministry, Dave would frequently blow on individuals for the purpose of healing. As I watched, incredible manifestations of healing followed as he released his breath. I believe that Dave was given a supernatural anointing to bring healing and freedom through the release of God's breath.

One of my favorite memories occurred while I was watching Dave minister at church. During the service, he called people to the altar for healing, and I remember Dave was laughing under the power of the Holy Spirit and joy. He turned his back on the person and on the congregation and said, "This is my ricochet shot." He then blew and thrust his arm toward the back wall of the church. The person behind him who was receiving prayer was immediately thrown back many feet under the power of the Holy Spirit into the arms of the deacons, completely healed and rejoicing in the power of God.

I watched many times over the years as Dave, under the power of the Holy Spirit, would blow on people, and they would receive their healing. I firmly believe that each of us has within us the capacity and gifting to release God's breath on this earth in the same way Jesus imparted the Holy Spirit to the disciples and Dave and brought healing to God's people.

MEDITATION AND PRAYER

Meditation, prayer, and breathwork often stand alone. However, I believe that biblical meditation was meant to partner with the power of the breath. Breathing is an autonomic function. We don't have to think about it. We just breathe. However, when we breathe with intentionality, we are partnering with the Spirit of God, inviting His power to flow through us and bringing enrichment to our lives. Biblical meditation always includes prayer, but prayer does not always include meditation. I have made a habit of using my commute time to pray and talk with God. Meditating and breathwork while driving is not something I recommend for many reasons. But prayer is something with which we can engage literally anywhere. Prayer does not have to be spoken; God knows our thoughts and our hearts.

The Lord—knows the thoughts of man, that they are but a breath (Psalm 94:11 ESV).

You know when I sit down and when I rise up; you discern my thoughts from afar (Psalm 139:2 ESV).

It is important to remember that in situations where praying aloud may be inappropriate, it is perfectly acceptable to pray through our thoughts. For example, perhaps you are witnessing a tense situation between two people, and it is escalating to a dangerous level. Wisdom would say to pray silently so as to avoid escalating the situation further. Or perhaps you are in a tranquil venue, and the Holy Spirit prompts you to pray. It is best to pray silently so as not to be a distraction.

BREATHWORK

I had just returned home from the office. It was a day filled with back-to-back meetings and a demanding schedule where I struggled to keep up with my task list for the day. My team was shorthanded, which created a staffing challenge that I needed to spend a great deal of time addressing (I paused to breathe intentionally). That led to an emergency meeting where senior management was asking for me to divert resources to deal with a high priority concern. Pulling resources from my team and re-tasking them, I was able to meet the needs of the shifted priorities (I paused again to intentionally breathe).

While I was addressing that concern, I missed an email from my boss requesting a timely response to an urgent matter (I paused here to breathe deeply again). I replied quickly to that email and, looking at the clock, realized that it was almost five o'clock and I had not moved from my chair, drank any water, or stopped for lunch. I also realized that I was feeling pretty lousy, sluggish, and exhausted (I paused again to breathe intentionally). I then decided to head home and start again tomorrow.

The 20-minute drive served as a playground for my thoughts as they attempted to relive each moment of the day, reminding me of everything I could have done differently. But rather than engage with my burdens, I began to pray (because meditating and breathing in the car is a bad idea). I prayed about my day, releasing my thoughts to God and letting Him renew my mind. By the time I reached my garage, instead of being tense and anxious, I was mentally prepared for an evening with my family. I parked the car, got out, and opened the back door.

The door would only open an inch; it was blocked. I pushed a little harder, "HEY!" said my oldest son, who was loading his laundry into the washing machine, and his clothes basket was blocking my entry. I waited for him to finish, and as I entered the house, I was immediately met by my three children. My youngest, Moriah, jumped on me, "Hold me, Daddy," she said. My second child, Judah, said, "Dad, can you come to play a game with me now?" and my oldest, Joash, said, "Dad, you told me you would play baseball with me today." My mind is ready, but suddenly, I am reminded that I am completely out of energy and exhausted from the day's events. I needed something to change for me to interact with my family physically and mentally in the capacity they needed me to.

I hauled all of the children into the living room, and we sat on the floor. I told them, "We are going to breathe." By now, my children are used to the concept of breathing as a restorative function. My children practice breathing and meditation each night at bedtime, which has greatly helped when their youthful energies ramp up right before lights out.

Sitting on the floor, I closed my eyes and started to breathe. In through the nostrils, counting 2, 3, 4, 5, out through the mouth, and repeating for several cycles with my children following along. After the last breath, I opened my eyes and noticed immediately that my mind was clear, I was filled with energy, and I was at peace. Even more remarkable, my children were at peace too, but also energized by the breathing! The rest of that evening, I held Moriah, and we danced through the living room; I played games with Judah and went outside with everyone to throw baseballs with Joash. My wife, Petra, and I finished the evening with our family around the dinner table. I was present for my family because I took the time to reset throughout the day through the power of my breath.

COUNSELING

It is not uncommon for me to see clients in deliverance ministry who, for numerous reasons, approach their appointments with great anxiety and nervousness. During the session, anxiety and the worry of what might happen become a hindrance preventing their ability to receive ministry. During one particularly significant session, my client, I'll call him Joe for confidentiality, arrived with so much nervousness that even the conversational task of interviewing him and building a foundational relationship was not possible. As I prayed inwardly for guidance, the Holy Spirit spoke to me clearly, "Breathe with Me." Transitioning from counseling into a moment of breathing with the Holy Spirit changed everything. Soft worship music filled the room as I invited the Holy Spirit to manifest His tangible presence.

Then we began to breathe, I instructed Joe to begin by closing his eyes and inhaling deeply as I counted to five. Then, holding the breath again for a count of five and releasing slowly for another count of five. We repeated this pattern four times with our eyes closed. With the final exhale, we rested and sat silently as the tangible presence of the Holy Spirit filled the room. His presence was palpable; all anxiety and worry were instantly dissolved, leaving only peace and an overwhelming sense of God's love that filled the room.

Great breakthroughs manifested in Joe's life as we continued to minister freedom. Even better was that through this experience, Joe was tuned to hearing the voice of God in his own life. Something that he had long struggled with. Not only did Joe receive the deliverance and freedom he was seeking, but he walked away with new wisdom and understanding that breathing with the Holy Spirit brings peace and prepares our hearts to hear His voice.

My stories illustrate how practical and beneficial small moments of breathwork can be. Breathwork can be done silently and just about anywhere, with the exception of driving or perhaps scuba diving. I often intentionally engage my breathing during worship at church, riding my bike, watching a movie, or on a conference call, and, of course, during every meditation session. Intentional and regular breathing, specifically through the nostrils, is what ancient Chinese writings describe as breathing through the "heavenly door," and that breath must be taken in through it. "Never do otherwise, for breath would be in danger, and illness would set in."[125] In the upcoming chapters, I offer breathwork activities that are both easy to perform and incredibly effective.

NOSE BREATHING

As my friend Greg Greenwood is fond of saying, "A man with an experience is never at the mercy of a man with an argument." A lot of valid research has been conducted in the area of breathing and the benefits of breathing through the nostrils. Yet the only way to truly benefit from this knowledge is to invest time in the practice of breathwork.

Every one of us has experienced it, the sudden realization that you are only able to breathe through one nostril. You may be realizing it right now: one of your nostrils may be blocked, leaving the other open and free flowing. You may have also noticed that, at times, your nostrils seem to switch roles. The left may be blocked now, but in an hour, the right is blocked, and the left is unblocked. This phenomenon is what the medical community calls the nasal cycle or ultradian rhythm. Most of the time we don't notice it, as this is a healthy function of the body to self-regulate. Early researchers of the nasal cycle believed that it was the result of sexual urges; others theorized that it was caused by the pull of the moon.

Eventually, pragmatic science began to reveal the true relationship between our bodies and the nasal cycle. It is now known that nasal tissues mirror the states of health. For example, when the body is imbalanced or sick, the nostrils would become inflamed. If infected, the nasal cycle is more pronounced and switches nostrils more frequently. In addition, drawing air in through the nasal passageways works like a ventilation system, regulating temperature and blood pressure and regulating the delivery of chemicals carried to the brain for the proper function of our sleep, mood, and emotions.[126] Other reasons include protection against infection or allergies and a mechanism to moisturize the nasal passageway.[127]

Another fascinating reason exists for the nasal cycle, one whereby we benefit tangibly. It stands to reason that if God created our bodies with a natural nasal cycle, that He would have done so with purpose. As we breathe air through our nostrils, our bodies are self-regulating both our energy levels and our relaxation states, and each nostril plays a separate role. Your right nostril initiates the sympathetic nervous system and functions as a throttle, waking you, heating you up, raising your heart rate, elevating your cortisol, and raising your blood pressure. All of these changes are designed to move our bodies into a state of readiness, full of energy, and a state of alertness and focus.[128] Taking air in through the right nostril stimulates the executive network within the prefrontal cortex, whose function it is to regulate our thoughts, actions, and emotions while contributing to effective decision making.[129]

Receiving air through the left nostril has the converse effect, generating a calming effect on our bodies. Breath taken through the left nostril activates the parasympathetic nervous system, initiating what is known as the rest and digest condition, triggering numerous calming functions within the body. Functions such as decreased heart rate, reduced blood pressure, salivary glands are activated, the stomach and intestines relax, and digestion improves, the gallbladder, pancreas, kidneys, and bladder become activated in a meaningful way, peristalsis is stimulated, which is the series of muscle movements that moves food through the digestive system.[130] Perhaps most importantly, nasal breathing delivers 20 percent more oxygen into the blood than through the mouth, keeping allergens out and decreasing the likelihood of catching a cold or flu.[131]

As with oxygen, our bodies also require a healthy amount of nitric oxide to support normal functions. Incidentally, nasal breathing is the only way nitric oxide is delivered, as it is produced and released only within the nasal cavity. With each breath taken through the nose, nitric oxide enters the flow of air and travels into the lungs, where it is distributed throughout the cardiovascular network.[132] Nitric oxide is responsible for regulating the opening and closing of the blood vessels, improving oxygen circulation throughout the body, and regulating blood pressure.[133] Nitric oxide is also responsible for the regulation of homeostasis, neurotransmission (communications within the brain), and the immune system, lowering cholesterol and preventing the clogging of arteries. All of which are helpful in the prevention of heart attacks and stroke.[134]

It should also be noted that each nostril also interprets smells differently. This means that during the nasal cycle, there is a "disparity of olfactory perception providing the olfactory system with two disparate images of the olfactory world. Each nostril is sensitized to different odorants."[135] Moreover, a research study conducted in 2015 focused on the impact of mouth breathing and hallucinations in an adult schizophrenic patient. The patient experienced a breathing pattern that favored the right nostril almost exclusively. Researchers began to introduce breathing exercises, increasing left nostril dominant breathing. As these practices continued for over three years, it was recorded that as her left logical nostril increased function, her hallucinations were subsequently significantly decreased.[136]

MOUTH BREATHING

As you now have come to understand, nose breathing is highly beneficial over mouth breathing, which has been known for centuries. Have you ever noticed that nearly all Egyptian statues are missing the nose? I used to notice it, and I rationalized it by believing that it was the result of mishandling or simple crumbling from age and that the nose was a more delicate part of the sculpture and, therefore, more prone to damage. In reality, there is a lot more to the story.

As it turns out, the reason carries a bit more purpose. Ancient Egyptians believed that the statues of deities or great leaders would become inhabited by their spirit or essence. Both mortals and deities were believed to inhabit their respective statues. It became an act of supernatural warfare to "deactivate an image's strength." The statues were believed to be a gathering place between the natural and supernatural realms. To cut off the nose of the statue meant that the spirit within no longer had the capacity to breathe, "effectively killing it."[137] I find it interesting that for the Egyptians, the nose and not the mouth represented life. I'll say it again: God had a purpose and certainly knew what He was doing when He chose to breathe life into Adam's nostrils.

Back to mouth breathing, scientists generally agree that regularly breathing through the mouth is dangerous and leads to several physical and mental complications. Problems resulting from mouth breathing range from inhaling unfiltered air to sleep problems, allergies, asthma, and bad breath. Tooth decay, sleep apnea, gum disease, jaw joint dysfunction, narrowing of the jaw and dental arch, crooked teeth, speech problems, enlarged tonsils, and more. It is a bigger problem than we realize, particularly due to the fact that: "The vast majority of health-care professionals are unaware of the negative impact of upper airway obstruction (mouth breathing) on normal facial growth and physiologic health."[138]

I don't want to overlook the obvious fact that, at times, breathing through the mouth is necessary. For example, situations such as total nasal congestion and medical reasons such as a deviated septum or small nostrils will increase the necessity for mouth breathing. These are causes, not symptoms, and can be resolved via proper medical attention. In one cruel and inhumane study in 1988, several monkeys were used as subjects in a mouth breathing experiment. The experiment would test whether mouth breathing had an adverse effect on facial development.

As you might have guessed, the results of the investigation yielded interesting findings. Each of the monkeys' noses was permanently plugged with silicone, preventing them from nose breathing entirely.

Over the course of the next six months, the length and shape of the faces changed, and a narrowing of the dental arch. Over the next two years, the monkeys' problems only worsened, and the monkeys' health continued to decline.[139] Further observations have shown that the same problems befall human mouth breathers. Mouth breathing, as it turns out, changes the physical body and transforms airways, all for the worse.

Great news for both the monkeys and us! After the removal of their nasal plugs, the monkeys fully recovered within six months. Their faces and air passages returned to their natural shapes and positions. Likewise, when people regain their capacity for nose breathing, they too are restored, and their bodies naturally return to the state in which they were created.[140] Our bodies were meant to breathe with the Spirit of God through our nostrils, as was demonstrated by Jesus and confirmed throughout Scripture and by medical research. Interestingly, while the Bible speaks a great deal about breath and breathing through the nostrils, it says nothing concerning taking breath through the mouth.

JOB UNDERSTOOD

The book of Job is not an easy read, but Job demonstrated a deep understanding of the *Ruach* and *Neshamah* breath of God and its role in his life and all of creation. Job speaks of the *Ruach* Spirit of God more than 14 times throughout the book. I've included several of the most pivotal moments where Job, in his defeated condition, still gave honor to the living *Ruach* breath of God.

> *In his hand is the life of every living thing and the breath of all mankind* (Job 12:10 ESV).

> *As long as my breath is in me, and the spirit of God is in my nostrils, my lips will not speak falsehood, and my tongue will not utter deceit* (Job 27:3-4 ESV).

> *But it is the spirit in a person, the breath of the Almighty, that gives them understanding* (Job 32:8 NIV).

> *The Spirit of God has made me, and the breath of the Almighty gives me life* (Job 33:4 ESV).

Each time Job uses this word, he is invoking and honoring the *Ruach* Spirit and attribute of God. As we breathe and also partner with the breath of God, we choose to honor the very breath that first gave life and continues to give life with each conscious breath we take.

> *Before the silver cord is snapped, or the golden bowl is broken, or the pitcher is shattered at the fountain, or the wheel broken at the cistern, and the dust returns to the earth as it was, and the spirit* [Ruach breath] *returns to God who gave it* (Ecclesiastes 12:6-7 ESV).

Even Solomon understood when he wrote in Ecclesiastes of the systems within the body. Solomon writes that the *Ruach* breath (that is received while in the womb) returns to God at the time of temporal departure.[141]

VAGUS NERVE

Research has demonstrated that emitting a sound while breathing out, like humming, can stimulate the vagus nerve and enhance the creation and dispersion of nitric oxide. These are two supplementary benefits.[142]

The vagus nerve is an advocate for the parasympathetic nervous system and is what helps us understand the physical effects of breathwork and meditative practices.[143] The vagus nerve is a system of nerves known as the vagal nerves. They are the primary nerves that make up the parasympathetic nervous system, controlling the "rest and digest" functions of the body. The vagus nerve is responsible for regulating essential functions like stress management, digestion, blood pressure, immune system responses, mood, and tactile sensations.[144]

Maintaining a healthy and activated vagus nerve system means maintaining the circuitry of the body and keeping our bodies running at top efficiency. The breathing exercises included later will activate your vagus nerve. However, it is likely that without knowing it, each of us already engages in regular practices that stimulate the vagus nerve system. Practices as simple as breathing slowly, singing, humming, laughing, stretching, or drinking cold water all serve to activate the vagus nerve system.[145]

The vagus nerve is the longest nerve in the entire body, connecting all vital organs. Its role is to ensure that our bodies remain in what is called homeostasis, or the ability to maintain balance in the body. As documented by *Frontiers in Psychiatry,* "The vagus nerve is an essential part of the brain-gut axis and plays an important role in the modulation of inflammation, the maintenance of homeostasis. Moreover, the vagus nerve plays an important role in the pathogenesis of psychiatric disorders, obesity, as well as other stress-induced and inflammatory diseases. Vagus nerve stimulation and several meditation techniques demonstrate that modulating the vagus nerve has a therapeutic effect, mainly due to its relaxing and anti-inflammatory properties." This is all due to how the vagus nerve communicates. The vagus nerve is responsible for the sending of information through what is referred to as the brain-gut axis and is critical in the stress response process.[146]

God masterfully crafted our bodies with the correct circuitry and communication methods for maintaining a healthy body. Science is now beginning to understand just how powerful our bodies are in the process of self-healing. As you intentionally breathe and engage your vagus brain-gut system, realize you are aiding your body as it brings healing and wellness to stress, obesity, relaxation, inflammation, digestion, mental health, blood pressure, immune response, mood, and increases the sensation of touch.

> *All he had to do was speak by his Spirit-Wind command, and God created the heavenlies. Filled with galaxies and stars, the vast cosmos he wonderfully made* (Psalm 33:6 TPT).

The same breath that gave Adam the first breath for all humanity is the same spirit-wind that spoke the heavens into existence. It is the same *Ruach* Spirit who creates life and replenishes the earth and is the same Spirit who is pleased when we choose to stop, be still, and meditate on His goodness. It is the same Spirit of God whose presence and glory surrounds every moment and thought as our minds and bodies rest under the covering power and protection of His pinions. Yet it is also the same breath that comes in like a rushing flood, bringing justice to the nations of the earth and exposing the holy from the profane.

And He is the same breath that blows the fire of wrath upon the wicked, and He is the violent blast of wind that overpowered the disciples and delivered the fire and power of the Holy Spirit, which engulfed them and filled each of them. It is the same breath of God living and working inside of every person who has chosen to call Him Lord. He is the breath of life.

> *When you release your Spirit-Wind, life is created, ready to replenish life upon the earth* (Psalm 104:30 TPT).

Be still, and know that I am God. I will be exalted among the nations, I will be exalted in the earth! (Psalm 46:10 ESV)

May you be pleased with every sweet thought I have about you, for you are the source of my joy and gladness (Psalm 104:34 TPT).

His breath is like an overflowing stream that reaches up to the neck... (Isaiah 30:28 ESV).

Suddenly they heard the sound of a violent blast of wind rushing into the house from out of the heavenly realm. The roar of the wind was so overpowering it was all anyone could bear! (Acts 2:2 TPT)

Then the Lord God formed the man of dust from the ground and breathed into his nostrils the breath of life, and the man became a living creature (Genesis 2:7 ESV).

TYING IT TOGETHER

"Meditation furnishes the mind somewhat with rest. It is the couch of the soul. The time that a man spends in necessary rest, he never reckons to be wasted, because he is refreshing and renovating himself for further exertion. Meditation, then, is the rest of the spirit."

—**Charles Spurgeon**

I have explained the importance of breathing for physical health, discussed technical aspects, and provided advice on breathwork. I have demonstrated that the Spirit and power of God are in the breath. It is for these reasons that intentional breathing is foundational to our meditation. Knowing how to use our breath helps us to attain deeper meditation, thereby creating space for the presence of the Holy Spirit as our bodies and minds become calm and at rest in His glory.

LET'S BREATHE!

Let everything that has breath praise the Lord! Praise the Lord! (Psalm 150:6 ESV)

- Pause for a moment now to breathe. Close your eyes, quietly thank the Holy Spirit for His presence, and welcome a tangible manifestation of His Spirit in your room. Invite Him to speak to you as you breathe.
- As you inhale, take notice.
- Are you breathing through your nose? If not, intentionally shift your breath to your nostrils.
- Which nostril do you notice more?
- Are you calm and breathing through your left nostril?
- Or are you energized and breathing through your right nostril?
- Do you need a moment of peace? Try breathing through your left nostril by closing your right.
- Do you need a bit of a pick-me-up? Try breathing through your right nostril by closing your left.

- As you take slow breaths in, you are activating your vagus nerve and triggering many positive chain reactions in your body for the better.

- Continue breathing deeply through your nostrils for a moment. Ask the Holy Spirit if He has anything He wants to talk about. Let Him take you through whatever thoughts come to your mind.

- When you are ready, begin to offer praise to the Lord, worship Him, and take time to remember how good He is and all He has done for you.

Stay in this moment as long as you need, then return to reading. I'll wait.

7

The SCIENCE *of* THOUGHTS *and* THINKING

Do not be conformed to this world, but be transformed
by the renewal of your mind, that by testing you
may discern what is the will of God, what is good
and acceptable and perfect (Romans 12:2 ESV).

What is a thought, and why does the Bible speak in such strong language on matters concerning our thoughts?

The Psalms are as descriptive as they are beautiful, describing the thoughts of God as precious and innumerable. This description also provides us with a view of how God sees our purpose and identity as precious and purposeful. How we perceive God ultimately informs the core of our identity and who we are. If you were to be asked, "Who are you?" what would be your response? This is an extremely hard question.

Yet, for those who have come to the full awakening of their identity and purpose in the Kingdom, it is surprisingly easy. Let's look at how we view God on a scale. On one end is the view of God in a hierarchical position where He is looking at each of us with an iron fist, waiting for each moment we fail to measure up. And in those moments, He strikes with rebuke, correction, and wrath, perhaps knocking us down through illness or injury with which to teach us. And on the other end of the scale is a view of God as somewhat distant, watching, and loving but mostly absent from the day-to-day.

And balanced right in the middle is Yahweh. The God who fiercely loves with the greatest jealousy. The God who defends us, protects us, and goes before us both in struggle and also in our joy. The God who is not waiting for us to mess up but ready when we do to pick us up, dust us off, and set us on the correct path with a gentleness of correction and rebuke. The God who never causes injury or illness but heals and restores us. He is the God who covets a deep relationship with us. A relationship not bound by walls of religious tradition but a genuine, vulnerable, and sincere connection. He waits daily for us to join Him in the Holy of Holies, if only for a moment. And at that moment, we lean into each other's company for an embrace and together rest in the glory. These holy moments are meetings that simultaneously occur in the secret places of our thoughts and in the abiding place of God in Heaven, where Scripture tells us we are also co-seated with Him.

> *But God still loved us with such great love. He is so rich in compassion and mercy. Even when we were dead and doomed in our many sins, he united us into the very life of Christ and saved us by his wonderful grace! He raised us up with Christ the exalted One, and we ascended with him into the glorious perfection and authority of the heavenly realm, for we are now co-seated as one with Christ!* (Ephesians 2:4-6 TPT)

What a fantastic perspective when we understand our time invested with God is not simply a thought exercise as the atheistic stoic philosophers once taught. Instead, we ought to consider each moment as holy and precious occurring within His presence. Scientific studies in quantum mechanics have demonstrated that thoughts are energy. That energy is in the form of electron particles in the brain. Electron particles have mass and can be measured.

In addition, theories such as particle duality, quantum entanglement, and superposition describe how our thoughts and our very being exist in multiple locations simultaneously! We really are present in the heavenly realm as much as we are in the natural world. Dr. Rainer Kaltenbaek at the University of Ljubljana, Slovenia, says, "Quantum physics does not put a limit on this in principle—it doesn't have a problem with me being here and over there at the same time."[147]

As I entered into meditation one morning, I understood biblically that I was seated in the heavenly realm. But something was different this time. I began to direct all of my thoughts toward the things above. The Holy Spirit took my mind back to a time when I was eleven years old and was caught up to Heaven.[148]

I walked with Jesus and watched as a sea of angels worshipped in the throne room of God. I was there again, but this time I was caught up while engaging in biblical meditation. Seated with Jesus, we just talked together and shared thoughts. He shared wisdom and unpacked a little more about the plans He has for me. It was a moment like no other, and I passionately believe that I was invited into that heavenly place because I was intentionally inviting the Holy Spirit to take me wherever He wanted in my mind and my thoughts.

Not only was this a holy moment, but God was demonstrating to me the biblical principle of existing in two places at once. I am in Heaven with Him while in my meditation on earth at the same time. This principle holds true for all believers, and my prayer is that as you come to this understanding, that you experience Heaven at a new level. Suddenly, meditation is not simply a healthy exercise but is a time set apart when we acknowledge our presence in the throne room and experience the glory of God's presence.

Please note that I am in no way acknowledging or lending credibility to the practice of astral projection. Astral projection is known as an out-of-body experience brought on through pharmaceuticals, hypnosis, occult rituals, and repressed traumatic experiences. Believers should not practice astral projection as it is not biblical. Sometimes, God Himself extends an invitation to our spirit as He did in my experience and in Revelation when John's spirit was invited by God into the throne room for the purpose of revealing knowledge. But this is not to be confused with the counterfeit astral projection.

> *Then suddenly, after I wrote down these messages, I saw a heavenly portal open before me, and the same trumpet voice I heard speaking with me at the beginning broke the silence and said, "Ascend into this realm! I want to reveal to you what must happen after this." Instantly I was taken into the spirit realm, and behold—I saw a heavenly throne set in place and someone seated upon it* (Revelation 4:1-2 TPT).

Any participation in astral projection is an open door to the demonic realm, requiring forgiveness, repentance, and renunciation.

As we enter into our meditation and align our thoughts with the Holy Spirit, Scripture tells us that our thoughts are elevated into a place where we bestow honor on God as we first consider His thoughts for us.

> *How precious to me are your thoughts, O God! How vast is the sum of them!* (Psalm 139:17 ESV)

This is not merely an implication of the thoughts of God. He is genuinely thinking about you and me to the degree that His thoughts cannot be counted. We are always on His mind. As our meditation time increases, our time in the glory also increases. And when our time in the glory rises, so also do our thoughts of Him increase.

Please take a moment now to consider alternatively how much God cares about our thoughts too. He does, and Scripture tells us that when we meditate with Him, He also considers our thoughts precious.

You perceive every movement of my heart and soul, and you understand my every thought before it even enters my mind (Psalm 139:2 TPT).

The Lord—knows the thoughts of man, that they are but a breath (Psalm 94:11 ESV).

Search me, O God, and know my heart! Try me and know my thoughts! (Psalm 139:23 ESV)

When we receive the eternal gift of salvation, we ask the Holy Spirit to not just share His thoughts with us but to purify and align our thoughts as well. As our thoughts become purified, the thoughts we think become His thoughts, and our desires become His desires. In the moment when the synergy of His thoughts and our thoughts coalesce, we experience a moment of delight in which our desires are met naturally and supernaturally.

Delight yourself in the Lord, and he will give you the desires of your heart (Psalm 37:4 ESV).

Be transformed. Those words from Romans that opened this chapter constitute the primary assignment for a renewed life. Restoration and redemption come from a renovated thought life. Transformation is a total life-altering event that occurs when we take our thoughts captive. Renewing the mind is a meditative process whereby we take our thoughts captive and intentionally train our minds to think about things of God. We meet the criteria of the primary assignment when our thoughts align with His thoughts concerning our identity. Our identity is a golden thread all throughout Scripture, beginning with our origin beautifully written by David in Psalms.

For you formed my inward parts; you knitted me together in my mother's womb. I praise you, for I am fearfully and wonderfully made. Wonderful are your works; my soul knows it very well. My frame was not hidden from you, when I was being made in secret, intricately woven in the depths of the earth. Your eyes saw my unformed substance; in your book were written, every one of them, the days that were formed for me, when as yet there was none of them. How precious to me are your thoughts, O God! How vast is the sum of them! If I would count them, they are more than the sand. I awake, and I am still with you (Psalm 139:13-18 ESV).

Each time we enter into meditation becomes an opportunity to truly know who we are, because of whose we are, and the perfection with which we were crafted. I recognize that viewing ourselves as "wonderful" or perfect may be difficult. When perhaps we may be experiencing a grueling day or even a grueling year, aligning with God's thoughts may seem out of sight. Yet, God never stops thinking of you as wonderful and perfect.

The act of simply entering into a solemn meditative moment with God and thinking about Him is enough to begin the healing and aligning process of restoring and transforming our minds. Leading neuroscientist Andrew Newberg, MD, concludes in research that "the more you think about God, the more you will alter the neural circuitry in specific parts of your brain. That is why I say with the utmost confidence that God can change your brain."[149] Let me state that these studies were not conducted from the viewpoint of a believer but rather from an academic performing secular research. That is precisely what makes these findings absolutely incredible and proves what Scripture tells us. When we contemplate the things of God, we become transformed.

MEET KARA

Let me introduce you to my friend Kara. She is a powerful deliverance minister, intercessor, and trusted friend in life and ministry. Kara has walked through this journey of learning and understanding biblical meditation with us for a few years. Her experiences in meditation have only increased her relationship with God and had the effect of improving her personal life as well. Here is her story.

> Meditation has helped me in a number of ways. I want to tell you about a recent experience involving a job interview. I have been diligently working toward a position in our Regulatory Department for a number of years. I have even interviewed previously. And although I had prepared and received coaching, I would still say things like: "I'm not good at math." I work in finance, so math is important. But when I think about math, I compare myself to other people (like my husband) who are calculus geniuses.
>
> This time was different. I was preparing to interview for the position I wanted once again. Instead of my normal pre-interview routine of last-minute reviewing of notes and self-talk, I decided to set my anxiety aside and meditate. I was only meditating for 5-10 minutes when the Lord brought to my mind Scriptures such as Philippians 4:13, I can do all things through Christ who strengthens me, and other words of encouragement. My anxiety was gone, and my mind was at peace. I was ready for the interview.
>
> The interview was quite short compared to others I've had. Not only was I offered the position, but I also began to hear from management such positive feedback. They told

me things like, "We didn't have to interview anyone else; we knew you were the perfect fit," and, "You have raised the bar for interviews in this department." Several other managers also congratulated me on performing so well in the interview.

Now, after ten years of hard work, I am in a position that I love. Meditation helped me to be calm confident, and to clearly communicate the things I had prepared to say instead of nervously stumbling over my words. Biblical meditation has given me a freedom from anxiety that otherwise would have been treated with medications.

Kara's story demonstrates that when we intentionally seek guidance from the Holy Spirit through meditation, our core beliefs, "I am not good at math," are able to be rewired in a moment of truth and clarity. Kara got her job not only because she meditated but also because she was prepared for the job, and she invited the Holy Spirit to speak the truth into her heart, removing all anxiety and stress. A new core belief was built for Kara in a ten-minute meditation that would have taken much longer otherwise. Kara's freedom came in the stillness as she practiced Psalm 46:10, and she fully knew the truth of God in her life.

LIES, BELIEFS, AND CAPTIVE THOUGHTS

Finally, brothers and sisters, whatever is true, whatever is noble, whatever is right, whatever is pure, whatever is lovely, whatever is admirable—if anything is excellent or praiseworthy—think about such things (Philippians 4:8 NIV).

This verse in Philippians is one of my favorite Scriptures! I like clear direction. I tend to struggle with abstract thought, and this verse could not be more straightforward. Here, we are given the road map for restoring our minds discussed in Romans 12:2. It's one thing to know the importance of renewing the mind; it is another to actually know precisely with what to replace the captive thoughts.

Over the last decade of ministry, I have ministered to hundreds of people who sought out freedom and deliverance from tormenting spirits in their lives. I am so grateful for the power of the Holy Spirit to deliver when we invite Him in. Yet for so many people, the torment in their lives is lodged directly within their minds and hearts. As lies become beliefs, beliefs become truth. An identity is then formed on the basis of the lies presented by the demonic assignments over a person.

I once ministered to an individual whom I will call Victor to maintain confidentiality in the ministry. Victor came to see me and my team for ministry because he had lost his ability to hear the voice of God. Victor held a position within the ministry, understood the Scriptures, and regularly taught in church. In a moment of high tension and stress, he began to emotionally and physically break down. As I ministered, I began to ask questions about his thought life and his beliefs.

We began to unpack his wrong beliefs, and as we did, we discovered that his identity was not rooted in what Scripture teaches. Instead, he had been listening to the demonic lies that infiltrated his mind and overpowered him. Beliefs such as, "I could never be good enough to please anyone," "It's just a matter of time before I fail again," "No one needs me," "I don't know what I'm doing," and "No one loves me." These may seem like obvious lies, but when a lie becomes rooted deep within the mind, it changes our identity and alters our perceptions of our personal efficacy.

As I began to pray with Victor, I walked him through forgiveness, both for himself and for anyone who has wronged him. The forgiveness revealed the doors that uncovered the roots of his wrong beliefs. One by one, Victor repented for partnering with the lies and renounced the demons who had gained entry to his mind and heart. And in that moment, like a rushing wind, Victor was instantly set free of the torment. His countenance brightened as he was beginning to transform.

I then guided Victor to invite the Holy Spirit to reveal the truth behind each of the lies he had believed. One by one, as Victor clearly heard the voice of the Lord, each lie was overturned as the truth was revealed. I quickly handed him a pad of paper and a pen, and he wrote the truths as the Holy Spirit revealed them. Victor now had a new list of beliefs. This time, truths from Heaven pierced his false identity and solidified him officially as a child of the most high God! From that moment forward, Victor's identity was not in question because he heard it from God Himself.

Victor was entirely transformed in that three-hour deliverance session. And just like Scripture tells us, when we think of things that are true, pure, right, excellent, praiseworthy, lovely, admirable, and noble, our minds are renewed, and our entire mind and body are transformed. What once was a false identity, formed on the basis of a demonic belief system, developed from the constant stream of lies in his thought life, was scrubbed clean in a moment with the Holy Spirit. The process really is that simple.

Regularly submit your thoughts to the Holy Spirit. Allow Him to guide you through forgiveness. Then present each belief, asking God to reveal the truth and dislodge the lies of the enemy, leaving you restored and purified.

STRONGHOLDS OF THE MIND

What I have been talking about and what Victor experienced is what is known as a "stronghold of the mind." It is essential to understand that deeply held false beliefs are not simply a construct of the human condition. They are targeted assignments from satan's dark realm. These assignments and thoughts are strategically focused on the most vulnerable portions of our identity. Once our identity is defeated, so also become the plans, purposes, and destinies of our lives. As my friend Becca Greenwood describes it, "A stronghold of the mind is based on a lie that satan has established in our thinking—a statement we count as true, but that is actually false. When we repeatedly listen to and entertain the lie, a stronghold is established."[150]

As believers in Jesus, we have the upper hand in our fight against these strongholds of the mind. The world turns to ungodly and unhealthy practices, looking for relief from destructive thoughts. Practices like yoga, hypnosis, neurolinguistic programming, and more are used in an attempt to retrain the brain. And to some degree, it can be argued, with a bit of success. But the key is that any success without God is limited and short-term at best. Instead, as believers, we can turn to Jesus and the Word of God for the truth, which defeats all lies.

THE SCIENCE OF BELIEF

"The fact is that harnessing the power of your mind can be more effective than the drugs you have been programmed to believe you need. [and the God given power of your mind] is a more efficient means of affecting matter than chemicals."

—Dr. Bruce Lipton

In a previous chapter, I discussed my own journey of healing from the diagnosis of type 2 diabetes. I made a choice within my conscious mind to be healed. As I walked through forgiveness, repentance, and breaking curses off my life, I was also instructing my subconscious mind what to believe. Our subconscious mind is more than a million times more powerful than our conscious mind.

> If the desires of the conscious mind conflict with the programs in the subconscious mind, which "mind" do you think will win out? You can repeat the positive affirmation that you are lovable over and over or that your cancer tumor will shrink. But if, as a child, you repeatedly heard that you were worthless and sickly, those messages programmed in your subconscious mind will undermine your best conscious efforts to change your life. The programs acquired by the subconscious mind shape 95 percent or more of our life experiences.[151]

I can hear my past clients now, "How do I control my subconscious?" "No matter how much I struggle to think good thoughts, nothing seems to change." "I try to lead a positive thought life, but my dreams are terrifying." You may have said something similar. We know what Philippians 4:8 says, but do we really live our life day to day thinking about those things? Control over our thoughts, both subconsciously and consciously, is achieved through time spent in the secret place of meditation, allowing the Holy Spirit to minister deeply into our subconscious thought life.

The moment our subconscious and our conscious mind come into alignment with truth is the moment our bodies begin to manifest the healing power from God. I could have declared that I was healed from diabetes and seen no physical response. It was the declaration, coupled with the tenacious and intentional, conscious thoughts of healing, partnered with the power of the Holy Spirit in meditation to retrain my subconscious mind to believe and manifest my total healing. The Bible spells this process out quite nicely.

> *Listen carefully, my dear child, to everything that I teach you, and pay attention to all that I have to say. Fill your thoughts with my words until they penetrate deep into your spirit. Then, as you unwrap my words, they will impart true life and radiant health into the very core of your being. So, above all, guard the affections of your heart, for they affect all that you are. Pay attention to the welfare of your innermost being, for from there flows the wellspring of life. Avoid dishonest speech and pretentious words. Be free from using perverse words no matter what!* (Proverbs 4:20-24 TPT)

The phrase "listen carefully," or in other translations, "be attentive," is not put forward as a suggestion. Anyone who has children knows a terrific way to get a child to pay attention is to look them in the eye, say their name, and say, "Listen to me." That is essentially what is happening in this passage of Scripture. A particularly important life skill is being imparted, and it is vital to our mental and physical health that we listen, understand, and act. Here, we are instructed not just to think but to fill our thought life with the words of God until they penetrate deep into our spirit. Biblical meditation is the vehicle by which we ponder the words of God as they fully overtake our conscious and subconscious minds.

The promise comes in Proverbs 4:22; after pondering these words, we receive true life and health in our bodies. Continuing, verse 23 tells us to guard the affections of our heart because they affect our entire being. Verse 24 provides the model for our ongoing maintenance to avoid dishonest, pretentious, and perverse speech. That includes how we are thinking and speaking about ourselves. Take a moment to inventory your thought life now. Are your thoughts void of dishonest, pretentious, and perverse thoughts? And are your thoughts filled with the promises of God, healing in your mind, body, and spirit, while exercising forgiveness and repentance regularly?

As I meditated through my own healing, my thoughts were constantly focused on the promises of God in my life. As I continued to spend time in the abiding place with Him, my thoughts began to align with truth naturally and organically. Some may perceive it as nonsensical, but in my meditation time, I would fill my mind with images of smiling, happy faces flooding my cells and blood vessels. I would visualize them traveling throughout my entire body, spreading the joy of the Lord, delivering health throughout my body, and training my subconscious mind to think accordingly.

> *A joyful, cheerful heart brings healing to both body and soul. But the one whose heart is crushed struggles with sickness and depression* (Proverbs 17:22 TPT).

CHANGING THE SUBCONSCIOUS MIND

If our subconscious mind governs 95 percent of our thinking patterns, how then can they be reprogrammed? Knowing that our subconscious is resistant to change helps us understand, to a small degree, why attempts to change mindsets are not a task easily undertaken. However, I will reveal the keys, which, when diligently applied, will serve to retrain the subconscious thought life and bring lasting change and freedom to a tormented mind and body. A child's first seven years, beginning in the womb, are spent soaking up everything around them, observing and forming the basis for identity, and programming their subconscious thinking.[152]

During this time, a child's mind has already received a generational inheritance via a download of emotions and memories through the process of epigenetic DNA transference.[153] Inherited emotions and memories form the roots of our belief system. If the root foundation is built on anxiety, stress, anger, rejection, or fear, the subconscious inheritance will follow its programming. Common root lies that become core beliefs appear in what is called automatic negative thoughts such as, "I am...." "People are...," and "the world is...." And if the root foundation is love, acceptance, freedom, and joy, the subconscious will likewise follow its programming. Each results in an outward lifestyle that reflects what is deeply rooted within each of us. These types of thoughts are the strongholds of the mind addressed earlier.

After seven years, and as we age, children and adults continue to program the subconscious through a series of habits, routines, repetitive practices, and trauma from life.[154] All of the original programming remains intact, serving to govern the day-to-day thought life until intentional, conscious action is taken to dismantle the lies and false beliefs.

Drawing from the Bible, my experience in ministry, and psychology research, I present the following techniques for changing the bad programming of our subconscious mind and taking authority over wrong beliefs in our minds. These are not presented in linear order except for the first three. These are crucial to displacing the root lies, twisted thinking, and core beliefs, which are strongholds of the mind. Feel free to navigate through the rest as you are led by the Holy Spirit.

PARTNER WITH THE HOLY SPIRIT FOR SPIRITUAL GUIDANCE

- Engage in Regular Biblical Meditation inviting the Holy Spirit to reveal and uproot all lies and replace them with truth. Refer to the worksheet in this book titled Identifying Wrong Beliefs.

Receive Inner Healing Ministry

- Inner healing cuts to the core of the false belief as the Holy Spirit reveals the truth, which overtakes the lies and destroys the strongholds of the mind.

Seek Personal Deliverance Ministry

- Submit to a thorough, balanced deliverance ministry with a credible deliverance ministry team. They will help identify false beliefs and use forgiveness and inner healing to bring healing and restoration to the root issues.

IDENTIFY CORE FALSE BELIEFS

Fill in the blanks for the following statements:

I am _____

People are _____

The world is _____

For each of these statements, ask yourself and the Holy Spirit the following questions to identify false core beliefs:

- What is the event/situation or mood/emotion that is connected to this belief?

- What does this say about me? Ask the Holy Spirit, is this true?

- What does this mean about me? Ask the Holy Spirit, is this true?

Identify new core beliefs by partnering with the Holy Spirit. He will reveal the truth to replace the lies.

I have provided a guide at the end of this chapter and at the end of the book to walk you through fully resetting false beliefs.

CONTINUE YOUR PROGRESS

Consciously notice when one of your false beliefs tries to surface. Simply, the act of noticing begins the healing process.[155] When one of your old core beliefs tries to return, take that thought captive and immediately replace it with the truth revealed by the Holy Spirit.

- Identify destructive mental or physical habits and intentionally develop new healthy habits. New habits become adopted into your subconscious mind and become part of your new day-to-day thought programming.

- Identify and eliminate unhealthy routines. Develop and practice new thoughts and lifestyle routines that bring joy and healing to your life.

- Feed your mind with truth from regular time spent reading the Word of God. And never stop asking the Holy Spirit to reveal the truth.

- Feed your body by adopting a nutritious lifestyle showing care for the temple of God. Our minds react to the fuel we give it.[156]

- Attend church and surround yourself with like-minded people who reciprocate support for a healthy thought life, see Hebrews 10:25.

- Plan to maintain progress through regular meditation, and be aware of the lies from the enemy, and listen to the Holy Spirit for truth in all matters.

THE POWER OF OUR THOUGHTS

What is a thought? Is a thought just an electrical impulse traveling through the brain? Where do they come from? Where are they going? And do thoughts only reside in the brain? Cognitive science and neuroscience have worked to answer these concepts for an exceptionally long time. Thoughts are real things, they are measurable, they are tangible; and as I've demonstrated, thoughts are powerful. In a study conducted at Heartmath Institute, test subjects were able to change the shape and expression of DNA using only intentional thoughts. By targeting thoughts of positive emotion, they were able to cause the DNA to unwind.[157] In another thought experiment, researchers conducted a triple-blind investigation to determine the power of intentional thought over great distances. For three days, 2,000 people located in Tokyo directed their thoughts toward water samples located in an electromagnetically sealed room in California. As water crystals began to form, they were rated and judged on a scale of beauty by independent judges. The astonishing results showed that the target water and resulting crystals were more "beautiful" than the control group of water used as a comparison. This thought experiment has since been replicated as a triple-blind study, yielding the same results.[158]

For researchers, a thought is difficult to define, but for this book, I've chosen to discuss thoughts from the biblical perspective. Biblically, a thought is both conscious and subconscious. A thought encompasses ideas, beliefs, reasonings, emotions, desires, and knowledge. Thoughts originate both from the heart and the mind and are used to reason, make decisions, respond to situations, and wrestle with moral and spiritual concerns.

SUPERNATURAL THINKING, MIND, AND GUT

For as he thinks within himself, so is he... (Proverbs 23:7 TPT).

But what comes out of your mouth reveals the core of your heart. Words can pollute, not food. You will find living within an impure heart evil ideas, murderous thoughts, adultery, sexual immorality, theft, lies, and slander. That's what pollutes a person. Eating with unwashed hands doesn't defile anyone (Matthew 15:18-19 TPT).

Have you heard the concept of the mind-gut connection? The Bible says in Proverbs 17:22 (ESV), *"A joyful heart is good medicine, but a crushed spirit dries up the bones."* The emotional state of our mind will affect the health and wellness of not only our gut but entire bodies, impacting our emotions and well-being.

Dr. Emeran Mayer has conclusively demonstrated through research how our bodies were created intentionally with what is called the gut-brain axis. The gut is connected to the brain through thick nerve cables that can transfer information in both directions and through communication channels that use the bloodstream: hormones and inflammatory signaling molecules produced by the gut signaling up to the brain, and hormones produced by the brain signaling down to the various cells in the gut, such as the smooth muscle, the nerves, and the immune cells, changing their functions. Many of the gut signals reaching the brain will not only generate gut sensations, such as the fullness after a nice meal, nausea and discomfort, and feelings of well-being, but will also trigger responses of the brain that it sends back to the gut, generating distinct gut reactions. And the brain doesn't forget about these feelings, either. Gut feelings are stored in vast databases in the brain, which can later be accessed when making decisions. What we sense in our gut will ultimately affect not only the decisions we make about what to eat and drink, but also the people we choose to spend time with and the way we assess critical information as workers, jury members, and leaders.[159]

As care is taken to nurture our supernatural thought life, our mind learns to feed healing signals of life, joy, and contentment throughout the entire nervous system. Our bodies receive these instructions and obediently begin to go to work restoring, healing, and renewing any and all damage throughout our entire bodies, all through our gut.

What are the thoughts in your mind at this moment? What thoughts occupy your mind most of the time? The Bible tells us in Romans 12:2 to be transformed by the renewing of our minds so that our minds are clear enough to discern the will of God. An incredible realization is that merely thinking about God has been proven to change the brain. This means that anyone who intentionally directs their thoughts to God will experience a renewal of the mind. It's that simple, folks! "The more you think about God, the more you will alter the neural circuitry in specific parts of your brain. God can [and will] change your brain."[160]

MEET JANE

Jane is a minister in our deliverance ministry; she is also a trusted friend and intercessor who has walked with us on this journey of biblical meditation. Jane's story demonstrates how anxiety in our thoughts and in the atmosphere can be brought to submission through meditation.

> My husband and I were having the privilege of taking care of our five-year-old and one-year old granddaughters for an overnight stay. We had never been asked to do this before and I had a little anxiety. They both can have nightmares, sometimes taking hours to recover. As I meditated, the Holy Spirit encouraged me in my heart repeatedly saying, "Do not fear." Both girls only woke up once, and neither had trauma. I know this was an answer to prayer and the result of my peace attained through meditation.
>
> I just had tooth work done. I was told I would need one molar prepared for a crown and another refilled. Normally, I do not even want to know I am there, so I requested nitrous oxide. However, it was expensive, and I decided to meditate instead to alleviate my anxiety. As the procedure began, I still had a small desire to request the nitrous oxide. But Jesus continued saying, "Don't you trust Me?" I began to breathe deeply in the meditation and became relaxed. I put in my headphones and turned on my worship music while continuing to meditate. As the dentist was finishing

up, I turned off the music. Noticing, the doctor said, "I don't know if you heard us discuss it, but one molar was not bad, and all we needed to do was to place a new filling in it; no crown is needed!" Also, the cost was about half of the original quote, and I was able to walk out an hour earlier!

Jane's stories show us that even in every circumstance, the Holy Spirit is waiting for a connection where He can bring not only peace but also healing and moments of joy as well.

DISTRACTIONS

We were in my office; James was explaining to me one of the greatest struggles he had been experiencing in his marriage of 40 years. "Ever since we were married, my wife likes to ask me what I am thinking about. I think she is looking for some deep revelation of thought. I think it's because I am silent or appear disengaged and peaceful. Much of the time, my response is 'nothing.' And that's where the problem begins. She becomes frustrated that I am not talking with her, or that I am withholding my feelings, or that I don't trust her with my deepest thoughts. But that's not it at all! I love my wife deeply and have no reservations about confiding in her my deepest thoughts. I just don't know what the problem is, and it has become a problem in my marriage. No matter how much I tell her, there is always a part of her that believes I am withholding something from her."

What James is experiencing is a story that I have heard many times in ministry. The good news is that the answer is fairly simple, actually. Men are not intentionally withholding thoughts or emotional discourse. The answer lies really in how God created the minds of men and women to be wonderfully different. A woman's brain is composed of almost ten times more white matter than a man's. White matter is a bundle of nerves that is interconnected across the entire brain. This connection acts like communication paths linking tasks, events, moments, and emotions together. This communication naturally makes the mind of a woman more connected and communicative, leading to more efficient multitasking. "Women's thought lives [are] almost like busy computers with multiple windows open and running all at once, unwanted pop-ups intruding all the time, and little ability to close out or ignore any of that mental or emotional activity until a more convenient time."[161]

Men's brains are quite different in this regard. With less white matter and fewer communication channels linking thoughts, events, and emotions, we have what is best described as a box system. As explained by marriage expert Mark Gungor, men store subjects of information in separate compartments or boxes. Once a topic is boxed, it may be shelved for a time or a long time. When men need to access the information contained in that box, it's pulled off of the shelf, opened, analyzed, put to use, and returned to the shelf with added information. For a man, connecting subjects to thoughts to emotions is intentional and often explains why men might recount a story with little emotional connectivity.

While men's subject categorization may seem like a gross oversimplification, it actually represents reasonably accurately what I have experienced both personally and in many years of ministry. That still leaves the question of why men think about nothing. Well, men have a special box that I'm told women don't have. This box happens to be my favorite box because there is nothing in it. Zero thoughts whatsoever. It's glorious like a mini vacation for the mind where no thoughts are occurring and no tasks are due. So, when asked, "What are you thinking?" for a man, the answer might in fact be "nothing."[162]

Research further supports this in an article published in *Medical News Today*. Men's and women's brains were observed using a technology called SPECT, which uses a form of light called gamma rays to measure blood flow in the brain. During this test, images were captured showing brain response differences between men and women. The study showed that during the trial, a woman's brain activity increased across sixty-five different brain regions. Men, on the other hand, showed an increase in only nine brain regions.[163] To further simplify, the mind of a woman is virtually illuminated while in thought. Whereas men must be consciously intentional when engaging in meaningful thinking.

Actively making the decision to close one thought box and move into another as needed by spouse, family, work, etc., must be intentional. For me, learning this concept has been incredibly freeing for me and my family. Whenever my wife or family needs my attention on an item, I know that I must shift from the box I'm currently in, to the box I need to be in to focus on their concerns. Although this is easily applied to the male brain, women likewise must take notice of their distractions and work to shift away from distractions as needs arise.

EMOTIONAL DISTRACTIONS

Whenever my busy thoughts were out of control, the soothing comfort of your presence calmed me down and overwhelmed me with delight (Psalm 94:19 TPT).

Once again, David is submitting his thought life to God. He recognizes that his thoughts have become emotionally distracted and out of his control. God honors him in his meditation and brings order to the chaos of his mind and restores his emotions.

Our emotions are made up of actual energy and, just like our thoughts, have a way of manifesting outwardly from our bodies. "Our emotions are literally energy in motion. When we find ways to block the energy from moving through our body, we end up storing emotions in our cells. Some ways that we learn to bypass our emotions include dissociating, addiction, perfectionism, judging ourselves, and being critical of others. Eventually, unprocessed emotions start showing up as physical symptoms or ailments."[164]

As David demonstrates for us, the moment he comes into the presence of the Lord, his emotions no longer control him as the Lord replaces the chaos with peace and delight. As the quote states, when we suppress our emotions, the negative emotional energy is stored in our cells and literally becomes part of our physical bodies. David's model of release perfectly demonstrates how we also can receive freedom from the onslaught of negative emotion and thought with which satan constantly bombards our lives.

As I have demonstrated both biblically and scientifically, the Bible is clear about what believers are to think about. There are some particularly good reasons why. In a study documented in *Science* magazine, researchers concluded that people spend nearly half (47 percent) of all waking hours being distracted. And they "found that people are thinking about what is not happening almost as often as they are thinking about what is and found that doing so typically makes them unhappy." And that "the ability to think about what is not happening is a cognitive achievement that comes at an emotional cost."[165]

The Bible agrees, and in Matthew, Jesus tells us, *"The* [seed] *sown among thorns represents the one who receives the message, but all of life's busy distractions, his divided heart, and his ambition for wealth result in suffocating the kingdom message and it becomes fruitless"* (Matthew 13:22 TPT). This is not an indictment of our distracted thinking but an opportunity to bring awareness and, from awareness, change. The practice of open biblical meditation, which I will explain later, allows the mind to flow with the Holy Spirit from thought to thought, moment to moment. Doing so provides a mechanism where distractions are addressed and thus disengaged from daily activity.

I CAN'T HEAR GOD'S VOICE

"For who has understood the mind of the Lord so as to instruct him?" But we have the mind of Christ (1 Corinthians 2:16 ESV).

As believers, we have been given the mind of Christ, and that mind, when nurtured, is perfectly aligned, healthy, and always listening to the voice of the Lord. I ministered recently with a young man, whom I will call John, who was dealing with a laundry list of self-defeating thoughts. His thoughts were the result of core beliefs that convinced him that he was not good enough, he was not loved, he was not valuable, he was a mistake, etc. His beliefs became so much a part of his internal thought life that outwardly, he appeared stooped over, depressed, sad, and unhealthy. John was in so much inner pain that even a lighthearted joke to break the tension in the room could not poke through. This young man was a believer in Jesus, but because he had nurtured his false beliefs, he could not hear the Holy Spirit speaking the truth.

I began to work with him, and as we identified each of his self-defeating core beliefs, we invited the Holy Spirit to reveal the truth. John's core belief was that because he was adopted, he was not wanted and not good enough. This thought pattern led him to constantly worry about his physical appearance and his work ethic. He worked harder to please people and vowed to never make a mistake in life. And because John was unable to discern the voice of the Holy Spirit, he always felt as though he was struggling with trying to be good enough just to measure up and not be rejected by friends, family, society, and even God. But what he soon learned is that through all of this effort, he had rejected himself along the way. By not acknowledging his identity as a child of God, holy, worthy, and accepted, he fell deeper into the snare of satan's lies. And satan convinced him that he was a mistake, that his identity was worthless and not good enough.

During counseling, I told this young man, "Before our session is over today, you will hear the voice of the Lord in your life." John looked at me with skeptical eyes and submitted himself to the counseling. As we reviewed each of his false beliefs, I would read them and ask, "Is this true?" If his answers were yes, he would write down his false belief on a new sheet.

Once we had a list of his false beliefs, we invited the Holy Spirit, who was already present, to manifest and reveal the truth to John. I spoke protection over his mind and the room and bound all demonic voices from influencing anyone. I had John pray and invite the Holy Spirit to reveal the truth behind each of the lies.

We sat in silence for a moment when suddenly, John began to write. The Holy Spirit was speaking to him, and it was coming like a flood. Over the next ten minutes, the Holy Spirit untwisted each of the lies on that paper and revealed the truth of his identity. Not only did the Holy Spirit reveal that John was accepted and loved, but that his adoption had nothing to do with his Kingdom identity or his inheritance as a son of God. As John continued to listen to the Holy Spirit, he soon understood that although he was born to a different earthly family, he was a child of God, born not of the flesh but of the will of God. This is a perfect example of our Kingdom identity as described by the Bible.

> *But to all who did receive him, who believed in his name, he gave the right to become children of God, who were born, not of blood nor of the will of the flesh nor of the will of man, but of God* (John 1:12-13 ESV).

In mere moments, John's life and identity were so totally restored, and I watched as years of rejection, hurt, and self-condemnation fell off. His countenance was bright and full of life and light; he smiled, and for the first time in many years, he accepted himself because he saw how God accepted him and nothing else mattered.

DELIVERANCE

For we do not wrestle against flesh and blood, but against the rulers, against the authorities, against the cosmic powers over this present darkness, against the spiritual forces of evil in the heavenly places (Ephesians 6:12 ESV).

Our thoughts are the foremost center of attack by the enemy. Satan and his demonic forces seek first to destroy the minds and hearts of God's children. Because in so doing, the power of God within each person becomes sufficiently diminished to the degree of uselessness in the Kingdom. But God is greater within each of us, and by bringing the strategies of satan into the light, we can pull down and destroy his advances on our minds.

As we develop a lifestyle of biblical meditation, our thoughts are aligned and tuned in with God's thoughts, and the demonic voices seeking to destroy the mind are tuned out and powerless. Shutting out the demonic voices and coming into agreement with the truth revealed by the Holy Spirit is a requirement for true, lasting deliverance from evil strongholds in our lives. Making biblical meditation a daily habit serves to reinforce all freedom and victory gained through deliverance from evil.

MULTIPLE CORE BELIEFS WORKSHEET

List each of the lies you've believed about yourself under My Beliefs. (Refer to the list at the back of this book for God's truth about you and write them in the Truth column.)

My Beliefs (lies I've believed about myself)	Truth

Answer the questions below as they relate
to your beliefs in the My Beliefs column.

What do my beliefs mean about myself?

What do my beliefs mean about other people?

What do my beliefs mean about the world?

What do my beliefs mean about God?

Confront Scriptures:

Read and meditate on the following Scriptures, comparing what they say to your beliefs: Psalm 139:13-18; John 1:12; Isaiah 49:9-10; Isaiah 42:5-6; Isaiah 54:17; Isaiah 55:8-9; Romans 5:8; 1 Timothy 2:3-4; Ephesians 2:4-5; Isaiah 45:22; Proverbs 23:23.

Pray:

> Holy Spirit, thank You for Your presence; You are magnificent, and You are welcome here. I invite You into my mind and my heart. Would You reveal the truth which has been hidden by the destructive lies of satan? I fully submit to You and choose today to align my mind and thoughts with Your mind and thoughts. I repent for believing lies and for accepting a false identity. I renounce all false beliefs and false thoughts about You, God, and I renounce all false beliefs and false thoughts about myself. I forgive myself for believing the lies of the enemy. I choose now to fully embrace what Scripture says, that I am a child of God, that I was fearfully and wonderfully created, knit together piece by piece in the secret place. I acknowledge that I have been called from the ends of the earth. You, God, have called me chosen, and You have called me a servant. I choose now to agree that I am accepted, wanted, and needed. I am not rejected, and now I speak to every demonic assignment over my life. I reject you, and I command you to come off my mind. I loose my heart and command you to LEAVE ME NOW! In the mighty name of Jesus. Holy Spirit, I invite You now to speak truth to my mind and heart.

Renew your mind:

As the Holy Spirit reveals truth, write it in the column labeled "Truth."

Maintain:

Meditate each day on these truths, bless yourself with them, and having displaced the lies of the enemy, they will become part of your renewed core belief system. If you are struggling to let go of a particular belief, then address that one separately on the worksheet titled Extensive Review of a Core Belief.

8

SOUNDS *of* MEDITATION

*So I will bless you as long as I live; in your name I will
lift up my hands. My soul will be satisfied as with fat and
rich food, and my mouth will praise you with joyful lips,
when I remember you upon my bed, and meditate on
you in the watches of the night* (Psalm 63:4-6 ESV).

THERE IS SOMETHING IN THE SOUND

It was 2014; I and a group of intercessors led by Becca Greenwood were strategically praying through the Iberian Peninsula, France, Spain, and Portugal. It was the assignment of a lifetime. I remarked that this assignment was a bucket list item that I never knew I had. Driving through the countryside, we prayed at castles and many strategic locations throughout the entire region to see God's Kingdom restored in the area.

This trip was remarkable for many reasons, but as it pertains to the topic of sound and meditation, it was eye-opening. Standing at the top of castle tower ruins, we would pray and seek God for this region and this country. We would pray that the people of this land would encounter Jesus and experience the love of the Father. As prayer typically does, the ebb and flow of prayer continued for many moments. Then, a wave of peace would settle in as the presence of the Holy Spirit increased, and we could feel the glory. We would all just stand or sit in the glory and silence of the Holy Spirit.

And the moment our assignment was complete without fail, somewhere nearby, a bell would chime. Each time was a different time of day and never aligned with the top or bottom of the hour. The timing of the ringing never made sense in the natural. But we knew instantly when we heard it that our assignment was fulfilled. As we meditated in the glory of God's presence, the sound would be a meaningful reminder that He was present and He was with us. More importantly, the sound signified that our assignment was significant and powerful. Sounds are often used by God in very symbolic ways, as He demonstrated with our group. The sound of a bell is not uncommon to hear when on these assignments, and I have experienced that on many more occasions since as God's way of saying, well done.

> *Whenever the spirit from God came on Saul, David would take up his lyre and play. Then relief would come to Saul; he would feel better, and the evil spirit would leave him* (1 Samuel 16:23 NIV).

Saul was under so much demonic torment that when David made music with the lyre, the tormenting spirit would leave him for a time and provide Saul with a respite. Music is a powerful weapon as much as it is a device for meditation. Scripture says here that when David would play, Saul experienced relief as the evil spirit would depart. The Hebrew word used for *relief* in this instance is *ravach,* which means to be refreshed.[166] At the sound of the music, Saul entered into a holy sound-induced meditation, one that was displeasing to tormenting spirits and renewing to his mind.

Culturally, this was not uncommon knowledge that evil spirits were disturbed by the sound of music. Earlier in 1 Samuel 16:16, Saul's attendants noticed the tormenting affliction on Saul. Using their knowledge of how the spiritual realm operates, they said to Saul, "Let our lord command his servants here to search for someone who can play the lyre. He will play when the evil spirit from God comes on you, and you will feel better." And so it was that David was called, and Saul was refreshed through the music.

Why did Saul experience such relief when David played? If the music turns away evil spirits, we should see people who are tormented by evil spirits receive freedom in the same way Saul did, right? Yes and no. Let's play a mind game for a bit and imagine that David was playing the lyre to the tune of Metallica's "Nothing Else Matters."[167] The song might sound great and have all of the right pitch, tone, and timbre in place to make for a beautiful arrangement. But the music would be vacant of any anointing or power of God to dispel any evil spirit.

David was anointed by God to play the lyre, and it was the music that came from David's anointing that set Saul free. Today, churches worldwide fill their sanctuaries with anointed music that provides a moment of refreshing in the spirits of those in attendance. Music has a way of either creating momentum and energizing the people or bringing a peace that soothes and calms the spirit. The instrument is less important than the anointing in this instance, and because David was anointed and obedient, Saul received momentary freedom.

Meditation, when married to anointed music, not only refreshes the spirit and settles the mind, but it also charges the atmosphere and welcomes the glory of God into the room. When the glory of God is present in meditation, a peace like nothing else envelops the body and mind, turning all thoughts toward the things of God and His plans and purpose for us. The anointing that Saul experienced when David played the lyre is the same anointing that is present when the Holy

Spirit is invited into our meditation accompanied by anointed worship music or sounds.

Theologian F.D. Maurice wrote of Saul's experience, "The music was more than a mere palliative. It brought back for the time the sense of a true order, a secret, inward harmony, an assurance that it is near every man and that he may enter into it. A wonderful message, no doubt, to a king or a common man, better than a great multitude of words, a continual prophecy that there is a deliverer who can take the vulture from the heart and unbind the sufferer from the rock. As the boy minstrel played, the afflicted monarch was refreshed, and the dark clouds rolled away."[168]

THE SHEMA YISRAEL MEDITATION

One of the most famous Jewish traditions is the ancient practice of meditation called the *shema* (pronounced sh'ma) based on Deuteronomy 6:4-9 and Numbers 15:37-41. It is known as the central affirmation of Judaism. An interesting fact is that during the recitation, it is customary to cover the eyes with the right hand as a way to ponder the meditation without visual distractions.[169]

> *Hear, O Israel: The Lord our God, the Lord is one. You shall love the Lord your God with all your heart and with all your soul and with all your might. And these words that I command you today shall be on your heart* (Deuteronomy 6:4-6 ESV).

> *The Lord said to Moses, "Speak to the people of Israel and tell them to make tassels on the corners of their garments throughout their generations, and to put a cord of blue on*

the tassel of each corner. And it shall be a tassel for you to look at and remember all the commandments of the Lord, to do them, not to follow after your own heart and your own eyes, which you are inclined to whore after. So you shall remember and do all my commandments, and be holy to your God. I am the Lord your God, who brought you out of the land of Egypt to be your God: I am the Lord your God" (Numbers 15:37-41 ESV).

The meditation of these passages was commanded by God to be practiced at least twice each day, intentionally keeping God at the forefront of the mind at all times. Rabbi Heschel Greenberg says this of the *shema* meditation, "One of the principle meditations in Judaism, particularly within the Chassidic tradition—which places an even greater emphasis on meditation—is on the oneness of God."[170]

This ancient, time-honored tradition is no longer required under the fulfillment of the law. However, the principle of keeping God at the forefront of the mind using verbal meditations and recitations acts as a vehicle aiding in the restorative alignment of our thoughts. Now, as Messianic believers, we can freely choose to engage in thoughtful meditation of Scripture, using it to heal and to inspire the outflow of God's character from us.

PRAISE AND WORSHIP'S ROLE IN BIBLICAL MEDITATION

One of my first experiences with biblical meditation was in 2010, and one of the first things I remember the Lord demonstrating was the practicality of meditation during a praise and worship experience. At the time, my wife, Petra, and I were attending Freedom church, pastored by Dutch Sheets in Colorado Springs. During one event, Rick Pino was invited to lead worship.

I remember as Rick primed the pump for an atmosphere of worship, I closed my eyes and began to take deep breaths through my nose. I immediately entered a meditative state that consumed me. I was at complete peace in my mind and my body. My thoughts were captured by the glory of God, which filled the atmosphere. I recall feeling like I could spend an incredible amount of time just resting in the glory. It was a feeling and an experience that I had never experienced prior to that moment. That moment signified the instant that I first touched the intimacy of a deep, meditative, and relational experience with Jesus. That experience is now part of my regular worship involvement.

This moment I just described was organic, and you have likely had similar experiences as well. What I did not know was that moment was the essence of biblical meditation. Just as with David's lyre, anointed praise and worship will usher in the glory of the presence and the power of the Holy Spirit. Once the glory arrives and our hearts are ready, God will encounter us in that moment to personally and privately welcome in the peace of God that can only come from His presence.

The Bible richly describes the involvement of music and worship within the context of our meditation. Psalm 63:5-6 (ESV) introduces us to singing praise and worshipping the Lord at night. *"My soul will be satisfied as with fat and rich food, and my mouth will praise you with joyful lips, when I remember you upon my bed, and meditate on you in the watches of the night."* And in Colossians 3:16 (ESV), an example is provided for singing and worshipping through thankfulness, which is a meditative posture: *"Let the word of Christ dwell in you richly, teaching and admonishing one another in all wisdom, singing psalms and hymns and spiritual songs, with thankfulness in your hearts to God."*

PRACTICAL APPLICATION

The next time you are at church or in your prayer room, and the anointing of the praise and worship begins to fill the room. Close your eyes and acknowledge the presence of the Holy Spirit. Breathe deeply, inhaling slowly through your nose and exhaling slowly through your mouth. Position your thoughts on Jesus and the words of the music glorifying Jesus. Invite Him in your mind to join you and be with you. Then just wait, breathe slowly, and allow the Holy Spirit to take your thoughts in that moment wherever He wants.

You will find that these times of worshipful meditation are the most restorative and peaceful times ever experienced. And that is because when the presence of God fills the room, all fear, worry, unbelief, anxiety, and stress suddenly disappear. After all, they cannot exist in the pure presence of the glory of God.

SOUNDS THAT HEAL THE LAND

Often, it is precisely the very evanescence of a sound that makes it all the more memorable or intense, such as the beauty of a musical phrase heard live, a remembered conversation, or even the silence of a shared moment.[171]

The use of various types of sound within meditation is quite common among every culture on earth. The primary reason, I believe, is due to the power inherent to audible tone and sound, which resonates healing vibration throughout our bodies and minds. The Buddhists use vocal mantras and ringing bells, which they believe promotes the right atmosphere for enlightenment. To a Buddhist, a bell or a mantra inspires contemplation and intense focus. To a Hindu, the transcendental sound of Om is believed to transform the mind and inspire elevated consciousness. To a Catholic, the rhythm of meditating through the rosary is part of the traditional thoughtfulness exercises. Bells, chimes, gongs, mantras, and repetitive sounds often fill the room with dissonant or discordant sounds of these secular meditation techniques.

All of these sounds have two primary aspects in common. First, they are unanointed sounds that have no spiritual impact beyond the emotional and neuropsychological level. And second, because the sounds are void of any anointing, the possibility for demonic affiliation intensifies with their usage, specifically in meditation. This should not be taken as an inditement on bells, chimes, and gongs, as the sounds of those instruments can be very beautiful. I am referring specifically to their intentional use to create an atmosphere of meditation. It is that atmosphere that invites the demonic through the open door by partnering with the evil roots of the secular meditation.

Believers in Jesus are encouraged to meditate with sounds of worship, praise, and vocal sound and musical instruments. The difference is that when a believer meditates through worship, or through the use of tongues, and even prayer, the sound is anointed. Anointed sound brings not only emotional healing but it also intensifies the spiritual connection to the throne room.

God created sound and the ability to make sound in different frequencies to serve as a vehicle for communication but also as entertainment and worship. As with all things, God's purpose in creation always has a deeper meaning. Sound is also used to heal, bring about transformation, and restore the desolation. When Elisha, the prophet, called for a musician to play in 2 Kings, the hand of the Lord touched him, and he prophesied a restoration to the dry pits. He declared they would be filled with water. Indeed, the water came, and the land was restored. The anointed sound of worship inspired Elijah to prophesy, which brought healing to the land.

"But now bring me a musician." And when the musician played, the hand of the Lord came upon him. And he said, "Thus says the Lord, 'I will make this dry streambed full of pools.'...The next morning, about the time of offering the sacrifice, behold, water came from the direction of Edom, till the country was filled with water (2 Kings 3:15-16,20 ESV).

As Paul and Silas found themselves imprisoned with their feet in stocks, they began to pray and sing songs to God. Again, the anointed sound of heart-focused worship brought a freedom that neither of them could have planned. Their meditations of worship and prayer invited the power of God, manifesting as an earthquake that destroyed the prison, opened the doors, and unlocked the chains that bound them. Yet, there is so much more to this event. Saving Paul and Silas was a gain, but God received the greater glory as the jailer and his family were brought into the Kingdom of God in that moment of destruction. It was the anointed sounds of Paul and Silas that ushered in the transforming power of God and brought a sinner and his entire family into eternal redemption.

After they were severely beaten, they were thrown into prison and the jailer was commanded to guard them securely. So the jailer placed them in the innermost cell of the prison and had their feet bound and chained. Paul and Silas, undaunted, prayed in the middle of the night and sang songs of praise to God, while all the other prisoners listened to their worship. Suddenly, a great earthquake shook the foundations of the prison. All at once every prison door flung open and the chains of all the prisoners came loose. Startled, the jailer awoke and saw every cell door standing open. Assuming that all the prisoners had escaped, he drew his sword and was about to kill himself when Paul shouted in the darkness, "Stop! Don't hurt yourself. We're all still here." The jailer called for a light. When he saw that they were still in their cells, he rushed in and fell trembling at their feet. Then he led Paul and Silas outside and asked, "What must I do to be saved?" They answered, "Believe in the Lord Jesus and you will be saved—you and all your family." Then they prophesied the word of the Lord over him and all his family. Even though the hour was late, he washed their wounds. Then he and all his family were baptized. He took Paul and Silas into his home and set them at his table and fed them. The jailer and all his family were filled with joy in their newfound faith in God (Acts 16:23-34 TPT).

The Bible has demonstrated the use of earthquakes to save God's people on more than one occasion. In the account of Jericho, Joshua led his army to march once around the entire city for six days. The foreboding sound of an army marching around the city while blowing loud rams' horn trumpets must have reverberated throughout the city, causing quite a lot of confusion among the inhabitants. On the seventh day, not only did they march and blow the trumpets, but people were released to shout for the victory and the destruction of the walls. In an instant and with a cacophony of shouting trumpets and a supernatural precision strike, God caused the walls of the fortress of Jericho to crumble. Again, anointed sound was used by God first to bring redemption through destruction.

As already noted, David is perhaps the most well-known biblical meditator, and his examples serve to demonstrate a pure model for biblical meditation. As such, David frequently engages in the use of sounds in the form of songs, prayer, and worship through the use of his voice and musical instruments.

Praise him with trumpet sound; praise him with lute and harp! Praise him with tambourine and dance; praise him with strings and pipe! Praise him with sounding cymbals;

*praise him with loud clashing cymbals! Let everything that
has breath praise the Lord! Praise the Lord!* (Psalm 150:3-6
ESV)

David continually demonstrates his vulnerability in the meditation
song of Psalm 63 as he longs for God in a dry and weary land. He speaks
with praise and remembers God. During his entire meditation in the
night, he uses the sound of his voice to praise the Lord.

FREQUENCY OF LIFE

*"At the heart of the universe is a steady, insistent
beat: the sound of cycles in sync."*[172]

The voice of God was the first sound, and it was the sound that
kickstarted the entirety of the universe, time, and space. His voice
created and propelled humanity into existence. The reverberations of
God's voice still resonates in every atom, and every cell in every living
thing, and every inanimate object in the universe. Even our cells and
DNA, which contain the building blocks for each of us, vibrate to a
sound frequency crafted by the voice of God. Furthermore, it has been
discovered that the entire human body resonates a unique frequency
signature. In a study performed at the University of California Santa
Barbara, human bodies resonate with unique and individual frequencies. And at the risk of dipping my toe in the esoteric, the study went
on to demonstrate that even consciousness resonates with a unique
frequency. The field of study is called general resonance theory or GRT.

According to the researchers, "All things in our universe
are constantly in motion, in process. Even objects that

appear to be stationary are, in fact, vibrating, oscillating, and resonating at specific frequencies. So, all things are actually processes. Resonance is a specific type of motion characterized by synchronized oscillation between two states. An interesting phenomenon occurs when different vibrating processes come into proximity: they will often start vibrating together at the same frequency. They "sync up," sometimes in ways that can seem mysterious."[173]

What does any of this have to do with meditation? It has everything to do with our capacity within meditation to draw close to God. As we meditate and join the Holy Spirit in the secret place, our imperfect human frequency, which has been subject to the inherited and intentional flaws of our lives, begins to sync up with His heart and, in that instant, resonates in sync with His. The feeling at the moment of synchronization is almost euphoric, like being surrounded by a bubble of perfect peace and love. Jesus Himself spoke of this synchronization, saying that as we sync up with Him, our lives will bear much fruit.

Abide in me, and I in you. As the branch cannot bear fruit by itself unless it abides in the vine, neither can you unless you abide in me. I am the vine; you are the branches. Whoever abides in me and I in him, he it is that bears much fruit, for apart from me, you can do nothing (John 15:4-5 ESV).

Now, with an understanding of the practicality of frequency and its connection within the abiding place, suddenly, the concept is not so esoteric, having firmly aligned with Scripture.

Further demonstrating the power of sound, scientists have concluded that using sound on plants and crops enhances plant immune systems, increases growth, and increases protective enzymes in plants. A technology that, when applied, reduces the need for herbicides and biocides by 50 percent and pesticides by as much as 25 percent. Ultimately, through the use of audible sound, plants are healthier and, as such, yield a higher quality product.[174]

In a study a little closer to home, scientists have successfully used the power of sound waves to grow bone from stem cells. RMIT University in Australia scientists concluded that "stem cells treated with high-frequency sound waves turned into bone cells quickly and efficiently."[175]

Just as David brought healing sound to Saul, and Elijah and the musician brought healing to the land, the human body was designed to respond to sounds. What happens to your body when listening to grinding heavy metal music? My younger self would have told you that it was enjoyable and fun to listen to. Having matured a bit, I know now that style of music generates feelings of angst, anxiousness, restlessness, and even anger.

Now, what happens in your body when listening to "Happy" by Pharrell Williams? The song naturally generates a state of joy and bright energy that inspires dancing. How about the song "It Is So" by Elevation Worship? Suddenly, a peaceful atmosphere fills the room. A worshipful calm sets in, creating an environment of meditation with the Holy Spirit. The music and words we feed our minds and bodies truly work to set the stage for our emotional, physical, and spiritual well-being.

According to 400 different published scientific articles, "music has mental and physical health benefits in improving mood and reducing stress. In fact, rhythm in particular (over melody) can provide physical pain relief." The power of sound has even been shown to significantly reduce feelings of anger, anxiety, and depression while increasing a sense of well-being. Additionally, researchers discovered that the sound stimulated touch fibers that affect pain perception, resulting in physical pain relief for people living with fibromyalgia to the degree that medications were significantly reduced.[176]

TONGUES

"Praying in tongues charges your spirit like
a battery charger charges a battery."

–Kenneth Hagin

Speaking in tongues or glossolalia is one of the special gifts given to believers when they receive the infilling of the Holy Spirit. Peter Wagner defines this gift as "The gift of tongues is the special ability that God gives to certain members of the body of Christ to speak to God in a language they have never learned, and/or to receive and communicate an immediate message from God to His people through a divinely anointed utterance in a language they have never learned."

The church received the gift of the tongues along with the presence of the Holy Spirit. At that time, tongues were unknown, and strange vocal utterances were seen to be the language of drunkards. Scripture tells us that the Holy Spirit gave them utterances that manifested as both strange new languages and also as new earthly languages previously unlearned. The gift of tongues is an ability designed uniquely for the purpose of meditation.

Peter Wagner also says that "the gift of tongues does not transmit the word of God. Rather, it transmits a word from God."[177] No other religion, cult, or belief in the world has been granted such a direct link to the throne room as believers in Jesus. The manifestation of utterances does appear in other religions, such as paganism and shamanism. It has also been recorded that the Oracle of Delphi spoke in a form of tongues inspired by the demonic spirit of Apollo, which possessed her. Only through the power of the indwelt Holy Spirit can a believer fully access the power of God through the righteous use of the gift of tongues. The Bible tells us that when we pray in tongues, our spirit prays, and we are personally edified, but our mind is unfruitful.

> *For if I pray in a tongue, my spirit prays, but my mind is unfruitful* (1 Corinthians 14:14 NIV).

Recent studies concerning speaking in tongues has revealed that when people speak in tongues, an observable decrease in activity is shown in the prefrontal cortex, which is the portion of the brain responsible for cognitive control. This decrease is marked by a relative increase of activity in the parietal lobe, which is the part of the brain linked explicitly to meditation and our sense of self and emotion. In simpler terms, "The words spoken in Glossolalia [tongues] originate from a source other than the mind of the individual speaking in tongues."[178] Again, Peter Wagner wonderfully summarizes the experience this way, "The gift of tongues does not transmit the word of God. Rather, it transmits a word from God."

When we speak in tongues, our minds quite literally get out of the way so that God can impart His word within us as we meditate. The gift of tongues is not a benign function of our bodies. This gift is truly our key to the throne room, and as we enter, we sit with the Father, and our spirit receives insight, truth, wisdom, and understanding. The Bible tells us in Proverbs 23:23 (ESV), *"Buy truth, and do not sell it; buy wisdom, instruction, and understanding."* This is the golden thread of meditation: How do we purchase truth? As we enter the secret place of meditation with the Holy Spirit, the gift of tongues unlocks the atmosphere and opens the door for God to speak directly to our spirit and bring healing and restoration.

Hear this! Believers, do not neglect your gift of tongues; it is the key you have been given within you that unlocks revelation knowledge directly from the Holy of Holies. And as we enter in, the thoughts of God are made known, and the purposes of God in our lives become clear. This gift is uniquely created to enhance and edify our times of biblical meditation. As we engage, our thoughts align, stress decreases, and blood pressure is reduced.[179] The gift of tongues benefits the entire body and spirit.

TRANSCENDENTAL MEDITATION (TM)

The gift of tongues is the righteous form of meditation, and the counterfeit is transcendental meditation. As referenced earlier, other demonic forms of tongues exist, but rather than edifying and providing access to God's Word, they serve to connect the user directly to demonic influence.

The creator of transcendental meditation, Mahesh Prasad Varma, received his revelation for the TM method during a two-year disappearance in the Himalayas, where he is said to have been in meditation and reflection. He emerged with a mission to evangelize the world with the philosophy of TM.

Transcendental meditation is a method of meditation that uses mantras and sounds to generate a meditative state. Further evidence shows that transcendental meditation and hypnosis share similar qualities, ultimately leading to "a decrease in the differentiation between the self and the external world."[180] TM incorporates chants and mantras, much of which originates from the dead languages of Pali and Sanskrit. During my visit to the Tibetan Buddhist temple, it was explained that during meditation, these Pali and Sanskrit phrases are used with no understanding of true meaning because of a lack of translation ability.

Ultimately, Transcendental Meditation is a direct counterfeit of true biblical meditation and the gift of tongues. As a practitioner of

TM navigates through their own maturity within the practice, a qualified TM master, yogi, or guru bestows secret mantras upon them, usually from the Sanskrit language. The use of the mantras are meant to transport the waking self or consciousness into transcendence. Because these mantras are secret and inaccessible, they must be repeated silently. It is taught that sharing or speaking a personal TM mantra removes its power, weakening its effectiveness.

This is a complete twisting of the righteous model provided for biblical meditation. The gift of tongues is not secret, nor is it a vehicle transporting our consciousness to another plane of existence. Instead, the gift of tongues was given for the edification and building up of the believers with power from Heaven. Boil TM down to ultimate simplicity, and it is escapism theology, where the goal is to pull away or run away from unpleasantness, emotions, suffering, and fears. Escapism theology is unbiblical, and suppressing unpleasant emotions, thoughts, and fears only serves to bring damage to the mind, will, and emotions. God came that we may have life everlasting! We are to experience that life now, and righteous biblical meditation aligns our thoughts with His and walks us safely through healing and restoration of inner wounds without suppression.

OM ॐ

The popular sound most of us are familiar with. As mentioned previously, Om is a sound made by combining the three audible sounds of A, U, and M to sound like (awe, oooh, mmmm) and a fourth sound which is silence. As the sound is chanted, each syllable is spoken in alignment with its meaning: A - what has been, U - what is, and M - what shall be. As defined in ancient Hindu texts, each sound of the Om chants brings honor and worship to the false gods of Brahma, the creator; Vishnu, the preserver; and Shiva, the destroyer. The very sound of Om is said to invoke these deities, which are known as the Hindu trinity called the Trimurti.

This is a blatant twisting of God's established Kingdom order. Where He is one God in three parts, Father, Son, and Holy Spirit, the Trimurti represents an unholy alliance of three separate demonic deities masquerading as a holy trinity. The symbol ॐ represents the chant and visually demonstrates the unholy trinity. The components of the symbol represent four states of consciousness in meditation. The unconscious, the waking, the dream, the absolute, and a fifth state called illusion, which prevents a peaceful state of consciousness. It is not a good outcome for a meditative moment.

For believers, meditation using Om or other transcendental mantras is forbidden by God. These practices are open doors that invite the demonic into the lives of the practitioner, which leads to destruction and a separation from God. While the Om represents the beginning, the middle, and the end, Jesus declares, *"I am the Way, I am the Truth, and I am the Life. No one comes next to the Father except through union with me. To know me is to know my Father too"* (John 14:6 TPT). Pure biblical meditation has no need or value for chants, rituals, or secret mantras. We have something better—freedom to be in God's presence as often as we desire. And better yet! He actually responds to us when we do! Shiva cannot respond, and if he could, I'm not sure I'd want to be experiencing my deepest emotions with "the destroyer of worlds."

CHANTING

I've addressed chanting as used in TM or with the Om already. Yet the practice of chanting is more broad than those applications, and we should be aware and discerning. Chanting is essentially the musical repetition of the names of gods or deities. As the names and words are chanted, the person chanting is working up to a whole body experience where, at times, they begin to vibrate throughout the entire body. As explained in Siddha yoga, "In the practice of chanting repetition focuses one's mind and energy on the names and qualities of god[s]. The focus achieved through repetition can support the chanter in becoming immersed in the sacred sound vibrations and in experiencing the qualities inherent in the names being sung." In the practice of yoga, chanting is a means to experience the divine within. This divine being is a reference to the Kundalini spirit discussed earlier.[181]

For believers, we should run from chanting or conjuring demonic vibrations within our bodies. This is not the righteous meditation we have inherited. Our inheritance of biblical meditation is a pure, almost effortless approach where our partnership with the living Holy Spirit alone brings total peace and comfort. All of these TM, om'ing, and chanting share the commonality of repetitious language or thought. In the Bible, Jesus Himself said it this way, *"And when you pray, do not heap up empty phrases as the Gentiles do, for they think that they will be heard for their many words"* (Matthew 6:7 ESV).

I realize this was contextually referring to the hypocrites standing in the synagogue shouting their prayers to be heard. Let's appreciate the principle of vain language and that it is an empty path. And in the case of pagan religion, it is very dangerous.

PRACTICAL APPLICATION: ABIDE IN HIM

This exercise incorporates aspects of biblical meditation, worship, and sound. This meditation should generally take 10 to 20 minutes, or as long as you desire to sit in the presence of God.

- Put on quiet praise and worship music and get into a comfortable, relaxed position.

- Anoint your forehead with fragrant oil. Anointing oil represents our consecration and dedication to the Lord and is a symbolic representation of the Holy Spirit in our lives. The use of oil will be discussed in a later chapter.

- Take a moment to ponder the goodness of God as you listen to the sound of the music.

- Close your eyes and breathe deeply in through your nostrils, exhaling slowly out of your nose.

- Begin to thank the Holy Spirit for His presence and invite Him into your thoughts.

- Invite Him into the room and ask for a tangible manifestation of His presence. He will honor your request, and the atmosphere will shift, and you may experience goosebumps commonly associated with His presence.

- Quietly begin to pray in tongues or release a prayer, either in your mind or out loud.

- Pray until you are at peace and feel the tangible presence of the Holy Spirit.

- Stop praying and be silent; let your body and mind rest in the silence as the Holy Spirit ministers to your thoughts.

- What is He saying? Where is He taking you?

- If He is taking you to a memory, you can trust that He will be with you, ensuring your safety. These moments are special, intimate times of healing. Soak them up.

Spend as long as you like in the presence of the Lord. There is no limit on time. Generally, after about 20 minutes, you may slowly return to normal breathing as you may have noticed that your breathing has slowed considerably.

Open your eyes and return to your day feeling refreshed and full of new life.

9

POSTURE, POSITION, *and* ANOINTING OIL

What delight comes to those who follow God's ways! They won't walk in step with the wicked, nor share the sinner's way, nor be found sitting in the scorner's seat. Their pleasure and passion is remaining true to the Word of "I AM," meditating day and night in his true revelation of light. They will be standing firm like a flourishing tree planted by God's design, deeply rooted by the brooks of bliss, bearing fruit in every season of their lives. They are never dry, never fainting, ever blessed, ever prosperous (Psalm 1:1-3 TPT).

O ur position before the throne means so much. I have heard people say, and I have asked it myself, "What if Jesus were in the room? What would your posture be?" But those questions do not give God the recognition that He deserves. Because He is, in fact, in the room. God declares in Jeremiah 23:23-24 (ESV): *"Am I a God at hand, declares the Lord, and not a God far away? Can a man hide himself in secret places so that I cannot see him? declares the Lord. Do I not fill heaven and earth? declares the Lord."* And in Acts, Paul makes it known that God is not contained within temples and places of worship: *"He supplies life and breath and all things to every living being."*

So Paul stood in the middle of the leadership council and said, "Respected leaders of Athens, it is clear to me how extravagant you are in your worship of idols. For as I walked through your city, I was captivated by the many shrines and objects of your worship. I even found an inscription on one altar that read, 'To the Unknown God.' I have come to introduce to you this God whom you worship without even knowing anything about him. The true God is the Creator of all things. He is the owner and Lord of the heavenly realm and the earthly realm, and he doesn't live in man-made temples. He supplies life and breath and all things to every living being. He doesn't lack a thing that we mortals could supply for him, for he has all things and everything he needs" (Acts 17:22-25 TPT).

COME AS YOU ARE

God is present in and at every moment of our existence, and He awaits our attention. Our mindset should not be on what posture we might take if He walked into the room. Rather, our mindset should lead us to the posture best suited for our moment with the ever-present King of glory. Because He is always present, our posture before Him will change accordingly. Be mindful also that your posture before the Lord does not become an idol in itself. Worrying about our stance or its appropriateness only serves to build walls around the genuineness and vulnerability of the moment in His presence. In Matthew, Jesus beautifully invites us in no matter what condition we are in:

Are you weary, carrying a heavy burden? Come to me. I will refresh your life, for I am your oasis. Simply join your life with mine. Learn my ways, and you'll discover that I'm gentle, humble, easy to please. You will find refreshment and rest in me. For all that I require of you will be pleasant and easy to bear (Matthew 11:28-29 TPT).

POSTURES

I always found the typical posture of meditation to be curious. Why do those who practice secular meditation typically sit cross-legged with a straight back? It seems incredibly uncomfortable over long periods of time that are supposed to be relaxing. I have discovered that physical posture is important, and scripturally, our posture before the Lord carries great significance. Our physical posture reflects our heart posture before the Lord. Matthew 15:18 (TPT) describes the importance of our heart posture, *"But what comes out of your mouth reveals the core of your heart. Words can pollute, not food."*[182]

While our posture is important, it is not meant to become a hindrance. We should always adopt a posture that is appropriate for our meeting with God and one that is pleasant and comfortable for our bodies. The manner in which we posture ourselves reflects the heart and the seriousness to which we give the moment. For most, doing what comes naturally is sufficient.

Let's look first at the practical aspects of posture in our meditation. Four primary positions are typically used in all forms of meditation. I've added two additional postures, walking and standing, for those who wish to meditate actively. Most of the positions are benign and simply provide a peaceful and comfortable posture for meditation. I will also address the positions to steer clear of as a biblical meditator. Keep in mind that these positions and postures are not meant to be a rule-based exercise. Instead, it is an opportunity to comfortably enter into a peaceful moment in any way you choose. You will find that the position that works best for you is the one that generally makes your body feel the most at peace and comfortable. The primary postures of biblical meditation, which we will cover in further detail, are sitting on a cushion or chair, kneeling, lying on the back, prostrating before the Lord, walking, or standing.

Sitting

Are you overwhelmed by the stresses of life and need calming peace and direction from the Holy Spirit? You may choose to sit cross-legged on a cushion or in a chair in a manner that is comfortable for the duration of the meditation. In Scripture, we see Mary, the sister of Martha, who, at the expense of so-called important duties, chose to sit at the feet of Jesus and listen. He said of her, "Mary has chosen the good portion." Let us all choose to devote time to sit before the Lord, just listening to what is on His heart.

> *Now as they went on their way, Jesus entered a village. And a woman named Martha welcomed him into her house. And she had a sister called Mary, who sat at the Lord's feet and listened to his teaching. But Martha was distracted with much serving. And she went up to him and said, "Lord, do you not care that my sister has left me to serve alone? Tell her then to help me." But the Lord answered her, "Martha, Martha, you are anxious and troubled about many things, but one thing is necessary. Mary has chosen the good portion, which will not be taken away from her"* (Luke 10:38-42 ESV).

As I write these words, I am sitting in a comfortable chair with my bare feet in the warm green grass. The sun's rays are providing a gentle heat. And as I look at the distance, I am overwhelmed by the beauty of the Rocky Mountains. It is a stunning view that showcases the majestic, creative nature of our God. My posture is focused and attentive but sprinkled with moments of awe and admiration of God's goodness as I write this fully enveloped within His presence.

Walking

Perhaps you seek to focus your mind on a task and need to align your mind and thoughts. A walking meditation may be the perfect position as it combines a light activity while allowing the Holy Spirit to minister to your mind. Walking while meditating may at first seem counterintuitive to the process. The truth is that when we consciously acknowledge God's presence in the midst of our activities and listen to His voice, we are truly fulfilling the essence of meditation. While walking, our minds are present with Him as we learn from Him, and our bodies become refreshed.

Standing

Perhaps you are joyful and wish to express your happiness in praise. Standing with arms raised and eyes heavenward represents your sign of total surrender as you submit and give it all up to God. Paul expresses his encouragement for people to raise holy hands in worship: *"There-fore, I encourage the men to pray on every occasion with hands lifted to God in worship with clean hearts, free from frustration or strife"* (1 Timothy 2:8 TPT).

David expressed his surrendered worship with lifted hands in a beautiful expression of an offering to the Lord: *"Let my prayer be as the evening sacrifice that burns like fragrant incense, rising as my offering to you as I lift up my hands in surrendered worship!"* (Psalm 141:2 TPT).

Walking and standing are excellent postures by which we can engage with God and maintain an alert focus on His creation and His glory.

Lying Prostrate, Face-Down

Are you broken before the Lord? Naturally, your posture might be lying prostrate before the Lord while He ministers healing and restoration to your mind and heart. Psalm 72:11 (ESV) calls all kings to fall down before the Lord: *"May all kings fall down before him, all nations serve him!"*

The Hebrew word for "fall down" in this context is *saha*, which means to bow down prostrate before the Lord.[183] Jesus fell down in this manner and made Himself prostrate before the Father as He prayed in Gethsemane: *"And going a little farther, he fell on his face and prayed, saying, 'My Father, if it be possible, let this cup pass from me; nevertheless, not as I will, but as you will'"* (Matthew 26:39 ESV).

Moses, in the ultimate act of humility, made himself lay prostrate before the Lord for forty days: *"Then I lay prostrate before the Lord as before, forty days and forty nights. I neither ate bread nor drank water..."* (Deuteronomy 9:18 ESV).

Lying prostrate before the Lord is often used when led by the Holy Spirit in an act of total surrender. Oftentimes, profound God encounters occur when we are prostrate before Him.

Kneeling and Bowing

Is your heart full of worship toward the Lord? Scripture shows us that bowing down and kneeling before the Lord signifies our worshipful posture and heart attitude. Kneeling is best with a cushion, meditation bench, or soft ground.

> *Come and kneel before this Creator-God; come and bow before the mighty God, our majestic maker! For we are the lovers he cares for, and he is the God we worship. So drop everything else and listen to his voice!* (Psalm 95:6-7 TPT)

Lying Down

Are you seeking mental rest and peace in his presence? A posture of lying down may suit you best. David occasionally describes his meditations as lying down and being silent before the Lord. Especially when he is angry and realizes that through his meditation (pondering), he will be restored: *"Be angry, and do not sin; ponder in your own hearts on your beds, and be silent"* (Psalm 4:4 ESV).

Lying on the back allows the body and mind to fully rest and reset. Be careful, though; lying on the back may lead to an unexpected nap as the meditative experience allows the body to relax completely.

As meditation becomes an integral part of daily life, your favorite posture will emerge organically and become second nature. Over time, postures even modify according to each person's style and level of comfortability. For example, as I meditate, my default position is sitting on a cushion, but as the glory increases in the room, I may move from sitting to kneeling as I am moved by the Holy Spirit in the moment. There is freedom in our expression before the Lord: experiment, be flexible, and never feel like there are rules when approaching the throne.

JOYCE'S STORY

Meet Joyce, one of the amazing deliverance ministers and intercessors on our team. Joyce has walked with us through the revelation and teaching behind biblical meditation for the past few years. Having incorporated it into her daily life, Joyce has found great peace and revelation. Here is how Joyce explains her experiences in biblical meditation:

> Many times, when I meditate, it is a time of intimacy with Jesus. We go for walks, or we sit together enjoying each

other's company. Also, I will focus on a Bible verse that directs my meditation time and conversation with Jesus. Meditating on the Father, or Jesus, or the Holy Spirit settles my soul and anchors the truth that is highlighted by them, becoming alive in my being and cannot be denied. This overflows in day-to-day living and my decision-making. It stimulates my imagination to see in the supernatural to believe in the reality of "the kingdom of heaven that is at hand," as Jesus teaches. Other times in meditation, the Lord will highlight an area that He wants changed in me, and being with Him makes it easy to yield to Him. Sometimes, I will even act out in the natural what I am seeing in the spiritual to anchor this surrender and change in me. I have found that obeying Philippians 4:8 is easily possible through biblical meditation.

So keep your thoughts continually fixed on all that is authentic and real, honorable and admirable, beautiful and respectful, pure and holy, merciful and kind. And fasten your thoughts on every glorious work of God, praising him always (Philippians 4:8 TPT).

Joyce's experiences in meditation demonstrate how the Holy Spirit loves to partner with us in any posture or position. Approaching Him without religious boundaries of posture or language allows us to experience the depth of His love without restraint.

AVOID

Believers practicing biblical meditation should *avoid* worshipful poses often used in secular meditations. Specific body postures are known as "asanas," while hand positions are called "mudras." It is a good practice to question an approach or pose in order to gain complete understanding. Knowing the roots, origins, and intent of a posture often reveals the hidden agenda of the positions.

The lotus pose, for example, is perhaps the most familiar. This is the pose where the legs are crossed, but rather than typical crossed-legged sitting, each foot rests on the top of the opposite thigh. This pose abnormally stretches and rotates the thigh ball-and-socket joint, often leading to joint pain. Additionally, the lotus pose typically involves the use of mudras or hand gestures, which are said to stimulate the different parts of the body. The lotus pose is a worshipful position created to bring honor and reverence to the false god Vishnu. It is believed by practitioners that the lotus flower grew from Vishnu's navel and forehead. The false god Brahma is believed to live at the center of the lotus flower within Vishnu. The false goddess Lakshmi is honored for originating from the lotus flower on Vishnu.

Another popular meditation pose is the Vajrasana or thunderbolt pose. It is performed in a kneeling position, but rather than simply kneeling, the ankles and toes are turned inward underneath while sitting on the heels of the inward-turned feet. This pose is responsible for a clinical condition known as yoga foot drop. This position cuts off oxygen to vital nerves in the feet, deadening the nerves.[184] The Vajrasana is a pose that represents a physical sacrifice to the false god Vishnu. According to Hindu legend, a sage known as Dadhichi entered into a deep meditative state, during which his spine was removed from his body and was made into a weapon known today as the vajra. This is a sacrificial pose offering the body as worship to false gods, as Dadhichi is said to have done.

In truth, meditation, prayer, and our approach before the Lord needs no specific posture, pose, or hand gestures. Biblical meditation is not about form or function, but rather, it is about benefiting our mind, body, and spirit through a connection with the Holy Spirit and the Bible. Posture before the Lord should always be guided by the heart. God spoke this to Samuel after rejecting Saul's kingship, *"...For the Lord sees not as man sees: man looks on the outward appearance, but the Lord looks on the heart"* (1 Samuel 16:7 ESV). And this message is confirmed as Jesus spoke and decreed the greatest commandment of all. Our approach to the throne room and our heart posture is all that matters. Don't let religious traditions and gestures corrupt the purity of simply approaching the Lord out of the pure desire to be in the restoring presence of His glory.

> *You are to love the Lord Yahweh, your God, with a passionate heart, from the depths of your soul, with your every thought, and with all your strength. This is the great and supreme commandment* (Mark 12:30 TPT).

ANOINTING OIL

It was an explosive weekend of teaching and impartation from anointed deliverance and inner healing ministries from all across the nation.[185] As I prepared to speak at this meeting of the International Freedom Group, the Holy Spirit urged me to bring my oil. *Curious,* I thought. I have used anointing oil in the past as a component of the ministry illustrated in Mark 6:13 (ESV), *"And they cast out many demons and anointed with oil many who were sick and healed them."* I have used this biblical principle to break the grip of the enemy in the lives of many demonized people. I've used it to anoint people as we entered into intercession before the Lord. But I have never used it in the context of a corporate meeting.

I had just received in the mail an order of oil mixed to the specifications and with ingredients described by God in Exodus 30:22-25. I thought this would be an excellent addition to our deliverance and inner healing ministry sessions. I did not realize that the Holy Spirit had a more excellent plan, which involved teaching me quickly about the use of anointing oil. I was obedient and brought the oil.

On the first day of the conference, worship was electric; our friends and worship leaders, Eric and Shuree Hoffman, opened the heavens before us as we worshipped the Lord. In the midst of our worship, Shuree declared prophetically a vision she was seeing, "A well of oil is opened in this place; step in." People began to experience a tangible manifestation of the Holy Spirit's anointing oil as they approached the altar. Some fell to their faces as the prophetic oil of the Lord began to wash over people and bring them into the Holy of Holies. It was beautiful watching the Holy Spirit manifest in this manner among the people. Then the Holy Spirit spoke to me, "Get your oil, and declare over the people their priesthood as sons and daughters of God."

> But you are God's chosen treasure—priests who are kings, a spiritual "nation" set apart as God's devoted ones. He called you out of darkness to experience his marvelous light, and now he claims you as his very own. He did this so that you would broadcast his glorious wonders throughout the world (1 Peter 2:9 TPT).

As I began to pray, the Holy Spirit instructed me to anoint every person in the room with the special anointing oil. As I began to share what the Lord had asked me to do, people immediately began to line up in front of me. It was as though the Holy Spirit had prepared their hearts to receive this anointing. I was broken and thankful to have acted in the obedience of the Holy Spirit. As I anointed every person in attendance, the worship was elevated, and a new dimension of the glory of God was reached in that moment. I anointed every person in the room, including the worship team.

People all over the auditorium were receiving fresh revelation, and everyone was rejoicing in the presence of the Holy Spirit. The portal of oil was indeed opened, and the manifestation of the Holy Spirit was prepared ahead of time as He instructed me to bring the oil I had just received. It was a powerful time of impartation in the glory of God. The next day, the worship team insisted that the oil be used to anoint the team for worship. I was overtaken as the worship team welcomed the presence of God, and almost immediately, the Glory was felt throughout the room.

This time was different; the manifestation was not a well of oil but of fire. What the Lord softened with oil on the previous day was burned and refined by the fire of the Holy Spirit palpably present in this moment. As the fire burned, people were awakened in their spirits. It was as though shackles had fallen off each person in the room, and a new level of freedom was released. All over the room, visions, revelations, decrees, and declarations were being released into the atmosphere. The kind of declarations that change regions and scatter the demonic presence.

Biblically, the use of anointing oil has deep meanings. Oil is used throughout Scripture to consecrate and dedicate people for the work of the Lord:

> *And you shall put them on Aaron, your brother, and on his sons with him, and shall anoint them and ordain them and consecrate them, that they may serve me as priests* (Exodus 28:41 ESV).

Then Samuel took a flask of oil and poured it on his head and kissed him and said, "Has not the Lord anointed you to be prince over his people Israel? And you shall reign over the people of the Lord, and you will save them from the hand of their surrounding enemies. And this shall be the sign to you that the Lord has anointed you to be prince over his heritage" (1 Samuel 10:1 ESV).

Then Samuel took the horn of oil and anointed him in the midst of his brothers. And the Spirit of the Lord rushed upon David from that day forward... (1 Samuel 16:13 ESV).

Anointing oil is a symbolic representation of the Holy Spirit. Jesus was anointed by God with the Holy Spirit. The word *anointed* in this instance refers to a custom at the time when the anointing was used to appoint, qualify, or to set apart for a special purpose. Jesus was anointed in this manner, as recorded in the book of Acts and also mentioned in the book of Luke:

...God anointed Jesus of Nazareth with the Holy Spirit and with power. He went about doing good and healing all who were oppressed by the devil, for God was with him (Acts 10:38 ESV).

The Spirit of the Lord is upon me because he has anointed me to proclaim good news to the poor... (Luke 4:18 ESV).

Oil is used for healing and restoration; believers are instructed to anoint the sick with oil.

Is anyone among you sick? Let him call for the elders of the church, and let them pray over him, anointing him with oil in the name of the Lord (James 5:14 ESV).

Oil is used for blessings and favor and as a symbol of overflowing and fervent joy.

> *You prepare a table before me in the presence of my enemies; you anoint my head with oil; my cup overflows* (Psalm 23:5 ESV).

> *You are passionate for righteousness, and you hate lawlessness. This is why God, your God, crowns you with bliss above your fellow kings. He has anointed you, more than any other, with his oil of fervent joy, the very fragrance of heaven's gladness* (Psalm 45:7 TPT).

Oil and Meditation

What does oil have to do with biblical meditation and aligning our thoughts spiritually? Each of these previous examples paints a picture of how the Holy Spirit manifests in our meditation. The time we spend in His presence is marked by changes in our expression of joy. An acceptance and symbol of our consecration as priests. A demonstration of our abundance of blessings and favor from God. And our complete healing and restoration in our bodies, hearts, and minds.

The Holy Spirit taught me about the oil and its specific use during meditation. I was sitting on a pillow, preparing to meditate in the presence of the Holy Spirit. Soft instrumental worship music was filling the atmosphere, and I prayed, inviting the tangible presence of the Holy Spirit in the room. As I prayed, the Holy Spirit interrupted me, saying, "Anoint yourself with oil." I thought, *I'm already comfortable and ready to rest in Your glory; do I really need oil?*

The Holy Spirit said again, "Anoint yourself with oil." Realizing suddenly how much I dislike having to tell my children to do something twice, I got up and retrieved a vial of anointing oil. Sitting back down, I thanked the Holy Spirit for His presence and anointed my forehead with the oil. Suddenly, I realized that I was the hands, but He was the One anointing my forehead.

Immediately, my body and my mind were at complete peace, and I felt as though my spirit was instantly elevated to a place and time that are not of this earth but to a place where time did not exist. My spirit was caught up in the presence of the Lord, where He spoke great revelation concerning the practice of biblical meditation, much of which has informed this book. My obedience to the Holy Spirit and submitting to Him as He anointed me with oil opened the portal of Heaven and invited me in, revealing great mysteries of His presence.

I was once skeptical that anointing oil was anything more than a bottle of liquid fat. I never questioned the power of anointing oil as it is represented in Scripture, being used to consecrate priests and anoint the temple. I began to ask the Holy Spirit for fresh revelation concerning my understanding. Since inquiring of the Holy Spirit, I have come through experiences like this story that unquestionably demonstrate the power of anointing oil as directed by the Holy Spirit. The truth and deep wisdom of the use of anointing oil have become evident to me. When used in meditation, anointing oil invites the presence of the Holy Spirit; it is an acknowledgment of our position as priests in the Kingdom, and it opens the atmosphere, allowing the Holy Spirit to minister directly to our minds and hearts.

Are you in need of healing? Anoint yourself with oil, and seek out others to pray over you and anoint you with oil. According to James 5:14 (ESV), *"Is anyone among you sick? Let him call for the elders of the church, and let them pray over him, anointing him with oil in the name of the Lord."*

Has your joy run low? Has it been stolen by the torment of the enemy? Are you in need of freedom from torment? Anoint yourself with oil, meditate with the Holy Spirit, and seek prayer for the casting out of demons according to Mark 6:13 (ESV), *"And they cast out many demons and anointing with oil many who were sick and healed them."*

Do you lack the feeling of acceptance as a child of God and have a hard time seeing yourself as righteous? Anoint yourself with oil and declare the truth of the word of God that you are the righteousness of God according to 1 Corinthians 1:30 (ESV): *"And because of him you are in Christ Jesus, who became to us wisdom from God, righteousness and sanctification and redemption."*

I strongly encourage you to incorporate the use of anointing oil within your biblical meditation, prayer time, intercession, and worship. Anoint your forehead and declare yourself as a consecrated royal priesthood, righteous before the Lord. As you meditate with the fragrance of the oil, invite the Holy Spirit to invade your thoughts and bring healing and relaxation to every corner of your mind.

10

The SENSES *of* MEDITATION

*I pray that the light of God will illuminate the eyes of
your imagination, flooding you with light, until you
experience the full revelation of the hope of his calling—
that is, the wealth of God's glorious inheritances that
he finds in us, his holy ones!* (Ephesians 1:18 TPT)

I was attending a deliverance conference where I planned to speak about forgiveness and inner healing to a group of leaders and deliverance ministers. As usual, the meeting began with enthusiastic praise and worship, setting a positive atmosphere and showing honor to the King of Glory. For me, the worship was not merely an exercise of singing and praising. My mind, emotions, and spirit at once engaged, bringing me to a place where I have transcended into the realm of the Holy Spirit. I am fully aware of the music and mindful of the presence of the Holy Spirit. The Glory is both tangible and palpable.

As I posture myself and sit before the Lord, I can feel His recognizable and unmistakable presence. At this moment, my mind is mentally grabbing hold of the Glory as one would embrace a loved one. Every fiber of my being feels alive with electricity from Heaven as waves of glory wash over me. I am touching Glory, hearing His voice speak to me as the worship creates a covering of sound surrounding me. I am experiencing a spiritual vision as the Holy Spirit guides my thoughts and leads me to the secret place.

Suddenly, a delightful scent fills the air, as if a new bouquet of roses has been placed before me. I am completely surrendered to the Holy Spirit at this moment as He prepares me to speak by guiding my thoughts, words, and ideas intended to be taught to those present. This was a moment of meditation for me before the Lord, which was initiated by the sound of surrendered worship.

The degree to which our spiritual senses are activated is directly proportional to our time spent in the presence of God. The Bible even speaks of the ability we have to taste the words of God, that they are sweet like honey in our mouth. David encourages us in Psalm 34:8 (NIV) to *"Taste and see that the Lord is good...."* And Psalm 119:103 (NIV) tells us, *"How sweet are your words to my taste, sweeter than honey to my mouth!"*

It is late, and I am sleeping in a hotel in Southern California, and I am teaching at a deliverance school the next morning. All of a sudden, I woke up to a dreadful odor that permeated my hotel room and made it hard to breathe. It was so intense that I had to get out of bed and turn the light on to figure out what was happening. The room was filled with a thick cloud of smoke that smelled like a burning dumpster. I decided to investigate the source of the smell.

Walking toward the hotel door, I noticed that the scent did not follow me. I walked to the other side of the room and stood by the window. The smell did not follow me. I must have been dreaming and walked back to my bed. The scent and cloud instantly returned and, this time, completely surrounded me and began to affect my breathing like smoke would when inhaled.

Once again, I walked around the room and noticed that the smell was getting more robust and invasive, filling the room and corrupting the atmosphere. I went into the hallway just to be sure something horrible had not occurred. The coast was clear, with no smell or smoke. Back in my room, I sat on my bed, prepared to pray. Suddenly, I heard the Holy Spirit say, "There is an unclean spirit in the room trying to intimidate and torment you. It is trying to disrupt your sleep and make you ineffective in your teaching." I sat for a moment and meditated with the Holy Spirit, thinking about what I should do to eliminate this unclean spirit. Then, the Holy Spirit reminded me of a story written about Smith Wigglesworth.

On one occasion, Wigglesworth awoke during the night aware of a satanic presence. Looking across the room, he saw the devil himself standing there. Wigglesworth said to satan, "Oh, it's only you." Then he turned over and went back to sleep.[186]

Pondering the words of the Holy Spirit, I was at peace and did not feel the need to battle the demonic entity in my room. My response to the demon was similar. "I don't have time for you, and I am going to bed." I crawled back into bed, and immediately the odor, cloud, and strained atmosphere in the room was gone. I was at perfect peace, and I was also at rest because I meditated before the Lord. Had I followed my carnal inclinations to wage war and cast the demon out of my room, I would have lost my rest and peace, which was the assignment of the demon who visited me. My obedience was achieved by first seeking God's presence through meditation and allowing Him to speak wisdom and guide me through the incident.

5-4-3-2-1

Lift up your eyes to the sky and see for yourself. Who do you think created the cosmos? He lit every shining star and formed every glowing galaxy, and stationed them all where

> *they belong. He has numbered, counted, and given each one*
> *a name. They shine because of God's incredible power and*
> *awesome might; not one fails to appear!* (Isaiah 40:26 TPT)

Anxiety is the most common mental disorder in the United States, affecting almost 30 percent of adults.[187] Anxiety is also one of the manifestations of the stronghold of fear in a person's life. It is commonly acknowledged that the root cause of general anxiety disorder is unknown. Therefore, the treatment options available aim only to alleviate its symptoms. This is to say that the only treatments for symptoms of anxiety disorders are through medications and what is called talk therapy or psychological counseling.[188] Both methods are used in counseling with mixed results.

Anxiety is also known to affect all five of the classic human senses: sight, smell, touch, taste, and sound. Documented studies show that anxiety increases symptoms of verbal hallucinations, which essentially means hearing voices without anyone actually speaking.[189] Increased stress affects taste perception. This means that states of anxiety have a direct impact on the modulation of the sweet and salt tastes, directly impacting the appetite.[190] Additionally, conditions of anxiety affect the way smells are perceived. Research shows that anxiety heightens sensitivity to foul odors, drawing focus to the negative.[191] Adrenaline released during states of anxiety is known to cause blurred vision and contributes to strange and unexplainable skin and touch sensations.

I have written this segment focused on anxiety because of the impact anxiety has on people and their health and well-being. As previously discussed, meditation soothes the effects of anxiety and brings a balance to the mind and body while allowing the Holy Spirit space to directly minister and comfort. One secular treatment method that seems to align with meditation and balancing our senses is the 5 4 3 2 1 method. This technique involves taking deep *Ruach* breaths through the nostrils and proceeding through the following sensory activations.

- Intentionally make a note of *five* things that can be seen.

- Focus on *four* things that can be touched.

- Notice *three* things that can be heard.

- Find *two* things that can be smelled.

- Focus on *one* thing that can be tasted.

Using this technique, especially during moments of high stress or anxiety, will bring the mind to a place of focus and calm, which can lead directly into a moment of meditation with the Holy Spirit or simply a calm, focused mind, which leads to more effective decision-making skills.

The Bible tells us to *"Pour out all your worries and stress upon him and leave them there, for he always tenderly cares for you"* (1 Peter 5:7 TPT). As I have explained, meditation is a space where we can seek guidance from God and release our worries to the Holy Spirit, allowing them to be lifted from our shoulders and freeing us from burdens. David writes, *"In the day that I am afraid, I lay all my fears before you..."* (Psalm 56:3 TPT).

THE BODY IS NOT ONE MEMBER, BUT MANY

I often hear from secular meditation experts and practitioners that sensory distractions must be eliminated for meditations to be genuinely effective. They teach that in mindfulness external stimuli must be eliminated through transcendence and trained states of intense focus, ultimately reaching a state of emptiness. The emptiness is a state of openness of the mind and body, eventually leading to demonic spiritual influence over the body and mind. For believers, the senses and all parts of the body were created to all work together, representing the temple of God.

> *In fact, the human body is not one single part but rather many parts mingled into one. ...Think of it this way. If the whole body were just an eyeball, how could it hear sounds? And if the whole body were just an ear, how could it smell different fragrances? But God has carefully designed each member and placed it in the body to function as he desires. A diversity is required, for if the body consisted of one single part, there wouldn't be a body at all! So now we see that there are many differing parts and functions, but one body* (1 Corinthians 12:14,17-20 TPT).

Emptying the mind is against biblical teachings and can invite demonic attachment and influence. There are no positive outcomes from having an empty mind. Instead, we should let the Holy Spirit guide us in processing our thoughts, bringing order to the chaos by addressing each thought with His help. The Bible does not instruct us to suppress our thoughts or emotions. Instead, it advises us to bring them to God and seek His assistance in constructively dealing with them.

> *Stop imitating the ideals and opinions of the culture around you, but be inwardly transformed by the Holy Spirit through a total reformation of how you think. This will empower you to discern God's will as you live a beautiful life, satisfying and perfect in his eyes* (Romans 12:2 TPT).

FREEDOM

This book has shown that there are no biblical meditation techniques that advocate for emptying oneself or disconnecting from emotions and senses while meditating. I have experienced incredible freedom when surrendering to God and participating with Him by using my senses when in His glory.

I often engage with the Holy Spirit through all of my senses, though not usually all at once. As you diligently devote time each day to meditate, you will experience the Holy Spirit in visions in your mind where you will see Him, be with Him, and interact with Him. You will engage with Him and do things that are pleasing and life-giving. Like the smell of roses I described earlier, you will be introduced to new fragrances, some supernatural and some natural. You will be enveloped in His magnificence, feeling the power of His presence as it permeates the space around you. Expect to hear the voice of God as you go deeper in your meditation time with Him. The words He shares with you are *"like a honeycomb, sweetness to the soul and health to the body"* (Proverbs 16:24 ESV).

FIVE SENSES MEDITATION

Pause for a moment from reading and meditate, intentionally engaging your senses. Pray this prayer:

> Holy Spirit, thank You for Your presence. You are wonderful, and I invite the tangible manifestation of Your glory. Lord, I invite You to interact with every part of my being, all of my senses, all of my mind, and all of my body. I specifically surrender each of my five senses for Your glory;

my smell, my taste, my hearing, my sight, and my touch are Yours. Holy Spirit, would You speak to me through my natural and supernatural senses today?

1. Close your eyes.
2. Take a deep breath through your nose.
3. Hold for 5 seconds, and release.
4. Repeat two more times and allow your body to become fully at rest.
5. Ask the Holy Spirit one or all of the following:

   ○ "Holy Spirit, what would You like to show me today?"

   ○ "What would You like to say to me today?"

   ○ "I invite You to interact with my sense of smell, taste, and touch. Show me Your glory, Lord."

6. Wait silently with your eyes closed for the Holy Spirit to take you on a journey through one or many senses.
7. Remain in His presence as long as you want, thanking the Holy Spirit for His presence and for the guidance He is providing in this secret place.

SECTION THREE

PRACTICAL
GUIDES *for*
MEDITATION

11

APPROACHING MEDITATION

Having now gained a strong understanding of righteous meditation rooted in biblical teachings, I invite you now to start incorporating this practice into your daily routines. Throughout this book, the many facets of biblical meditation have been introduced and taught from a place of purity, uncorrupted by the ideologies and methodologies of secular meditation, from setting the atmosphere with music, prayer, and oil to breathing.

I've discussed welcoming and hosting the Holy Spirit and the natural science behind our thoughts and meditation. I've taught the importance of finding a favorite posture and tuning in with the senses while engaging your supernatural thinking through the gift of tongues.

Biblical meditation truly is a holy moment set aside between you and God. There are no rules other than to love and honor God with your presence. This chapter presents the basic approach to your biblical meditation. This will work, and you will be immensely blessed if, and only if, all religious hindrances and prior experiences of secular meditation are removed.

This principle is summarized by Moses when he said, *"The Lord will fight for you, and you have only to be silent"* (Exodus 14:14 ESV). And again, in the verse that defines our meditation, David writes, *"Surrender your anxiety. Be still and realize that I am God. I am God above all the nations, and I am exalted throughout the whole earth"* (Psalm 46:10 TPT).

PURIFY YOURSELF

None of what has been taught in this book or its methods has been informed by or received any guidance from secular meditation techniques. This is an important distinction as the pure form of biblical meditation is explored without any corruption or deceit. Suppose during the reading of this book, you realize that your prior participation in other religious forms of meditation may cloud your experiences or hinder you in some way. In that case, I invite you to pray the cleansing prayer of release from yoga and unrighteous meditation found in the back of this book now and come in alignment with the power of a supernatural thought life and Kingdom meditation.

Having prayed the prayer of release from yoga and unrighteous meditation, you are now delivered from the religious entanglement and are welcome to meditate with the Holy Spirit, free from all distracting and accusing voices and thoughts of the enemy.

GETTING READY

I have come to learn over many years of practice that biblical meditation can occur anywhere and at about any time when you have a moment to pause. I have also become convinced that setting aside a place that is solely purposed for meditation and prayer is vital, if it can be accomplished. I have a space in the corner of my home office reserved for prayer and meditation. I usually sit on a large floor pillow or lie on my back with my head on the pillow. The environment should be as relaxing and free from outside distractions as possible. Experiment with your comfort. Sitting on a large floor pillow might be best. Perhaps a deep, comfortable chair is suitable where you can sink deeply into the moment. Maybe a meditation bench designed for both kneeling and sitting comfortably works for you. Simply lying back with your head on a pillow may be precisely what is needed. While less common, standing and walking around as you meditate may be the most comfortable.

The point is to experiment and experience all of the different options as you build your favorite meditation technique. You may find it helpful to your meditation to start with soft worship music in the background. Avoid loud music. You don't want to overpower the relaxing peace of the moment. As meditation becomes part of your daily lifestyle, you will discover that your preference for silence versus music will ebb and flow. Sometimes, sitting in silence with the Holy Spirit is more restorative. At other times, the anointing of the soft worship music sets the perfect atmosphere. Be free to experiment and learn what comes naturally.

BEGIN

The environment is set, and the space is prepared; it is time to begin. Gently close your eyes and open them with a simple prayer. Note that the opening prayer is vital to hosting the Holy Spirit and entering into the secret place. The prayer also creates a protective blood covering, shielding the mind from all demonic attempts to influence this holy time in the Lord's presence.

Holy Spirit, thank You for Your presence; You are welcome here to have Your way in my mind, emotions, heart, and the entirety of my being. Thank You for Your protective covering over my thoughts. Holy Spirit, I ask for and welcome the tangible manifest glory of God both in the natural and supernatural. I choose to be present in this moment with You. Teach me and guide me into all truth and understanding. Holy Spirit, I ask for the release of supernatural thoughts, total peace, and rest. Wash over me now with Your waves of glory and love as I turn my attention toward Your abiding peace and rest.

Close your eyes and begin to breathe the *Ruach* breath of life deeply, four seconds in through the nostrils, filling up the belly, holding for two seconds, and releasing for four seconds. Repeat four to five times or for as long as three minutes.

ENTER IN AND GO DEEP

Keeping your eyes closed allows your thoughts to ebb and flow without hindrance. Do not try to push away thoughts or external sounds. Follow the Holy Spirit through your thoughts without feeling the pressure to take any action or do anything in this moment. Allow your mind to take the journey, and your imagination will fill in the blanks. You might find yourself engaging in a fun activity with the Holy Spirit or walking and talking with Him on a cool afternoon as you visualize the moment within your mind. Try asking the Holy Spirit, "What do You want to tell me or show me at this moment?" Be prepared to hear His voice immediately.

Tune your mind and your senses, intentionally asking, *What am I focused on now? Am I thinking about anything? What are the ambient sounds around me? Are they joyful, neutral, or chaotic? What are the smells around me, and how do they make me feel? Comfortable, peaceful, uneasy? What taste, if any, am I experiencing?*

Now, tune in to your spiritual senses. What are you hearing, seeing, feeling, smelling, and touching as you participate in your mind?

None of the conclusions you reach are wrong. They represent the areas in your mind where the Holy Spirit is ministering new comfort, and your mind is establishing new healthy neural pathways, allowing you to manifest outwardly the benefits of your time spent in meditation.

OPTIONS?

Distractions account for 47 percent of our waking hours. Harvard researchers conclude that a wandering, distracted mind is an unhappy one.[192] That's terrible and underpins our need for regular meditation. But you should also be aware that the basic formula for meditation I have provided is only a jumping-off point. If you are an avid lover of the outdoors, try hiking and intentionally enter into meditation as you consciously connect with creation. Breathing deeply in the nostrils, listen carefully to the sounds of wind in the trees, babbling creek, or chirping birds. Smell the crisp mountain air, and observe the wonder of creation surrounding you. Perhaps take your shoes off and allow your bare feet to connect with God's beauty. Feel the softness of the grass, dirt, or water beneath your feet.

Note: I am not referring to spiritual grounding as it is often taught in some forms of yoga. The Bible references on more than one occasion that the act of taking off shoes consecrates holy ground. Walking around your home, outdoors, etc., is an excellent opportunity to exercise the principle of taking the territory for the Kingdom. Are you a musician? You might choose to meditate with your instrument and connect with the musical nature of the Spirit. Whatever your preference, diligent devotion to your biblical meditation will inspire changes in your mind and in your life inspired by the Holy Spirit.

Stay as long as you like in the place of biblical meditation. There are no limitations and time restrictions unless you set them yourself. Don't force the time to be longer than necessary. When you feel a release in your spirit, gently open your eyes and return to the tasks of the day.

STICK WITH IT, MAINTAIN IT, AND RECEIVE YOUR HEALING

So you have practiced biblical meditation, now what? You are off to a great start. As you deepen your relationship with the Holy Spirit, your encounters will become even more powerful and purposeful. In the beginning, you are still working through the questions: *Am I doing it right? What if I can't relax? What if I have a negative thought? I feel ridiculous. Or, I have had great and wonderful experiences already, but how do I keep it up?* These questions are all coming from a place of insecurity. I taught earlier that the changes to your thought life are meant to be as simple as building new habits. I taught that the most important thing is maintaining a connection with the Holy Spirit. Everything else comes from that relationship.

But if you are like me, you might like lists and processes that make it easier to follow your progress. The following list is a guide our ministry has developed and used for many years to help maintain the incredible progress realized through biblical meditation and a supernaturally charged thought life. These are not linear and are not meant to be a strict guide but more of a model for ongoing maintenance. These same steps are used for walking out healing as well. This was my process as I walked out of my healing from diabetes.

- *Engage in daily biblical meditation, including visualization and imagination, taught in this book.* Meditation is not about treating symptoms but allowing God to uncover the root source of an issue. Once the root source is identified, healing can begin.

- *Develop a lifestyle of true and right forgiveness.* Go beyond the words and begin truly walking in forgiveness. Our model of forgiveness is recorded in our book, *The Science of Deliverance.*

- *Seek out deliverance and inner healing.* Close any open doors you might have that would allow the enemy to invade your thoughts.

- *Foster an environment to renew the mind and bring healing.* This is accomplished by following the wisdom of Romans 12:2 and Philippians 4:8.

- *Exercise regularly* as physical activity has been shown to have many positive effects on our thought life. According to Harvard Medical School, "The parts of the brain that control thinking and memory are larger in volume in people who exercise than in people who don't. Even more exciting is the finding that engaging in a program of regular exercise of moderate intensity over six months or a year is associated with an increase in the volume of selected brain regions."[193]

- *Pray regularly and seek God for revelation, wisdom, and understanding.*

- *Ensure a proper diet and nutrition.*

- *Live a lifestyle of blessing.* Bless others, and bless yourself (see Proverbs 22:9 and Romans 12:4).

- *Surround yourself with a community of healthy life-giving relationships.* These will nurture you and provide an outlet for you to nourish others (see Hebrews 10:24-25).

SUMMARY OF ESSENTIALS AND BREATHING TECHNIQUES

The following is a basic summary outline of the biblical meditation process for quick reference:

(Refer to the next chapter for specific meditations for different purposes.)

- Find a quiet space and get comfortable. Establish your posture before the Lord.
- Play soft, ambient worship music, or choose silence.
- Open with prayer, inviting the manifest presence of the Holy Spirit into the room and to your thoughts.
- Close your eyes.
- Breathe deeply, repeating the following for 3 minutes or less.

  ◦ In through the nostrils slowly for 4 seconds.
  ◦ Hold for 2 seconds.
  ◦ Release slowly for 4 seconds.

- Allow thoughts to come and go in your mind, taking no action on any of them now.
- Ask the Holy Spirit:

  ◦ What do You want to tell me now?
  ◦ What do You want to show me in this moment?

- Wait and follow Him; you will hear His voice.
- Tune in to your senses, both spiritual and natural.

    °   What do you feel, smell, touch, or see in the spirit?

Experiment with this bulleted pattern beginning with the fifth bullet and the following alternate options: Note that the numbers indicate a pattern for counting while inhaling and exhaling. For example, the pattern 4,6 means to inhale for four counts and exhale for six counts. Similarly, 4,6,8 indicates inhaling for four counts, holding breath for six counts, and exhaling for eight counts. 4,4,6,3 follows the pattern of inhaling for four counts, holding breath for four counts, exhaling for six counts, and holding breath for three counts.

- Calming (4,6) – Inhale for 4 seconds, exhale for 6 seconds. Repeat for one to three minutes.

- Relieve Stress (8,8) – Inhale for 8 seconds, exhale for 8 seconds. Repeat for one to three minutes.

- Energize yourself (1,1) – Inhale for 1 second, exhale for 1 second. Repeat 20 times.

- Fall Asleep (4,16,8) – Inhale for 4 seconds, hold for 16 seconds, exhale for 8 seconds. Repeat for one to three minutes.

- Lower heart rate and relieve stress (4,4,6,3) – Inhale for 4 seconds, hold for 4 seconds, exhale for 6 seconds, and hold for 3 seconds. Repeat for one to three minutes.

- Reduce blood pressure (4,7,8) – Partially close both nostrils, inhale for 4 seconds, hold for 7 seconds, and exhale for 8 seconds. Repeat up to 30 times.

12

MEDITATION TECHNIQUES
and SUPERNATURAL
THINKING

Throughout this journey, I have prepared you and provided the necessary tools and understanding to experience the freedom of biblical meditation. Your mind is about to undergo a remarkable metamorphosis that will lead you to think beyond the natural and embrace supernatural thinking. It's time to step forward and welcome a mental, physical, and spiritual revival that will initiate an incredible relationship with Jesus. Equip yourself to move ahead and experience this essential transformation.

The meditations on the following pages are only the starting point as you journey with the Holy Spirit through your thoughts while He ministers healing and incredible power in your life. And they are also for those who have already developed a beautiful relationship with the Holy Spirit. These techniques will breathe new life into your abiding time with Him, adding substance as you explore your senses. Depth, as you discover the compassionate power of God's heart. Width, as you journey through your thoughts and imagination with the Holy Spirit. And height as you soar with God, experiencing the explosive power of His magnificence.

It's important to keep in mind that supernatural thinking does not require a completely clear mind, a perfectly tidy home, or absolute silence. Those are all nice to have, and do at times enhance the experience. God has the ability and desire to be present with you during any chaotic or cluttered moment. He can help you settle your emotions, calm your nerves, and provide His love directly to your spirit. No formula is required, and the techniques on the following pages should not become rote religious exercises.

Instead, use them to get to know the process. Then, from your heart, you will begin to meditate naturally in any moment, emotion, or state of mind when it is needed. You will find your flow, and the Holy Spirit will meet you in the way He knows you best. Expect each moment of your meditation to bring vitality to your spirit, soul, and body. God is honored when we devote time for Him and ourselves as we care for the temple He created and purposed for greatness.

MENO IN DAMAM—A QUIET, ABIDING MOMENT WITH THE HOLY SPIRIT

I am standing in absolute stillness, silent before the one I love, waiting as long as it takes for him to rescue me. Only God is my Savior, and he will not fail me (Psalm 62:5 TPT).

Biblical grounding:

Based on Psalms 62:5, 37:7, and John 15:5-8. Pronounced as written, *damam* means stillness, while *meno* means to abide and be present. This meditation encourages *meno* to abide from a posture of *damam* stillness.

Purpose:

An abiding encounter with the Holy Spirit in the quiet and stillness as you experience His glory.

Environment:

This meditation is best suited for a restful moment of silence.

Posture:

Position yourself comfortably in a manner best suited to relax your body and mind. Sitting on a pillow on the floor or lying down on your back may be most comfortable. Feel free to transition from one posture to another as the Holy Spirit's presence increases.

Open with prayer:

> Holy Spirit, thank You for Your presence and glory. I invite You to join me, and I ask for a tangible manifestation of Your glory as I meditate with You now. Thank You, Holy Spirit, for the blood of Jesus that covers me and my thoughts. I bind and cancel all attempts of the enemy to distract me. I submit my mind and body to You, and I declare this time is set apart and holy before You.

Breathe:

Close your eyes and breathe deeply of the *Ruach* breath of God.

- Inhale through your nose for 4 seconds.

- Hold for 2 seconds.

- Slowly exhale through your mouth for 6 seconds.

- Repeat 6 times.

- Return to normal breathing.

- Avoid the urge to push nagging thoughts away or silence the noises in the room. Just let your mind process and jump from one thought to another.

Meditate:

As you breathe, focus your thoughts on the Holy Spirit and His presence.

- Now, ask the Holy Spirit: What do You want to tell me? Have a short conversation with the Holy Spirit and go to whatever thought(s) He takes you. Allow your body and mind to experience peace. Feel and notice your mind and body relax.

- Can you feel His presence? There is no rush; stay as long as you want and soak in the glory.

- Think about His goodness.

- Think about the ways He has blessed you.

- Stay with the Holy Spirit for several minutes; there are no time limits other than those you set yourself.

- Take a moment to notice what your current state feels like consciously.

- How does your head feel?

- How does your body feel?

- How about your mind?
- Did you notice anything different about the atmosphere in the room?
- Did you notice an increase in peace and calm within your mind?

Perhaps you are feeling uncomfortable and strange. These feelings and questions are perfectly normal and exactly how our minds and bodies are designed to process this experience. The more time you devote to hosting the presence of the Holy Spirit, the greater you will experience His glory.

OPEN-THOUGHT MEDITATION

Biblical grounding:

Based on Psalm 46:10, this meditation encourages an atmosphere of quiet rest within the glory of God.

Purpose:

A calming meditation releases anxiety and tension, increases blood oxygen, and reduces blood pressure and heart rate. A moment of rest in which your mind is allowed to process thoughts and ideas freely.

Environment:

This meditation will work in any environment. From a busy office to a calm break in the day. Try to practice this during a lunch break or when a mental break is needed.

Posture:

Position yourself comfortably, perhaps with a nice chair, pillow on the floor, or lying down.

Open with prayer:

> Holy Spirit, thank You for Your presence; I invite You to join me in my thoughts. Bring peace and rest to my mind as I give You complete control of my thoughts. Take me where You want to go.

Breathe:

Close your eyes and breathe deeply of the *Ruach* breath of God.

- Inhale through your nose for 4 seconds.
- Hold for 2 seconds.
- Slowly exhale through your mouth for 6 seconds.
- Repeat 6 times.
- Return to normal breathing.

Meditate:

Mentally take note of the sounds, smells, and senses in your environment. This will help you become present with the Holy Spirit at this moment.

- Remain at peace and allow your mind to wander. Remember, you gave the Holy Spirit permission to take you where He needs you to go.

- Allow your thoughts to come and go unhindered, and be open to the Holy Spirit if He pauses on any idea.

- Avoid any verbal speaking. Allow the Holy Spirit to guide your thoughts.

- Remember, meditation is not prayer—it is a mindful focus of thoughts and listening. Focus your thoughts on whatever is pure, right, excellent, pleasant, lovely, admirable, and noble.

- Wait in the stillness; the Holy Spirit will speak to your heart and mind.

- Continue breathing regularly and remain at peace as long as you desire.

- After a comfortable time of peaceful rest, ask the Holy Spirit: What do You want to say to me or show me?

- Remain peaceful and listen to the Holy Spirit if He speaks.

- If the Holy Spirit is silent, it's okay. That means you need to rest and be at peace in His presence.

- Open your eyes when you feel the meditation has been completed. Usually 10-15 minutes initially, gradually increasing your time as desired. Caution: This meditation can put you to sleep if not prepared.

DAVIDIC MEDITATION – BASED ON DAVID'S MEDITATIONS IN THE PSALMS

Biblical grounding:

Based on Psalms 104:34, 39:1-13, and 40:1-3.

Purpose:

This recharging meditation provides a safe place for the passionate expression of emotions and thoughts. You are rightly aligning your mind to the attributes of God. Ultimately, you are waiting on the Lord to lift you and restore joy as you honor Him. This meditation stimulates the vagus nerve and recharges the mind and body through increased CO_2.

Environment:

This meditation is best practiced in the privacy of your prayer room.

Posture:

Begin this meditation while sitting upright or kneeling on a pillow— transition to lying down as the Holy Spirit begins ministering to your spirit.

Open with prayer:

Holy Spirit, thank You for Your presence...

The Davidic model of meditation allows for freedom of emotions, thoughts, and expressions while focusing on the things listed above for alignment in thinking, restoration, and healing of the mind.

Connect with your deep emotions. Are you experiencing joy? Perhaps you are in anguish or neutral in emotion. Regardless, this is when you will receive a touch from God.

Breathe:

Begin with the *Ruach* breath of God designed to recharge your mind, body, and spirit.

- Sit up straight to open the diaphragm.
- Inhale for 4 seconds through the nose.
- Hold your breath for 4 seconds.
- Exhale the breath for 4 more seconds.
- Hold for 4 seconds.
- Repeat 5 times.
- Return to natural breathing.

Meditate and draw your attention to one or two of the following questions. As you ponder these, wait as the Holy Spirit quickens your spirit with the answers:

- What has He done for you?
- What has He asked of you?
- What are His promises to you, both fulfilled and unfulfilled?
- What has He accomplished that seemed impossible?
- What has God decreed over you?

- What is He asking you to do?
- How have you benefited from His goodness?
- What are His defining qualities that minister to you?

Consciously direct your thoughts to the nature of God. Choose something to focus on that falls within David's meditations, which he wrote in the Psalms. Be creative with these.

- God's attributes – Psalm 103:8
- God's word and statutes – Psalm 119:15,78,99, Psalm 1:2
- God's mighty deeds and wonders – Psalm 119:27, Psalm 145:5
- Personal experiences and emotions – Psalm 39
- Sin and forgiveness – Psalm 51:1-7
- God's presence and refuge – Psalm 16:1,11
- God's promises – Psalm 119:148
- God's decrees – Psalm 119:23
- God's ways – Psalm 119:15

As you ponder this thought, allow God's thoughts to penetrate your heart as He speaks to your spirit:

- Wait in silence for a minute.
- Release your voice audibly or in thought to the Lord as the passion stirs and burns within you.
- Wait and rest in silence, taking whatever posture you desire before the Lord.
- There is no rush; when ready, open your eyes and thank the Lord for His goodness.

VISUALIZATION MEDITATION

Biblical grounding:

Based on Psalm 34:8; Ephesians 3:20; Colossians 3:2; 2 Corinthians 10:5.

Purpose:

An energizing meditation designed to give life to the imaginations of your mind while partnering with the Holy Spirit to breathe new life into them. This is an excellent meditation for waking up in the morning or re-energizing for a long afternoon.

Environment:

Since this is an energizing meditation, it can be done anywhere comfortable and distraction-free.

Posture:

Sitting or lying on your back are excellent postures for this meditation.

Open with prayer:

> Holy Spirit, You are welcome here; I present myself to You for meditation. I instruct my mind and thoughts to focus on You. I speak protection over my mind and declare that my mind, will, and emotions are open to the guidance of the Holy Spirit. I cancel every assignment of the enemy

over my mind, will, and emotions. I bind every demonic entity in this room from interacting with me and tell you to go from this place. Thank You, Jesus, for Your protection, and I give myself entirely to You. Have Your way.

Breathe:

- Close your eyes and take two deep breaths quickly through your nose.
- Next, inhale and exhale quickly through your nose. One second in and one second out.
- Repeat 10-20 more times.
- Resume normal breath.
- Meditate and begin to visualize.
- Using your imagination, select from the following and begin to picture it.

  ○ Healing in an area where you might need a breakthrough.

  ○ Success in an upcoming assignment.

  ○ Worshipping the Lord in His throne room.

  ○ Are you fatigued? Visualize yourself full of life and energy.

  ○ Visualize enough energy to play with your children after work.

  ○ Visualize mental strength to accomplish a challenging task late at night because the day is filled.

You are the director of your visualization; when you engage your mind to create an atmosphere of success internally, your physical brain will adapt and follow suit.

Partner with the Holy Spirit; He will guide your imagination and show you what you are capable of. Just let the imagery play out in your mind. No need to rush; your brain is learning. Remain here for as long as you need. When you have concluded your meditation, open your eyes, thanking the Holy Spirit for His presence and guidance.

MEDITATION FOR CHILDREN

Biblical grounding:

Based on Psalms 131:2, 46:10; Acts 2:17; and Matthew 19:14.

Purpose:

To invite the calming presence of the Holy Spirit to a child and teach them to abide with Jesus.

Environment:

Encourage your child to find and hold their favorite stuffed animal. Dim the lights and speak softly.

Posture:

It is best to sit comfortably, or if at bedtime, lie down on their bed.

Open with prayer:

Have them repeat after you, "Holy Spirit, thank You for Your presence. I love You, and You are welcome in my room. I ask for peace and comfort in my mind and my dreams. I welcome You to speak to me and show me what You want me to see.

Breathe

- Begin breathing; ask them to inhale through their nose as deeply as possible into their belly.
- Ask them to exhale very slowly through their open mouth (like blowing out through a straw.)
- Repeat three times.

Meditate

- With eyes closed, instruct them to imagine doing their favorite activity.
- Then have them ask the Holy Spirit, "Holy Spirit, please join me in my imagination."
- They may play together for a moment; there is no need to rush this moment.
- After a moment, have them ask the Holy Spirit, "Holy Spirit, what do You want to tell me?"
- In most cases, the Holy Spirit will speak to their spirit.
- When the meditation concludes, they may want to tell you what they saw or heard. Share in their joy and excitement of what they experienced with the Holy Spirit.

SUPERNATURAL-THINKING MEDITATION

Take a moment to think supernaturally.

Biblical grounding:

This meditation is based on Proverbs 4:20-23.

Purpose:

To train the mind in supernatural thinking by intentionally focusing on God and His words. As His words penetrate your heart, new life flows from you. Repetition is the key to this meditation. As your thought life develops a habit of right thinking, the outflow of your life becomes a reflection of your heart and mind.

Environment:

This meditation is best performed in a calming space, allowing your mind to ponder. Play a soft worship song, perhaps instrumental (optional).

Posture:

Begin by bending. Stretching out, extending yourself, and spreading out as your posture before the Lord. (Alternatively, remaining seated or lying down is acceptable.) Having a Bible nearby for reference may be helpful.

Open with prayer:

Thank the Holy Spirit for joining you, and ask for a tangible manifestation of His glory to fill the room.

Breathe:

- Close your eyes, take a slow, deep breath through your nose, and hold it for 5 seconds.
- Exhale slowly through your mouth, speaking in tongues on the exhale.**
- Repeat five times.
- Return to normal breathing, remain silent, soaking in the presence of the Holy Spirit for 2-10 minutes.
- Open your eyes slowly when you are ready.

Meditate:

- Open the Bible to Proverbs 3:13, read the words, and set it aside.*
- In silent reflection, focus on the following words from this Scripture and contemplate them in your mind.
- *"Blessed is the one who finds wisdom, and the one who gets understanding"* (Proverbs 3:13 ESV)
- Close your eyes once again and breathe deeply.
- Say, "Holy Spirit, I'm listening; what are You saying to me in this verse?"

- Continue in this intimate moment with the Holy Spirit as He counsels you; remain as long as you need.

- These are words of instruction promising life and healing for your body.

- Stay in the quiet moment of abiding for several minutes.

- Having done this, you are being prepared for the outward expression of God's glory in your life resulting from your meditation.

*Later, choose any Scripture or prophetic word you wish to contemplate.

**Alternatively, if you do not yet have the gift of tongues, you can utter any phrase of thankfulness. Example: "Thank You, Holy Spirit, for Your presence." Or make a declaration over your life such as, "I am blessed and highly favored." Or simply, "Yahweh."

BREATHE TO LOWER BLOOD PRESSURE

Maintaining optimal blood pressure levels can be achieved through effective breathing techniques, which have been proven to be as beneficial as medications. One such technique is IMST Breathing—a clinically researched method that is highly recommended for its therapeutic benefits.[194]

Pray and Declare Healing from Scripture:

Psalm 103:2-3 (TPT): *"Yahweh, you are my soul's celebration. How could I ever forget the miracles of kindness you've done for me? You kissed my heart with forgiveness, in spite of all I've done. You've healed me inside and out from every disease."*

Declare:

I speak to my cardiovascular system and declare the promises of God are true. I receive healing for my blood pressure and command my body to be restored in the name of Jesus.

Breathe:

- This technique uses the 4-7-8 model.
- Begin by holding both nostrils partially closed. Inhaling should be difficult.
- With the mouth closed, inhale deeply for 4 seconds.
- Hold your breath for 7 seconds.
- Exhale from the mouth slowly for 8 seconds.
- Repeat this pattern up to 30 times per sitting to reduce blood pressure immediately and to maintain healthy blood pressure.

MEDITATION *in* DELIVERANCE *AND* INNER HEALING

"Everything we do must come from His presence,
His spirit, His anointing fire, and His glory!"

—Becca Greenwood[195]

I still hear it frequently, "What does meditation have to do with the ministry of deliverance?" I'll admit that when the Lord began guiding me to start asking Him how to incorporate the techniques in this book in deliverance, I was skeptical. In my early days of researching and practicing meditation, I was struck by how easily and quickly I was able to host the glory of the Lord in my times of abiding.

Over the years, it was not uncommon for me to close my eyes, invite and experience His presence wherever I am. I've brought His glory to the gym as I exercised, and I've sat in His glory as I relaxed in the eucalyptus steam room. I have brought His glory to the office as I sat at my desk, closing my eyes, breathing, and resting in His presence for a moment. But I still wondered, *How do I incorporate meditation meant to host the presence of God into a deliverance, inner healing, and counseling session?* I said to the Lord, "I need You to teach me how You want me to do this in a way that brings glory to You, brings healing, and sets the captives free."

REVEALED!

> *"The first thing we notice about the glory realm is the ease*
> *it brings. The glory brings an ease in every dimension*
> *of ministry. The glory brings an ease, for instance, in*
> *the Ministry of Healing. We may have prayed for the*
> *sick in one dimension, but when we move into the glory*
> *realm, healing just happens. There is no struggle."*
>
> —Ruth Ward Heflin[196]

One of the most profound lessons I have learned is to let God be God, and when we do, everything works out according to His plan. The same holds true for the deliverance ministry. The more we struggle and fight, the tighter the enemy holds, and the harder it becomes to bring freedom and cast out demons.

But when we step back as a deliverance minister and welcome the presence of God to lead, that becomes the "suddenly" when the breakthrough occurs. Once the glory of God enters the room, the ease by which ministry occurs can leave us feeling as though we are not doing enough or working hard enough. We believe we must possess all the answers, speak wise words, and perform the right spiritual actions. After all, we have the experience, right?

However, these things have limited spiritual significance and are more relevant to satisfying the needs of the soul rather than truly becoming transformative and bearing spiritual fruit. Conversely, the breakthrough happens when we host the Glory and allow the Holy Spirit to provide direction through prophecy, visions, and actions.

During my early years in ministry, seeing clients for deliverance was a powerful time of ministry. But it could have been much more. We would set up the room, usually five chairs, in a semi-circle around the ministry recipient. We'd open the ministry time with prayer, binding any spirits and commanding them to leave. Then we would move into the deliverance ministry, tearing down strongmen and casting out demons. It was a wonderful time of freedom and victory in many areas for so many people.

Looking back with fondness, I recall having a process and a method to navigate the ministry of deliverance and inner healing. One, pray, two forgive, three repent and renounce, four cast it out. I would often encounter a demon that was more difficult and rebellious. During these times, we would follow the process, and eventually, we would see victory. But therein lies the problem that God was urging me to solve. The Holy Spirit said to me, "You are working at it too hard. Let Me show you."

I remember when it happened, I was leading a not particularly difficult deliverance session. It was going well for the most part. Until we got to the issue of unforgiveness. I began to counsel this person through the process of true repentant, heartfelt forgiveness when we hit a block. He was unable to remember anyone or anything that required forgiveness. Even traumatic issues in his life were distant, and he was unable to think. Believing that we were likely dealing with a mind-binding or deaf and dumb spirit, I immediately began to call the demons up and bind them from interfering. Nothing changed.

Then, I remembered my assignment from the Lord to bring the presence of God into the room through biblical meditation. I paused the session, and as I listened to the Holy Spirit, I felt Him guide me to have the client close his eyes, lead him through meditation, and breathe the *Ruach* breath of God.

"Close your eyes," I said, and "repeat after me. Thank You, Holy Spirit, for Your presence here. You are welcome here. I ask You to manifest Your tangible presence in this place for wisdom, healing, and revelation." Immediately, the atmosphere of the room shifted. The glory of God's presence fell so strongly that we looked at each other in acknowledgment and confirmation. I then instructed him to take a deep *Ruach* breath of air in his nostrils and release it through his mouth. We did that four more times while in the presence of the Holy Spirit. We were caught in a glory moment from which none of us wanted to leave.

But the Holy Spirit was in a teaching mood that day. He told me to ask him to bring to his mind the people he needs to forgive at this moment for his freedom today. Side note: Often the list of people we need to forgive can be overwhelming, and working through forgiveness for each of them can take a significant amount of time. The Holy Spirit has proven gentle in this area.

Asking the Holy Spirit to reveal only the people standing in the way of today's healing feels almost like taking a shortcut. But that's how the Holy Spirit operates. All powerful, without the pain. No sooner did the person say the words than vivid faces and names began appearing to him. It was all I could do to keep up with my pen as he spoke the names of people. Over the next hour, not only did the Holy Spirit teach us how to achieve a breakthrough in an area, but He also taught us how to incorporate biblical meditation in the ministry of deliverance and inner healing.

Our ministry has steadfastly acknowledged the guidance of the Holy Spirit during every session of deliverance, inner healing, and counseling, and this commitment remains absolute. I honor Him for the guidance that has led to great physical healing, forgiveness, and healing from trauma in the lives of His people. He is present and invited in all areas of our ministry. We will not conduct ministry without first hosting the glory of God by charging the atmosphere with His tangible presence.

DELIVERANCE BY WAY OF THE HOLY SPIRIT

*"The Holy Spirit is a healing spirit. When the
Holy Spirit is present, anything is possible."*

—Reinhard Bonnke

I led a team of deliverance ministers on an assignment in Georgia several years ago. The assignment was to train an advanced deliverance school by equipping leaders across the state to begin building deliverance teams in their churches and areas. The school was outstanding, and many people received great freedom. Typically, we would offer a question-and-answer session following each ministry session or lesson. The number-one question we would get asked is, "How do we know what demon, curse, or infirmity we are dealing with if the client does not know?" This question came as the students watched my team flow in ministry and prophetically address demons and infirmities that the client was unaware of, which resonated deeply within their spirits. Our answer was always the same. "You must first rest in the Holy Spirit and always listen to His direction. Anything else is the result of the flesh."

*"It is important to discern the difference between acts of
the understanding and those of the will. Understanding
with the mind is of little value. The intent of the heart
is all important. We should concern ourselves only
with loving and delighting ourselves in God."*

—Brother Lawrence[197]

Proverbs 4:7 tells us to get wisdom, but at all costs, get understanding. There is great wisdom in praying for people and seeing captives set free. There is great wisdom in forgiveness, inner healing, and breaking generational curses. But all of those practiced without the understanding granted only by the tangible presence of the Holy Spirit are simply good sounding words.

Hosting the glory of His presence establishes the atmosphere for His divine wisdom and understanding. As the Scripture says, there is a cost in gaining understanding. What is the price we pay? The immeasurable time in His presence opens doors, breaks barriers, drives out demons, breaks curses, and sets the captives free.

Have you ever said, "I struggle to find even fifteen minutes for prayer daily"? Or perhaps, "I find it hard to pray for as long as I should." These are not excuses; they are shining a spotlight on the one deficiency you have in your relationship with Jesus. Try to recall an event where you sat at a table with strangers. You try to have a conversation but realize that because you don't really know these people, relatability is challenging outside of time spent together. So, generally, small talk wins the moment and saves everyone from the uncomfortable, socially unacceptable awkwardness of public silence.

Now recall an event where you were with a group of your peers or friends. You've known these people for a long time and have experienced many good times together. The conversation flows naturally from a place of knowing. Each of you understands the other, and the conversation comes easy because the breadbasket of friendship has been filled. The presence of God operates on this same principle. Those who have not first rested in His presence are the ones who uncomfortably sit in their prayer time with nothing but small talk to get them by.

This entire book is based upon Psalm 46:10, *"Be still, and know that I am God."* Those who have rested in the presence of God have developed the mind of Christ and have, over time, come to truly know the Holy Spirit's presence, personality, nuances, and even His humor. Perhaps the reason why praying poses a challenge to some individuals is due to the insufficient fostering of their relationship with the Holy Spirit.

If this resonates with you in any way, I urge you to be silent and still. The Lord will speak from that stillness, enabling you to develop a profound relationship with your King. Explore a fresh approach to connecting with God that allows you to let go of the pressure to pray for an extended period. Remove that clock, and give Him your silence. Soon, you will find your relationship blooming with depth and understanding. From that understanding comes the most incredible wisdom direct from the throne room of Heaven.

I was attending a conference of the International Freedom Group in Colorado alongside many prominent deliverance ministers. Pasqual Urrabazo always ministers powerfully and under the great anointing of the Holy Spirit. As is typical during deliverance conferences, space is given for God to move and for deliverance to break out in the meeting. As ministry began to occur among the people, Pasquale could be heard saying, "Take a deep breath, and release it. One of the ways demons come out is by the breath." As soon as the person he spoke to obeyed, the demon released its grip, and the person was free. While this example is not directly related to meditation per se, this demonstration highlights the principle addressed earlier in this book that in partnership with the Holy Spirit, the *Ruach* breath of God brings healing.

I CAN'T HEAR GOD'S VOICE

That was where we were stuck. I will refer to this person as Sally. As we were ministering deliverance over her, it was revealed that she was dealing with a spiritual blockage. She said, "I can't hear God's voice anymore." Having lived her life for the last several years in the quiet, she has been unable to truly connect with the voice of God. It had been devastating for her. Sally is a believer and knows the voice of her Father, but through unhealed trauma and involvement in unrepentant sin, she became unable to hear His voice clearly.

Though other spiritual concerns brought her in to see me, it was clear that the Holy Spirit wanted to restore this relationship. As we began to pray and minister, I told Sally, "Before this session is over, you will hear the voice of the Lord." I am so confident that my declaration is not coming from a place of hopefulness; I genuinely believe that she will hear again in the following moments of ministry. Following the guidance of the Holy Spirit, we walked through forgiveness, repentance, renunciation, and breaking strongholds in her life. Sally received great freedom, and we were watching a transformation of spirit, soul, and body right in front of us. But that was only the groundwork for what the Lord ultimately wanted to accomplish in Sally's life.

Next, I began to guide her through a basic biblical meditation right there in the session. The Holy Spirit's presence fell tangibly, and the glory filled the room. I then guided Sally through a peaceful breathing exercise, in through her nostrils for four seconds, then releasing slowly, welcoming the *Ruach* breath of God in her life and inviting peace into her spirit.

"With your eyes closed and feeling peaceful, I want you to ask the Holy Spirit to speak to you and to tell you what He wants you to know. Say, Holy Spirit, I'm listening; what do You want to say to me now?" After a brief pause, Sally's countenance shifted. Her eyes were still closed, but she was filled with joy and peace that radiated from her face.

After a brief moment, I asked, "What did He say to you?"

Smiling, Sally said, "He said I am His beloved; He has missed our times together, and He has never, nor will He ever leave me." Sally received the greatest gift that day—she received her freedom from demonic torment; but what made this experience even more significant was that it brought her closer to her Creator and Father through a restored relationship. Sally now has the freedom and understanding to nurture her rekindled relationship with the Holy Spirit.

Sally's story does not represent a singular event. I am so confident that the Holy Spirit will speak that I set an expectation with every client that they will experience the voice of the Lord during each session. The Holy Spirit has always been gracious to meet us when we honor Him and faithfully host His presence.

> *"When honor is given it unlocks our heavenly*
> *Father's glory. What a beautiful world our*
> *honoring words and actions can create."*
>
> —Rebecca Greenwood, *Glory Warfare*[198]

INNER HEALING

> *They all got into a boat and began to cross over to the other side of the lake. And Jesus, exhausted, fell asleep. Suddenly a violent storm developed, with waves so high the boat was about to be swamped. Yet Jesus continued to sleep soundly. The disciples woke him up, saying, "Save us, Lord! We're going to die!" But Jesus reprimanded them. "Why are you gripped with fear? Where is your faith?" Then he stood up and rebuked the storm and said, "Be still!" And instantly it became perfectly calm* (Matthew 8:23-26 TPT).

"I am" are the words the Lord spoke to me as I meditated in His presence. I had asked Him for direction concerning the application of meditation to the ministry of inner healing. "I am," was all He said to me. This is to say He exists everywhere, He is present in all time, and He is the personification of abiding. Then I was given a vision of Jesus sleeping as the boat He was on was caught in the storm. I used to believe that Jesus must have been below deck lying on a comfortable bed, and the waves may have lulled Him to sleep. But the Bible mentions nothing about the boat having a cabin or room beneath the deck. According to Mark's account in chapter 4, verse 38, Jesus was on the stern of the boat when He fell asleep. When the disciples approached Him during the storm, we are told that Jesus stood up and rebuked the storm. Jesus was not below deck, aloof to His surroundings. He was in the midst of it, likely being pummeled along with everyone else. Yet He was at peace, resting from His exhaustion. When Jesus rebuked the storm, He said, "Be still," and the waters were immediately calm from obedience.

What does this tell us about inner healing? First, Jesus is our Anchor, and He is the Foundation on which everything else is built. Jesus's presence will always calm the storm, bringing healing and restoration to the tumult and trauma of life. Bringing the presence of God into your moments of pain and grief always calms the storm and opens the door for Him to reveal and heal any trauma, wound, or pain.

When the disciples approached Jesus, they were distraught and incredulous toward Jesus. They acted as though the answer to their problem was ignoring the situation. In truth, Jesus taught them and us a valuable lesson that day. In the midst of our storms, He is present. In the midst of our chaos, He is here, and in the midst of our pain, He is waiting for us to come to the place of rest with Him on the stern of the boat and let Him remove the trauma, pain, and chaos from our hearts.

The stern of a boat holds significance as this is the place commonly used for lounging, resting, and sitting. But more importantly, this is the location from which the boat is steered and controlled. Jesus was in the very seat of control He needed to be in at that moment. He was modeling the principle for us that when we rest in Him, He will partner with us to command our storms to "be still" and provide direction through the chaos.

From that lesson comes the practice of inner healing. It is almost too simple and a process that can be done at any time in the privacy of your prayer room. As discussed, the process begins with deep *Ruach* breaths through the nose. Invite the Holy Spirit and say, "Holy Spirit, thank You for Your presence; You are welcome here. You are welcome in my mind, and my trauma, and my memories. Would You show me an area You would like to heal today?"

Perhaps you already have a moment that you would like the Holy Spirit to heal. Trust Him, and let Him take you to the area He directs. He might directly address the moment on your mind, but be obedient and go with Him wherever He leads. A deeper connection is likely to exist, possibly one of which you are unaware. Do not relive the memory or ask Jesus to join you in the memory. He is already present with you on the stern of the boat.

Ask the Holy Spirit what He wants to reveal about this moment. He will uncover any lies that have crept in and taken residence in your heart. Are there any people involved in this moment that require forgiveness? Now is the time to forgive and unlink yourself from the pain of the moment. Forgiveness allows the Holy Spirit to come in and replace the lies with truth. Once the Holy Spirit has uncovered the lie you believed in the moment of trauma, ask Him, what is the truth? Allow Him to gently reveal the truth as He removes the lie and heals the pain of the wound. Healing begins and concludes with an understanding of I AM. The understanding comes when we partner with Him in the stillness, intentionally quieting our mind and inviting Him into the darkest areas to shine brightly.

PHYSICAL HEALING
AND DELIVERANCE

The miraculous healing that I have received and documented through this book is a testament to the healing power of the glory of God. Isaiah tells us that when our thoughts are tuned to God, and we wait on Him, He is faithful to strengthen us with supernatural energy and vitality of youth.

> *He gives power to the faint, and to him who has no might he increases strength. Even youths shall faint and be weary, and young men shall fall exhausted; but they who wait for the Lord shall renew their strength; they shall mount up with wings like eagles; they shall run and not be weary; they shall walk and not faint* (Isaiah 40:29-31 ESV).

This promise speaks to physical endurance and strength. I do not believe this verse is symbolic in any way. It is a decree from Heaven that anyone of any age and physical condition will be strengthened and renewed, providing we do one thing. Isaiah says, *when* we wait on the Lord, *then* God will renew strength and enable us for the run set before us with supernaturally natural energy. The key has always been to rest and wait in silence before the Lord in His presence. How much less obligatory does it get?

Put simply, God is literally saying to us, His children, "Sit down and be quiet. I know, and I understand. Let Me help you." It's the golden thread woven throughout all of the inspired Scripture. *"Be still and know that I am God"* is the call to a deeply bonded relationship with Him abiding in the stillness. And *"the Lord will fight for you; you need only to be silent"* is the call for total unrestrained, surrendered silence before Him.

"I thought I was meeting you for a deliverance session today." I have heard that statement several times now, and I chuckle each time. People expect deliverance to be what is shown on TV or based on previous experiences from well-meaning but unrighteous deliverance methods. The truth is that deliverance comes through perfect love, allowing the Holy Spirit's presence to permeate the atmosphere and our total surrender and repentance of all sin and iniquity in our lives.

My deliverance prayer sessions are not uneventful. The demonic still tries to put on a show and often peacocks around, hoping to gain the upper hand. But demons flee the moment we are obedient, offering complete surrender, abiding in the glory of the Holy Spirit's presence, and letting Him fight for us. I hope you realize that this model of deliverance often happens in the stillness of your meditation.

HEALING

Throughout Jesus's ministry, we watch Him perform many acts of deliverance. In every instance, the demonic is subject to Jesus's word and authority, and it leaves. Yet, there is one component present in Jesus's deliverance ministry that must not be overlooked. Every person whom Jesus set free from demonic torment also received physical healing in their bodies.

In Matthew chapter 8, Jesus is witnessed casting out many demons and healing everyone who was sick. In Luke chapter 11, Jesus casts out a demon that was causing a man to be mute. The man was instantly healed and immediately spoke.

> *At that very hour some Pharisees came and said to him, "Get away from here, for Herod wants to kill you." And he said to them, "Go and tell that fox, 'Behold, I cast out demons and*

perform cures today and tomorrow, and the third day I finish my course'" (Luke 13:31-32 ESV).

Jesus persisted steadfastly in His mission to cast out demons and cure the sick despite the Pharisees' cautionary words about Herod's intentions to kill him. We can learn from this that setting people free from demonic torment and healing them physically stands out among other forms of ministry, even in the face of risk.

PHYSICAL AND SPIRITUAL HEALING

It is in vain that you rise up early and go late to rest, eating the bread of anxious toil; for he gives to his beloved sleep (Psalm 127:2 ESV).

The mortal body that has been entrusted to us by God requires rest and meditation with Him. This verse beautifully illustrates how much our physical bodies require downtime and rest. I believe this is one reason God demonstrated to us the principle of rest on the seventh day of creation and established the Shabbat. From a research perspective, "The essence of rest is being in harmony in motivation, feeling, and action. The essence of non-rest is being in disharmony in motivation, feeling, and action. If one continues with an activity for a long time without breaks for rest, one becomes drained of bodily and mental resources."[199] "In order to see gains in fitness, in order for the body to keep doing what you want it to do, you have to give it enough rest to repair itself."[200]

Once again, we encounter a biblical truth credited by secular research. God tells us to abide, meditate, rest, and be healed. The world says to meditate, rest, and be restored. It's relatively common knowledge now that the doctor will prescribe a period of rest during a time of physical healing.

> *Now, because of you, Lord, I will lie down in peace and sleep comes at once, for no matter what happens, I will live unafraid!* (Psalm 4:8 TPT)

> *He offers a resting place for me in his luxurious love. His tracks take me to an oasis of peace near, the quiet brook of bliss. That's where he restores and revives my life. He opens before me the right path and leads me along in his footsteps of righteousness so that I can bring honor to his name* (Psalm 23:2-3 TPT).

Spiritual healing derives from biblical meditation and rest, bringing healing to the physical body, mind, and spirit. During the ministry of deliverance, introducing moments of biblical meditation and supernatural thinking serves to invite a healing moment going far beyond simply casting out a malevolent demon.

May this book have opened your eyes to the immense power of biblical meditation and supernatural thinking. My ultimate desire is that you can implement this knowledge in your everyday life and witness the countless rewards of connecting with Heaven through meditation, abiding time, thoughts, and rest. Then, from your own healing and restoration, become an outward representation of God's light in you, bearing much fruit.

> *Are you weary, carrying a heavy burden? Come to me. I will refresh your life, for I am your oasis. Simply join your life with mine. Learn my ways and you'll discover that I'm gentle, humble, easy to please. You will find refreshment and rest in me. For all that I require of you will be pleasant and easy to bear* (Matthew 11:28-30 TPT).

APPENDIX

CONFRONTATIONAL SCRIPTURES

COMMON FALSE CORE BELIEFS

MULTIPLE CORE BELIEFS WORKSHEET

PRAYER OF RELEASE OF YOGA AND DEMONIC MEDITATION

CONFRONTATIONAL
SCRIPTURES

R ead the following Scriptures and meditate on them. What do they say to you? What is God revealing to you through these Scriptures? What do these Scriptures say about you? Do you have any beliefs that do not agree with the written Word of God in these Scriptures? Meditate on them and ask the Holy Spirit for the truth that drives out the lies of the enemy.

Psalm 139:13-18 NIV

For you created my inmost being; you knit me together in my mother's womb. I praise you because I am fearfully and wonderfully made; your works are wonderful, I know that full well. My frame was not hidden from you when I was made in the secret place when I was woven together in the depths of the earth. Your eyes saw my unformed body; all the days ordained for me were written in your book before one of them came to be. How precious to me are your thoughts, God! How vast is the sum of them! Were I to count them, they would outnumber the grains of sand— when I awake, I am still with you.

Isaiah 41:9-10 NIV

I took you from the ends of the earth, from its farthest corners I called you. I said, "You are my servant"; I have chosen you and have not rejected you. So do not fear, for I am with you; do not be dismayed, for I am your God. I will strengthen you and help you; I will uphold you with my righteous right hand.

Isaiah 42:5-6 NIV

This is what God the Lord says—the Creator of the heavens, who stretches them out, who spreads out the earth with all that springs from it, who gives breath to its people, and life to those who walk on it: "I, the Lord, have called you in righteousness; I will take hold of your hand. I will keep you and will make you to be a covenant for the people and a light for the Gentiles."

Isaiah 54:17 NIV

"No weapon forged against you will prevail, and you will refute every tongue that accuses you. This is the heritage of the servants of the Lord, and this is their vindication from me," declares the Lord.

Isaiah 55:8-9 NIV

"For my thoughts are not your thoughts, neither are your ways my ways," declares the Lord. "As the heavens are higher than the earth, so are my ways higher than your ways and my thoughts than your thoughts."

Jeremiah 1:4-5 NIV

The word of the Lord came to me, saying, "Before I formed you in the womb I knew you, before you were born I set you apart; I appointed you as a prophet to the nations."

Jeremiah 29:11 NIV

"For I know the plans I have for you," declares the Lord, "plans to prosper you and not to harm you, plans to give you hope and a future."

John 1:12-13 NIV

Yet to all who did receive him, to those who believed in his name, he gave the right to become children of God—children born not of natural descent, nor of human decision or a husband's will, but born of God.

COMMON FALSE
CORE BELIEFS

Refer to this list of common lies and false beliefs as a possible starting point when completing the following worksheets. Partner with the Holy Spirit for wisdom and listen as false beliefs are revealed.

I am _____

People are _____

The world is _____

I am all alone.

I don't matter.

God has forsaken me.

I can't trust anyone.

I can't trust church leaders.

Everything is out of control.

Not even God can help me.

The pain is too great to bear.

I don't know what to do.

I'm pulled from every direction.

I'm too small to do anything.

I'm not loved, needed,
cared for, or important.

I was a mistake.

He, she, they are coming back.

I can't stop this.

I'm so stupid.

I was a participant.

I felt pleasure, so I must have wanted it.

I kept going back.

I am bad, dirty, shameful, sick, nasty.

It was all my fault.

I'm just in the way.

I'm too weak to resist.

I can't get away.

I'm overwhelmed.

God could never love me.

There is no way out.

I allowed it.

I will never feel clean again.

There are no options for me.

Nothing good will ever come of this.

They don't need me.

I'm in the way; I'm a burden.

I'm not acceptable.

Everything is confusing.

There is nothing good for me.

It is never going to get any better.

I have no reason to live.

I am unimportant.

Money is the root of all evil.

I'm not worthy of love.

I'm a failure in life.

I will never be happy.

I've been overlooked.

I don't have any purpose.

I should have known better.

No one ever really cares.

No one will be able to really love me.

I'm worthless and will never become successful.

I should never have been born.

I deserved it.

MULTIPLE CORE BELIEFS WORKSHEET

L ist each of the lies you've believed about yourself under My Beliefs. These are your core false beliefs.

My Beliefs (lies I've believed about myself)	Truth

Answer the questions below as they relate
to your beliefs in the My Beliefs column.

What do my beliefs mean about myself?

What do my beliefs mean about other people?

What do my beliefs mean about the world?

What do my beliefs mean about God?

Confront Scriptures:

Meditate on the following Scriptures, comparing what they say beside your beliefs: Psalm 139:13-18; John 1:12; Isaiah 49:9-10; Isaiah 42:5-6; Isaiah 54:17; Isaiah 55:8-9; Romans 5:8; 1 Timothy 2:3-4; Ephesians 2:4-5; Isaiah 45:22; Proverbs 23:23.

Pray:

Holy Spirit, thank You for Your presence, You are magnificent, and You are welcome here. I invite You into my mind and my heart. Would You reveal the truth that has been hidden by the destructive lies of satan? I fully submit to You and choose today to align my mind and thoughts with Your mind and thoughts. I repent for believing lies and for accepting a false identity. I renounce all false beliefs and thoughts about You, God, and I renounce all false beliefs and thoughts about myself. I forgive myself for believing the lies of the enemy. I choose now to fully embrace what Scripture says. That I am a child of God, that I was fearfully and wonderfully created, knit together piece by piece in the secret place. I acknowledge that I have been called from the ends of the earth. You, God, have called me chosen, and You have called me a servant. I choose now to agree that I am accepted, wanted, and needed. I am not rejected, and now I speak to every demonic assignment over my life; I reject you, and I command you to come off my mind. I loose my heart and command you to LEAVE ME NOW! In the mighty name of Jesus. Holy Spirit, I invite You now to speak the truth to my mind and heart.

Renew your mind:

As the Holy Spirit reveals truth, write it in the column labeled "Truth."

Maintain:

Meditate each day on these truths, bless yourself with them, and having displaced the lies of the enemy, they will become part of your renewed core belief system.

If you are struggling to let go of a particular belief, then address that one separately on the worksheet titled Extensive Review of a Core Belief.

EXTENSIVE REVIEW *of a* CORE BELIEF WORKSHEET

Working with the Holy Spirit, identify a false core belief (lie), acquire truth, and create a new core belief based on truth.

My Belief (the lie that I believed)

What is the primary emotion or situation connected to this belief?

What does this belief mean about me or my life?

What does this belief mean about the world?

What does this belief mean about other people?

What does this belief mean about God?

Confront Scriptures:

Thoughtfully and meditatively read each of the following Scriptures in your Bible. Weigh them beside your answers above.

- Psalm 139:13-18 – You are fearfully and wonderfully made.

- John 1:12 – You are called a child of God, an inheritance with positional power and authority.

- Isaiah 49:9-10 – You are chosen, you are called servant, you are accepted.

- Isaiah 42:5-6 – You are called to righteousness; you are a covenant.

- Isaiah 54:17 – You have the heritage of the Lord; you will refute the false accusations.

- Isaiah 55:8-9 – God's thoughts for you are greater than you can imagine.

- Romans 5:8 – God loves us so much that Christ died for us.

- 1 Timothy 2:3-4 – God desires all people to come to the knowledge of truth and be saved.

- Isaiah 45:22 – God desires that the entire world would turn to Him and be saved.

- Proverbs 23:23 – Purchase truth and do not sell it.

Review:

Discover that the beliefs (lies) written on this page do not agree with what God's Word says.

Identify a new core belief:

Invite the Holy Spirit into your space, invite Him into your mind, and invite Him into the depth of your heart and ask Him to reveal the truth.

Pray the following prayer:

> Holy Spirit, thank You for Your presence, You are magnificent, and You are welcome here. I invite You into my mind and my heart. Would You reveal the truth that has been hidden by the destructive lies of satan? I fully submit to You and choose today to align my mind and thoughts with Your mind and thoughts. I repent for believing lies and for accepting a false identity. I renounce all false beliefs and thoughts about You, God, and I renounce all false beliefs and thoughts about myself. I forgive myself for believing the lies of the enemy. I choose now to fully embrace what Scripture says. That I am a child of God, that I was fearfully and wonderfully created, knit together piece by piece in the secret place. I acknowledge that I have been called from the ends of the earth. You, God, have called me chosen, and You have called me a servant. I choose now to agree that I am accepted, wanted, and needed. I am not rejected, and now I speak to every demonic assignment over my life; I reject you, and I command you to come off my mind. I loose my heart and command you to LEAVE ME NOW! In the mighty name of Jesus. Holy Spirit, I invite You now to speak the truth to my mind and heart.

Wait and listen silently for the Holy Spirit to reveal the truth to your mind and spirit.

As the Holy Spirit reveals the truth for the false belief listed, write it in the space below.

_____

_____

_____

_____

_____

_____

_____

_____

_____

_____

_____

_____

_____

NEXT STEPS

This new truth is a new core belief, and it is to become a daily personal declaration over your life.

Every day during meditation, bless yourself with this newly restored truth over your life and become transformed from the inside out totally and completely by the renewing of your mind.

Repeat this process for each false core belief in your life.

MULTIPLE CORE BELIEFS
WORKSHEET

U sing the list of false core beliefs, write your beliefs below under My Beliefs:

My Beliefs
(lies I've believed about myself)

Answer the questions below as they relate
to your beliefs in the My Beliefs column.

What do my beliefs mean about myself?

What do my beliefs mean about other people?

What do my beliefs mean about the world?

What do my beliefs mean about God?

Confront Scriptures:

Thoughtfully read each of the Scriptures in your Bible.

- Psalm 139:13-18 – You are fearfully and wonderfully made.
- John 1:12 – You are called a child of God, an inheritance with positional power and authority.
- Isaiah 49:9-10 – You are chosen, you are called servant, you are accepted.
- Isaiah 42:5-6 – You are called to righteousness; you are a covenant.
- Isaiah 54:17 – You have the heritage of the Lord; you will refute the false accusations.
- Isaiah 55:8-9 – God's thoughts for you are greater than you can imagine.
- Romans 5:8 – God loves us so much that Christ died for us.
- 1 Timothy 2:3-4 – God desires all people to come to the knowledge of truth and be saved.
- Isaiah 45:22 – God desires that the entire world would turn to Him and be saved.
- Proverbs 23:23 – Purchase truth and do not sell it.

Review:

Discover that the beliefs written do not agree with what God's Word says.

Identify new core beliefs.

Pray and invite the Holy Spirit into your space, invite Him into your mind, and invite Him into the depth of your heart and ask Him to reveal the truth.

Pray the following prayer:

> Holy Spirit, thank You for Your presence, You are magnificent, and You are welcome here. I invite You into my mind and my heart. Would You reveal the truth that has been hidden by the destructive lies of satan? I fully submit to You and choose today to align my mind and thoughts with Your mind and thoughts. I repent for believing lies and for accepting a false identity. I renounce all false beliefs and thoughts about You, God, and I renounce all false beliefs and thoughts about myself. I forgive myself for believing the lies of the enemy. I choose now to fully embrace what Scripture says. That I am a child of God, that I was fearfully and wonderfully created, knit together piece by piece in the secret place. I acknowledge that I have been called from the ends of the earth. You, God, have called me chosen, and You have called me a servant. I choose now to agree that I am accepted, wanted, and needed. I am not rejected, and now I speak to every demonic assignment over my life; I reject you, and I command you to come off my mind. I loose my heart and command you to LEAVE ME NOW! In the mighty name of Jesus. Holy Spirit, I invite You now to speak the truth to my mind and heart.

Silently wait and listen:

The Holy Spirit will begin to speak to you, revealing the truth.

Identify new core beliefs:

As the Holy Spirit reveals the truth for each of the false beliefs listed, write them in the Next Steps table.

NEXT STEPS

Tear or cut out and shred the old false core beliefs on page 274.

Every new truth written on this page is to become a daily personal declaration over your life.

Every day during meditation, bless yourself and declare these newly restored truths over your life and become transformed from the inside out, totally and completely by the renewing of your mind.

Truths and New Core Beliefs

PRAYER *of* RELEASE *of* YOGA *and* DEMONIC MEDITATION

FORGIVE

Father God, I acknowledge Your lordship over my life; I believe in Your Son Jesus and that He willingly gave His life for mine on the cross. I believe that He rose again, having conquered sin and death while forgiving me and rescuing me from all my sins—past, present, and future. I believe that I am a child of God created in Your image. I acknowledge that I have participated in evil actions that have dishonored You and my body. I ask for and receive Your forgiveness now, according to 1 John 1:9. I also choose to forgive myself and loose myself from the bondage and torment caused by my actions.

If we confess our sins, he is faithful and just to forgive us our sins and to cleanse us from all unrighteousness (1 John 1:9 ESV).

I REPENT FOR MY WILLING PARTICIPATION WITH:

Hinduism	Yoga	Tai chi
Mudras	Asanas	Christian yoga
Gurus	Yogis	Kundalini
Honoring the gods Brahma Vishnu Ganesh Kali And all other Hindu, Buddhist, and Egyptian gods, goddesses, and so-called ascended mortal beings.	Emptying myself through yoga-inspired breathing techniques.	Guided imagery and partnering with spirits or energy.
Trance and hypnotism	The manipulation of energy through prana, mantras, chants, chakras, asanas, mudras, and especially kundalini.	Vipassana
Narcissism and the belief that transcendence comes from within.	Transcendental meditation	Loving Kindness meditation
Qigong (pronounced chi-gong)	Zazen (Zen) meditation	Mantra meditation
Pranayama meditation		

I RENOUNCE ALL OF MY INVOLVEMENT WITH:

Words, chants, and mantras spoken in honor of false gods.	Om (AUM)	Namaste
Brahman	Ishvara	Shiva
Shakti	Surya	Chandra
Vishnu and the Lotus	Hanuman	Krishna
Kali and all other Hindu false deities	Prana	Chakras
Nadis (72,000 psychic channels)	The serpent and force of Kundalini	Royal yoga (raja)
Ashtanga (eight limbs)	Bhakti yoga and the supreme spirit	Any acquired celestial knowledge or benefit received from participation in yoga or worldly meditation.
Consciousness manipulation	Union with the primal essence of consciousness	Krishna consciousness
The false wisdom of hatha and raja yoga	Mental suppression	Infirmity brought on through ignorant participation in "harmless yoga."
The subtle body and the gross body	All forms of yoga, jnana, bhakti, Hatha, and karma,	

BREAK

- I break the power of all yoga, meditation, Hinduism, and Buddhism in my life.

- I break the legal hold, access, and influence over me by participating in these evil activities.

- I break the power of kundalini from the base of my spine to the top of my head.

- I break the power of all honor I bestowed on the previously renounced demon gods and goddesses in my life.

- I break the power of all honor I bestowed on ascended mortal beings.

- I break the power of every demon spirit that gained access to my life to influence me and my actions.

- I break the power of infirmity over my life, specifically in my joints, back, internal organs, mind, and central nervous system, causing fibromyalgia, joint pain, and other undiagnosed problems.

- I break the associated trauma caused by kundalini, yoga, and demonic meditation on my life. I command all trauma attached to my DNA to be removed and to fall off now. I command my genes to forget the trauma and to be healed now in Jesus's name.

- I now command every evil spirit in the name of Jesus to leave me now! Your only assignment is to go now, touching and harming no one.

RECEIVE

- God, I now receive the blessing of Your healing power of love and acceptance. I receive the blessing of authentic, pure biblical meditation in my life as a healing gift from You.

- I offer the quiet stillness of my meditation times to You. Holy Spirit, have Your way in my life; open my eyes and ears to hear, see, and experience more of You.

- I declare that my biblical meditation is time set apart for my healing and restoration, as commanded in Psalm 46:10.

Thank You, God, for restoring my life and filling me with truth and wisdom that overpowers the demonic thoughts of satan and his demons. I declare that I am free, healed, and restored, and Holy Spirit, I choose now to meditate only with You, amen.

NOTES

1. Strong's Concordance H7503 *raphah*.

2. Strong's Concordance H3045 *yada*.

3. Statistic found at: https://www.cdc.gov/diabetes/library/spotlights/diabetes-facts
    -stats.html; accessed October 15, 2023.

4. May 6, 2023, reported using a Dexcom continuous glucose wearable monitor.
    Readings are recorded every 5 minutes.

5. Shashank S. Sinha, Ajay K. Jain, et.al., "Effect of 6 Months of Meditation on Blood
    Sugar, Glycosylated Hemoglobin, and Insulin Levels in Patients of Coronary Artery
    Disease," *International Journal of Yoga,* May-Aug 2018, 11(2), 122-128; https://doi
    .org/10.4103/ijoy.IJOY_30_17; and https://www.ncbi.nlm.nih.gov/pmc/articles/
    PMC5934947/; accessed October 15, 2023.

6. Elder F.E. Mullan, ed., *The Spiritual Exercises of St. Ignatius of Loyola* (Boston: P.J.
    Kennedy & Sons, 1914).

7. Don Inigo Lopez de Loyola changed his name to Ignatius of Loyola prior to founding
    the Jesuit order.

8. Mehmet Bulut, "Ignatius of Loyola: Founder of Jesuit Order," *Daily Sabah*, December
    22, 2021; https://www.dailysabah.com/arts/portrait/ignatius-of-loyola-founder-of
    -jesuit-order; accessed October 15, 2023.

9. "Depression Facts, *Hope For Depression Research Foundation,* January 25, 2021);
    https://www.hopefordepression.org/depression-facts/; accessed October 15, 2023.

10. Michael Hyatt and Megan Hyatt Miller, *Mind Your Mindset: The Science That Shows
    Success Starts with Your Thinking* (Grand Rapids, MI: Baker Books, 2023).

11. Strong's H1897 *hagah* and H7878 *siah*.

12. Roger Crisp, editor and translator, *Aristotle, Nicomachean Ethics* (Cambridge University Press, 2014).

13. Strong's H6026 *anog*.

14. Martin Caparrotta, et.al., "What Is the Purpose of Meditation? (12 Experts Explain)," HumanWindow, May 4, 2023; https://humanwindow.com/what-is-the-purpose-of -meditation/; accessed October 15, 2023.

15. If you struggle with your identity as a child of God, or have never accepted Jesus as your Savior, please read Psalm 139:13-16 and Romans 10:8-10. Contact our ministry at www.engagemin.org.

16. Aimee Semple McPherson, "This is my task," speech in Los Angeles at the Angelus Temple, March 1939.

17. Daniel Goleman and Richard Davidson, *Altered Traits* (New York: Penguin 2018).

18. American Psychological Association; APA Dictionary of Psychology; https:// dictionary.apa.org/mindfulness; accessed October 15, 2023.

19. Joaquín Selva, "Gratitude Meditation: A Simple but Powerful Intervention," PositivePsychology.com, April 21, 2017; https://positivepsychology.com/gratitude -meditation-happiness/; accessed October 16, 2023.

20. "Six common misconceptions about meditation," News and events: Bangor University, March 19, 2018; https://www.bangor.ac.uk/news/archive/six-common -misconceptions-about-meditation-36207; accessed October 16, 2023.

21. Duncan Riach, "Meditation is not about quieting the mind," Medium, June 6, 2019; https://medium.com/swlh/meditation-is-not-about-quieting-the-mind -8c50efc2f6e1; accessed October 16, 2023.

22. Giovanni Dienstmann, *Practical Meditation: A Simple Step-by-Step Guide* (New York: Dorling Kindersley Limited, 2018).

23. The Norwegian University of Science and Technology (NTNU), "This is your brain on meditation: Brain processes more thoughts, feelings during meditation, study shows," ScienceDaily, May 15, 2014; www.sciencedaily.com/ releases/2014/05/140515095545.htm; accessed June 22, 2023.

24. Eileen Luders, Nicolas Cherbuin, Christian Gaser, "Estimating brain age using high-resolution pattern recognition: Younger brains in long-term meditation practitioners," *NeuroImage,* Volume 134, July 1, 2016, pages 508-513; https://doi .org/10.1016/j.neuroimage.2016.04.007; accessed October 16, 2023.

25. Strong's G3191 *meletaō*.

26.   Strong's H7881 *sichah.*

27.   Strong's H7878 *siach.*

28.   Strong's G3191 *meletaō.*

29.   Strong's G3306 *menō.*

30.   Strong's H1897 *hāḡâ.*

31.   Strong's H7503 *rāp̄â.*

32.   Strong's H7742 *śûaḥ.*

33.   Strong's H5375 *nāśā'.*

34.   Strong's H7878 *śîaḥ.*

35.   Strong's G1189 *deomai.*

36.   Strong's G3870 *parakaleō.*

37.   Goleman, *Altered Traits,* 44-45.

38.   Miguel Farias and Catherine Wikholm, "Has the science of mindfulness lost its mind?" *BJPsych Bulletin,* December 2016; https://www.ncbi.nlm.nih.gov/pmc/articles/PMC5353526/; accessed October 16, 2023.

39.   David Hamilton, "Harvard Study finds that Meditation Impacts DNA," April 19, 2011; https://drdavidhamilton.com/harvard-study-finds-that-meditation-impacts-dna/; accessed October 16, 2023.

40.   Manoj Bhasin, Marie G. Joseph et.al., "Genomic counter-stress changes induced by the relaxation response," *PLoS ONE,* 3(7); https://doi.org/10.1371/journal.pone.0002576; accessed October 16, 2023.

41.   Miguel Porta, *Entropy, A Dictionary of Epidemiology* (Oxford University Press, 2014); https://www.oxfordreference.com/view/10.1093/acref/9780199976720.001.0001/acref-9780199976720-e-628; accessed July 2, 2023.

42.   Strong's G3306 *menō.*

43.   US National Library of Medicine, "FKBP5 FKBP prolyl isomerase 5 [Homo Sapiens (human)]"; *National Center for Biotechnology Information,* Gene ID: 2289, updated October 10, 2023; https://www.ncbi.nlm.nih.gov/gene/2289; accessed October 16, 2023.

44.   US National Library of Medicine, "SLC6A4 solute carrier family 6 member 4 [Homo Sapiens (human)]"; *National Center for Biotechnology Information,* Gene

ID: 6532, updated October 10, 2023; https://www.ncbi.nlm.nih.gov/gene/6532; accessed October 16, 2023.

45.   Siresha Bathina, and Undurti N. Das, "Brain-derived neurotrophic factor and its clinical implications," *Archives of Medical Science,* December 10, 2015; https://www .ncbi.nlm.nih.gov/pmc/articles/PMC4697050/; accessed October 16, 2023.

46.   Sabrina Venditti, et.al., "Molecules of Silence: Effects of Meditation on Gene Expression and Epigenetics," *Frontiers in Psychology,* August 11, 2020; https://www .ncbi.nlm.nih.gov/pmc/articles/PMC7431950/; accessed October 22, 2023.

47.   Strong's H1826 *dāmam.*

48.   Covered later, silence is not required for all meditations. This reference demonstrates the benefits of silence versus the requirement.

49.   Kris Acheson, "Silence as gesture: Rethinking the nature of Communicative Silences," *Communication Theory,* 18(4), 535-555, October 29, 2008; https://doi.org/10.1111/j.1468-2885.2008.00333.x; accessed October 16, 2023.

50.   Ibid.

51.   Strong's H1827 *demamah.*

52.   Keith H. Basso, *Wisdom Sits in Places* (University of New Mexico Press, 1996), 82-83.

53.   Shahram Heshmat, "5 Benefits of Imaginative Thinking," *Psychology Today,* April 14, 2022; https://www.psychologytoday.com/us/blog/science-choice/202204/5 -benefits-imaginative-thinking; accessed October 16, 2023.

54.   Monique Farmer, "Channeling childhood creativity to achieve professional success," *Public Relations Society of America Inc.,* March 2022; https://www.prsa.org/article/ channeling-childhood-creativity-to-achieve-professional-success; accessed October 16, 2023.

55.   George Land, "The Failure of Success," *TEDxTucson YouTube,* 2011; https://youtu .be/ZfKMq-rYtnc; accessed July 3, 2023.

56.   Coert Engels, "We are born creative geniuses and the education system dumbs us down, according to NASA scientists," Ideapod, November 14, 2022; https://ideapod .com/born-creative-geniuses-education-system-dumbs-us-according-nasa-scientists/; accessed October 16, 2023.

57.   "Research Paper: Neuro-Science Behind Visualization," *International Coach Academy,* December 3, 2013; https://coachcampus.com/coach-portfolios/research-papers/bala-kishore-batchu-neuro-science-behind-visualization/2/; accessed October 16, 2023.

58. "Imagery," *Johns Hopkins Medicine,* June 7, 2021; https://www.hopkinsmedicine.org/health/wellness-and-prevention/imagery; accessed October 16, 2023.

59. Tim Blankert and Melvyn R.W. Hamstra, "Imagining Success: Multiple Achievement Goals and the Effectiveness of Imagery," *Basic and Applied Social Psychology,* 39(1), 60-67, published December 7, 2016; https://doi.org/10.1080/01973533.2016.1255947; accessed October 16, 2023.

60. C. Frank, et.al., "Mental Representation and Mental Practice: Experimental Investigation on the Functional Links between Motor Memory and Motor Imagery," *PLoS ONE, 9(4),* 2014; https://doi.org/10.1371/journal.pone.0095175; accessed October 17, 2023.

61. Vinoth K. Ranganathan, et.al., "From mental power to muscle power—gaining strength by using the mind," *Neuropsychologia* (2014), 42(7), 944-956; https://doi.org/10.1016/j.neuropsychologia.2003.11.018; accessed October 17, 2023.

62. Hsiao-Hsien Lin, et.al., "Influence of Imagery Training on Adjusting the Pressure of Fin Swimmers, Improving Sports Performance and Stabilizing Psychological Quality," *International Journal of Environmental Research and Public Health* (2021), 18(22), 11767; https://doi.org/10.3390/ijerph182211767; accessed October 17, 2023.

63. Joseph Guarino, "Prepping for Public Speaking with Creative Visualization," *Institute of Public Speaking*; https://www.instituteofpublicspeaking.com/prepping-for-public-speaking-with-creative-visualization/; accessed October 17, 2023.

64. Strong's H2938 *taam.*

65. Strong's H7200 *raah.*

66. "The Scary Truth about How Zombie Scrolling Impacts Mental Health," *Newport Institute* (September 26, 2022); https://www.newportinstitute.com/resources/mental-health/zombie_scrolling/;accessed October 17, 2023.

67. David S. Black and George M. Slavich, "Mindfulness meditation and the immune system: A systematic review of randomized controlled trials, *Annals of the New York Academy of Sciences* (2016), 1373(1), 13-24; https://doi.org/10.1111/nyas.12998; accessed October 17, 2023.

68. "Latest federal data show that young people are more likely than older adults to be experiencing symptoms of anxiety or depression," *KFF,* March 27, 2023; https://www.kff.org/coronavirus-covid-19/press-release/latest-federal-data-show-that-young-people-are-more-likely-than-older-adults-to-be-experiencing-symptoms-of-anxiety-or-depression; accessed October 17, 2023.

69. "How meditation helps with depression," *Harvard Health,* February 12, 2021; https://www.health.harvard.edu/mind-and-mood/how-meditation-helps-with-depression; accessed October 17, 2023.

70. "Meditation: A simple, fast way to reduce stress," *Mayo Foundation for Medical Education and Research,* April 29, 2022; https://www.mayoclinic.org/tests -procedures/meditation/in-depth/meditation/art-20045858; accessed October 17, 2023.

71. Lydie A. Lebrun-Harris, et.al., "Five-Year Trends in US Children's Health and Well-being, 2016-2020," *JAMA Pediatrics,* March 14, 2022, 176(7); https://doi .org/10.1001/jamapediatrics.2022.0056; accessed October 17, 2023.

72. "Stress Management: Breathing Exercises for Relaxation," *MyHealth.Alberta.ca,* February 9, 2022; https://myhealth.alberta.ca/Health/pages/conditions .aspx?hwid=uz2255; accessed October 17, 2023.

73. Goleman and Davidson, *Altered Traits,* 2018.

74. "Change Your Mind: Meditation Benefits for the Brain," Ask The Scientists, July 20, 0222; https://askthescientists.com/brain-meditation; accessed October 17, 2023.

75. Rimma Teper and Michael Inzlicht, "Meditation, mindfulness and executive control: The importance of emotional acceptance and brain-based performance monitoring," *Social Cognitive and Affective Neuroscience,* May 12, 2012, 8(1), 85-92; https://doi .org/10.1093/scan/nss045; accessed October 17, 2023.

76. Asfandyar Khan Niazi and Shaharyar Khan Niazi, "Mindfulness-based stress reduction: A non-pharmacological approach for chronic illnesses," *North American Journal of Medical Sciences,* January 3, 2011, 3(1), 20; https://pubmed.ncbi.nlm.nih .gov/22540058/; accessed October 17, 2023.

77. "Mindfulness-Based Cognitive Therapy"; https://www.psychologytoday.com/us/ therapy-types/mindfulness-based-cognitive-therapy; accessed October 17, 2023.

78. "What is cognitive behavioral therapy?" *American Psychological Association,* 2017; https://www.apa.org/ptsd-guideline/patients-and-families/cognitive-behavioral; accessed October 17, 2023.

79. Dennis Greenberger, et.al., *Mind Over Mood* (New York: Guilford Press, 2015).

80. E. Patterson, LPC, "Important facts and statistics about stress: Prevalence, impact, &; more," *The Recovery Village Drug and Alcohol Rehab*, September 5, 2022; https:// www.therecoveryvillage.com/mental-health/stress/stress-statistics; accessed October 17, 2023.

81. Sara Lindberg, "Eustress: The Good Stress," Healthline, January 3, 2019; https:// www.healthline.com/health/eustress#good-stress; accessed October 17, 2023.

82. "What is Stress?" *The American Institute of Stress,* March 30, 2022; https://www .stress.org/daily-life; accessed October 17, 2023.

83. Farias and Wikholm, "Has the science of mindfulness lost its mind?" *BJPsych Bulletin.*

84. Danah Henriksen, et.al., "Mindfulness and creativity: Implications for thinking and learning," *Thinking Skills and Creativity* (September 2020), 37, 100689; https://doi.org/10.1016/j.tsc.2020.100689; accessed October 17, 2023.

85. Elizabeth A. Hoge, et.al., "Mindfulness-Based Stress Reduction vs Escitalopram for the Treatment of Adults with Anxiety Disorders," *JAMA Psychiatry,* November 9, 2022, 80(1), 13; https://doi.org/10.1001/jamapsychiatry.2022.3679; accessed October 17, 2023.

86. Strong's H3966 *mod* and H2896 *tob.*

87. Jo Nash, PhD, "The History of Meditation: Its Origins & Timeline," PositivePsychology.com, May 27, 2019; https://positivepsychology.com/history-of-meditation/#how-old-is-meditation; accessed October 17, 2023.

88. Muata Ashby, *Egyptian Yoga: The Philosophy of Enlightenment* (Cruzian Mystic Books/Sema Institute, 2005).

89. Muata Ashby, *Meditation: The Ancient Egyptian Path to Enlightenment* (Cruzian Mystic Books/Sema Institute of Yoga, 2005).

90. Nirbhay N. Singh, *Psychology of Meditation* (Nova Science Publishers, 2016).

91. Giovanni Dienstmann, *Practical Meditation: A Simple Step-by-Step Guide* (London: Dorling Kindersley Limited, 2018).

92. Chan-Young Kwon, "Research and Public Interest in Mindfulness in the Covid-19 and Post-Covid-19 Era: A Bibliometric and Google Trends Analysis," *International Journal of Environmental Research and Public Health,* February 21, 2023; 20(5), 3807; https://doi.org/10.3390/ijerph20053807; accessed October 17, 2023.

93. Inna Belfer and David Shurtleff, eds., "Yoga: What you need to know," *NIH, National Center for Complementary and Integrative Health,* August 2023; https://www.nccih.nih.gov/health/yoga-what-you-need-to-know; accessed October 17, 2023.

94. *The Gale Encyclopedia of Senior Health: A Guide for Seniors and Their Care Givers* (Gale, Cengage Learning, 2015).

95. "All About Kundalini," Kundalini Yoga, May 2, 2020; https://kundalini-yoga.co.uk/about-kundalini; accessed October 17, 2023.

96. Gurmukh Kaur Khalsa; *Kundalini Rising: Exploring the Energy of Awakening* (Self-Publishing: Sounds True, 2009).

97. "What is Kundalini Awakening? (Symptoms and Dangerous)" Fitsri, December 10, 2022; https://www.fitsri.com/articles/kundalini-awakening; accessed October 17, 2023.

98. A. Valanciute and L.A. Thampy, "Physio Kundalini syndrome and mental health," *Mental Health, Religion & Culture,* 2011, 14(8), 839-842; https://doi.org/10.1080/13674676.2010.530648; accessed October 17, 2023.

99. https://youtu.be/wymi3AxcqnU; accessed October 17, 2023.

100. "Kundalini Yoga—Why is it dangerous?" Official website of Sadhguru, *Isha Foundation,* January 2, 2023; https://isha.sadhguru.org/yoga/yoga-articles-yoga/kundalini-yoga-beneficial-or-dangerous/; accessed October 17, 2023.

101. "Kundalini Syndrome: The Dangers of Unpreparedness" October 25, 2020; https://saiayurvedic.com/blog/kundalini-syndrome-the-dangers-of-unpreparedness.aspx; accessed October 17, 2023.

102. "History and Spread of Vipassana.," *Vipassana Research Institute*; https://www.vridhamma.org/History-and-Spread-of-Vipassana; accessed October 17, 2023.

103. M. Saydaw, "Fundamentals of Vipassana Meditation," *Tathagata Meditation Center.*

104. Dienstmann, *Practical Meditation,* 2018.

105. https://youtu.be/vuDkvBTKbQ4; accessed October 17, 2023.

106. Bradford Hatcher, *The Book of Changes = Yijing, Word by Word,* Hermetica.info (2009); https://hermetica.info/Yijing1+2.pdf; accessed October 17, 2023.

107. Yanlong Guo, "Iconographic Volatility in the Fuxi-Nüwa Triads of the Han Dynasty," *Archives of Asian Art,* April 1, 2021, 71(1), 63-91; https://doi.org/10.1215/00666637-8866680; accessed October 17, 2023.

108. "Fuxi Origin, Creation Myth & Contributions," Study.com, December 26, 2022; https://study.com/academy/lesson/fuxi-origin-creation-myth-significance.html; accessed October 17, 2023.

109. Irving Yee, "How to Make Your Mind as Clear as Water," *The Art Of Tai Chi* (January 11, 2022); https://artoftaichi.com/blog/how-to-make-your-mind-as-clear-as-water/; accessed October 17, 2023.

110. B. Nykyforiak, "The Four Brahmavihāras (Divine Abodes)," *Team Higher Ground,* September 9, 2019; https://www.teamhigherground.com/blog/2019/9/9/the-four-brahmavihras-devine-abodes; accessed October 17, 2023.

111. Doug Smith, "Secular Buddhist Association," *Secular Buddhist Association,* May 1, 2017; https://secularbuddhism.org/on-metta/; accessed October 17, 2023.

112. Numbered Discourses 4.67 "The Snake King," *SuttaCentral;* https://suttacentral.net/an4.67/en/sujato?lang=en&;layout=plain&;reference=none&;notes=asterisk&;highlight=false&;script=latin; accessed October 17, 2023.

113. Guides: Ignatian Resources: The Spiritual Exercises, *Regis University;* https://libguides.regis.edu/c.php?g=882343&;p=6379574; accessed October 17, 2023.

114. Elder Mullan, *The Spiritual Exercises of St. Ignatius of Loyola* (England: Aziloth Books, 2012).

115. D. Borohhov, "What Is the Meaning of AUM?" Ananda, April 26, 2023; https://www.ananda.org/yogapedia/aum/; accessed October 17, 2023.

116. Strong's H5186 *natah* (incline).

117. Strong's H3824 *lebab* (heart).

118. Strong's H7307 *Ruach* (Spirit of God).

119. Strong's H7363 *rachaph*.

120. Strong's H5397 Neshamah, breath of God.

121. Maria Victoria Fraga and Susan Guttentag, "Lung development," *Avery's Diseases of the Newborn* (2012), 571-583; https://doi.org/10.1016/b978-1-4377-0134-0.10042-3; accessed October 18, 2023.

122. Brian J. Koos and Arezoo Rajaee, "Fetal Breathing Movements and Changes at Birth," *Advances in Fetal and Neonatal Physiology* (January 1, 2014), 89-101; https://doi.org/10.1007/978-1-4939-1031-1_8; accessed October 18, 2023.

123. John 1:12 TPT: *But those who embraced him and took hold of his name he gave authority to become the children of God!*

124. "Dave Duell prayed...people were physically healed!"; https://sidroth.org/television/tv-archives/dave-duels/; accessed October 18, 2023.

125. Jane Huang and Michael Wurmbrand, *The Primordial Breath: An Ancient Chinese Way of Prolonging Life Through Breath Control* (Original Books, 1987).

126. James Nestor, *Breath: The New Science of a Lost Art* (New York: Penguin Books, 2020).

127. Nachum Soroker, et.al., "Measuring and Characterizing the Human Nasal Cycle," *PLOS ONE* (2016), 11(10). https://doi.org/10.1371/journal.pone.0162918; accessed October 18, 2023.

128. Nestor, *Breath: The New Science of a Lost Art.*

129.   Amy F.T. Arnsten, "Stress signalling pathways that impair prefrontal cortex structure and function," *Nature Reviews Neuroscience* (June 2009), 10(6), 410–422; https://doi.org/10.1038/nrn2648; accessed October 18, 2023.

130.   Jacob Tindle and Prasanna Tadi, "Neuroanatomy, Parasympathetic Nervous System," *NIH National Library of Medicine* (October 31, 2022); https://www.ncbi.nlm.nih.gov/books/NBK553141/; accessed October 18, 2023.

131.   Carolyn Farnsworth, "Nose breathing vs. Mouth Breathing: What to know," *Medical News Today* (February 17, 2023); https://www.medicalnewstoday.com/articles/nose-breathing-vs-mouth-breathing#nose-breathing-vs-mouth-breathing; accessed October 18, 2023.

132.   Patrick McKeown, *The Oxygen Advantage: Simple, Scientifically Proven Breathing Techniques...*" (New York: William Morrow/HarperCollinsPublishers, 2016).

133.   Ruth Allen, "The health benefits of nose breathing," *Lenus, The Irish Health Repository* (January 2015); http://hdl.handle.net/10147/559021; accessed October 18, 2023.

134.   McKeown, *The Oxygen Advantage.*

135.   Noam Sobel, et.al., "The world smells different to each nostril," *Nature* (1999), 402(6757), 35-35. https://doi.org/10.1038/46944; accessed October 18, 2023.

136.   David Shannahoff-Khalsa and Shahrokh Golshan, "Nasal cycle dominance and hallucinations in an adult schizophrenic female," *Psychiatry Research* (2015), 226(1), 289-294; https://doi.org/10.1016/j.psychres.2014.12.065; accessed October 18, 2023.

137.   Julia Fiore, "Why do so many Egyptian statues have broken noses?" Artsy, March 8, 2019; https://www.artsy.net/article/artsy-editorial-egyptian-statues-broken-noses; accessed October 18, 2023.

138.   Ruth Allen, "The health benefits of nose breathing."

139.   Peter A. Shapiro, "Effects of nasal obstruction on facial development," *Journal of Allergy and Clinical Immunology* (May 1988), 81(5), 967-971; https://doi.org/10.1016/0091-6749(88)90162-5; accessed October 18, 2023.

140.   Nestor, *Breath: The New Science of a Lost Art.*

141.   Neil K. Kaneshiro, MD, "Changes in the newborn at birth," *NIH National Library of Medicine: MedlinePlus,* December 10, 2021; https://medlineplus.gov/ency/article/002395.htm; accessed October 18, 2023.

142.   Patrick McKeown, "How to stimulate the vagus nerve with breathing exercises," Oxygen Advantage (April 10, 2023); https://oxygenadvantage.com/science/vagus-nerve-stimulation/; accessed October 18, 2023.

143. Roderik J.S. Gerritsen and Guido P.H. Band, "Breath of life: The respiratory vagal stimulation model of contemplative activity," *Frontiers in Human Neuroscience* (October 9, 2018), 12; https://doi.org/10.3389/fnhum.2018.00397; accessed October 18, 2023.

144. "Vagus nerve: Gastroparesis, Vagus Nerve Stimulation; Syncope," *Cleveland Clinic,* January 1, 2022; https://my.clevelandclinic.org/health/body/22279-vagus-nerve; accessed October 18, 2023.

145. Jim Donovan, MEd, "Saved by Sound: One Musician's Story of Illness and the Healing Sounds That Saved Him," https://www.donovanhealth.com/; accessed October 18, 2023.

146. Sigrid Breit, et.al., "Vagus Nerve as Modulator of the Brain-Gut Axis in Psychiatric and Inflammatory Disorders," *Frontiers in Psychiatry* (March 13, 2018), 9; https://doi.org/10.3389/fpsyt.2018.00044; accessed October 18, 2023.

147. Leah Crane, "Large-scale quantum effects," *New Scientist,* April, 15, 2023, 258(3434), 10; https://doi.org/10.1016/s0262-4079(23)00643-7; accessed October 18, 2023.

148. This is a correction. In *The Science of Deliverance* my age was mistakenly written as 8 years old.

149. Andrew Newberg and Mark Robert Waldman, *How God Changes Your Brain: Breakthrough Findings from a Leading Neuroscientist* (New York: Ballantine Books).

150. Rebecca Greenwood, *Defeating Strongholds of the Mind* (Lake Mary, FL: Charisma House, 2015).

151. Bruce Lipton, *The Biology of Belief: Unleashing the Power of Consciousness, Matter and Miracles* (Hay House, 2016).

152. Ibid.

153. June Javelosa, "Scientists have discovered how memories are inherited," *World Economic Forum,* December 4, 2018; https://www.weforum.org/agenda/2018/12/memories-can-be-inherited-and-scientists-may-have-just-figured-out-how/; accessed October 18, 2023.

154. Bruce H. Lipton, "Is there a way to change subconscious patterns?" BruceLipton. com; March 13, 2023; https://www.brucelipton.com/there-way-change-subconscious-patterns/; accessed October 18, 2023.

155. Weizmann Institute of Science, "Quantum Theory Demonstrated: Observation Affects Reality, ScienceDaily, February 27, 1998; https://www.sciencedaily.com/releases/1998/02/980227055013.htm; accessed October 18, 2023.

156.   Lisa Andrews, "Better Food, Better Mood?" *Communicating Food for Health;* https://search.ebscohost.com/login.aspx?direct=true&;AuthType=shib&;db=ccm &;AN=157168247&;site=eds-live&;scope=site&;custid=s8856897; This resource is only accessible through the university library. Or to the public through the paid site https://www.foodandhealth.com/blog/better-food-better-mood. If you would like to view the document, I am happy to provide a PDF copy on request.

157.   Rollin McCraty, Dana Tomasino, Mike Atkinson, "Modulation of DNA Conformation by Heart-Focused Intention," *HeartMath Research Center, Institute of HeartMath;* Boulder Creek, CA, 2003; http://www.aipro.info/drive/File/224.pdf; accessed October 18, 2023.

158.   Dean Radin, Gail Hayssen, et.al., "Double-Blind Test of the Effects of Distant Intention on Water Crystal Formation," *ScienceDirect EXPLORE,* September 2006, 2(5), 408-411; https://doi.org/10.1016/j.explore.2006.06.004; accessed October 18, 2023.

159.   Emeran Mayer, *The Mind-Gut Connection* (New York: Harper Wave/HarperCollins Publishers, 2018).

160.   Newberg and Waldman, *How God Changes Your Brain.*

161.   Shaunti Feldhahn and Jeff Feldhahn, *For Men Only: A Straightforward Guide to the Inner Lives of Women* (New York: Multnomah Books, 2016).

162.   Paula Gallagher, "Confused or Frustrated by Your Man? Science Can Explain What He's Thinking," *Evie Magazine,* March 22, 2020; https://www.eviemagazine.com/post/confused-or-frustrated-by-your-man-science-can-explain-what-hes-thinking; accessed October 18, 2023.

163.   Daniel G. Amen, et.al., "Gender-Based Cerebral Perfusion Differences in 46,034 Functional Neuroimaging Scans," *Journal of Alzheimer's Disease* (2017), 60(2), 605-614. https://doi.org/10.3233/jad-170432; accessed October 18, 2023.

164.   N.K. Gill, "Responding to Feelings," *Visions,* 2021, 16(4), 12-13; https://www.heretohelp.bc.ca/visions/responding-to-feelings-vol16; accessed October 18, 2023.

165.   Matthew A. Killingsworth and Daniel T. Gilbert, "A Wandering Mind Is an Unhappy Mind," *Science,* November 12, 2010, 330(6006), 932-932; https://doi.org/10.1126/science.1192439; accessed October 18, 2023.

166.   Strong's 7314, *ravach.*

167.   "Metallica - Nothing Else Matters" (Harp Twins) Electric Harp Metal; *YouTube;* https://youtu.be/CvI5oy25QO4; accessed July 31, 2023.

168.   "Ellicott's Commentary for English Readers," BibleHub; https://Biblehub.com/commentaries/ellicott/1_samuel/16.htm; accessed October 18, 2023.

169.   *Shulchan Aruch,* Orach Chaim 61:5.

170.   Rabbi Greenberg, "Outline of the faith"; https://rabbigreenberg.com/read/judaism/outline-of-the-faith/; accessed October 18, 2023.

171.   Nicholas Hammond, *The Powers of Sound and Song in Early Modern Paris* (Pennsylvania State University Press, 2021).

172.   Steven Strogatz, *Sync: How Order Emerges from Chaos in the Universe, Nature, and Daily Life* (New York: Hachette Books, 2004).

173.   Tam Hunt, "The "Easy Part" of the Hard Problem: A resonance theory of consciousness," *Authorea,* January 4, 2019; https://doi.org/10.22541/au.154659223.37007989; accessed October 18, 2023.

174.   Reda Hassanien, Tian-zhen Hou, et.al., "Advances in Effects of Sound Waves on Plants," *Journal of Integrative Agriculture* (February 2014), 13(2), 335-348; https://doi.org/10.1016/s2095-3119(13)60492-x; accessed October 18, 2023.

175.   Gosia Kaszubska, "Sonic advance: How sound waves could help regrow bones," *RMIT University,* February 22, 2022; https://www.rmit.edu.au/news/all-news/2022/feb/sound-waves-stem-cells; accessed October 18, 2023.

176.   Marlynn Wei, MD, "The Healing Power of Sound as Meditation," *Psychology Today,* July 5, 2019; https://www.psychologytoday.com/us/blog/urban-survival/201907/the-healing-power-sound-meditation; accessed October 19, 2023.

177.   C. Peter Wagner, *Your Spiritual Gifts Can Help Your Church Grow* (Ventura, CA: Regal Books, 2005).

178.   Andrew B. Newberg, et.al., "The measurement of regional cerebral blood flow during glossolalia: A preliminary SPECT study," *Science Direct Psychiatry Research: Neuroimaging,* November 2006, 148(1), 67-71; https://doi.org/10.1016/j.pscychresns.2006.07.001; accessed October 19, 2023.

179.   Christopher Dana Lynn, "Glossolalia influences on stress response among apostolic pentecostals," Dissertation, University of Alabama, 2009.

180.   Gabriele Penazzi and Nicola De Pisapia, "Direct comparisons between hypnosis and meditation: A mini-review," *Frontiers in Psychology,* July 15, 2022, 13; https://doi.org/10.3389/fpsyg.2022.958185; accessed October 19, 2023.

181.   "The Practice of Chanting," Australia 2014; https://www.siddhayoga.org/practices/chanting/caqs; accessed October 19, 2023.

182.   Matthew 15:18 TPT.

183.   Strong's H7812, *šāḥâ.*

184. Joseph Chusid, "Yoga Foot Drop," *JAMA,* August 9, 1971, 217(6), 827; https://doi .org/10.1001/jama.1971.03190060065025; accessed October 19, 2023.

185. International Freedom Group is a professional association of credible, accountable, and balanced deliverance ministries; www.christianharvestintl.org; accessed October 23, 2023.

186. Albert Hibbert, *Smith Wigglesworth: The Secret of His Power* (Tulsa, OK: Harrison House, 2009).

187. P.R. Muskin, "What are anxiety disorders?" Psychiatry.org; https://www.psychiatry .org/patients-families/anxiety-disorders/what-are-anxiety-disorders; accessed October 20, 2023.

188. "Anxiety Disorders," *Mayo Clinic, Mayo Foundation for Medical Education and Research,* May 4, 2018; https://www.mayoclinic.org/diseases-conditions/anxiety/ diagnosis-treatment/drc-20350967; accessed October 20, 2023.

189. Matthew Ratcliffe and Sam Wilkinson, "How anxiety induces verbal hallucinations" *ScienceDirect,* January 2016, *Consciousness and Cognition,* Vol. 39, 48-58; https://doi .org/10.1016/j.concog.2015.11.009; accessed October 20, 2023.

190. Esin Ileri-Gurel, Bilge Pehlivanoglu, Murat Dogan, "Effect of Acute Stress on Taste Perception: In Relation with Baseline Anxiety Level and Body Weight," *Chemical Senses,* January 2013, Vol. 38(1), 27-34; https://doi.org/10.1093/chemse/bjs075; accessed October 20, 2023.

191. Denise Chen and Pamela Dalton, "The Effect of Emotion and Personality on Olfactory Perception," *Chemical Senses,* May 2005, Vol. 30(4), 345–351; https://doi .org/10.1093/chemse/bji029; accessed October 20, 2023.

192. Killingsworth and Gilbert, "A wandering mind is an unhappy mind," *Science,* 330(6006), 932-932.

193. "Exercise can boost your memory and thinking skills," *Harvard Health,* February 15, 2021; https://www.health.harvard.edu/mind-and-mood/exercise-can-boost-your -memory-and-thinking-skills; accessed October 20, 2023.

194. Daniel H. Craighead, et.al., "Time-efficient inspiratory muscle strength training lowers blood pressure and improves endothelial function, no bioavailability, and oxidative stress in midlife/older adults with above-normal blood pressure," *Journal of the American Heart Association*, June 29, 2021, 10(13); https://doi.org/10.1161/ jaha.121.020980; accessed October 20, 2023.

195. Becca Greenwood, International Freedom Group Annual Meeting, August 2023, International Freedom Group, Aurora, Colorado.

196.   Ruth W. Heflin, *Glory: Experiencing the Atmosphere of Heaven* (Hagerstown, MD: McDougal Publishing, 2000).

197.   Brother Lawrence and Marshall David translator, *The Practice of the Presence of God in Modern English* (2013).

198.   Rebecca Greenwood, *Glory Warfare: How the Presence of God Empowers You to Destroy the Works of Darkness* (Shippensburg, PA: Destiny Image Publishers, 2018).

199.   Margareta Asp, "Rest: A Health-Related Phenomenon and Concept in Caring Science," *Sage Journals, Global Qualitative Nursing Research,* 2, 233339361558366; https://doi.org/10.1177/2333393615583663; accessed October 22, 2023.

200.   Rick Ansorge, "Rest and recovery are critical for an athlete's physiological and psychological well-being," *UCHealth Today;* https://www.uchealth.org/today/rest -and-recovery-for-athletes-physiological-psychological-well-being/; accessed October 20, 2023.

ABOUT JAREB NOTT

JAREB NOTT is a teacher, author, and co-founder of Engage Deliverance & Training. His focus is on equipping others for a transformative journey toward freedom and purpose through dynamic teaching and activation. Since 2010, he has operated in the realms of biblical teaching and training, personal deliverance, and strategic spiritual warfare. Along with his wife, Petra, he is the co-author of *Engage your Destiny* and *The Science of Deliverance.* Jareb currently leads services and teaches regularly for both Engage Ministries and Christian Harvest International in Colorado Springs, founded by Becca and Greg Greenwood.